CHRISTMAS COOKIES

From Your Favorite Brand Name Companies

 Duncan Hines®   **HERSHEY'S®**   ®   ®   **LAND O LAKES®**

and many more

CHRISTMAS COOKIES

PUBLICATIONS INTERNATIONAL, LTD.

Cover photo credit: Sanders Studio, Inc., Chicago, IL

Pictured on cover: Almond Shortbread Bars *(page 64)*; Chocolate Cherry
Brownies *(page 60)*; Chocolate Cookie Sandwiches *(page 45)*; Chocolate
Pistachio Fingers *(page 84)*; Chocolate Tassies *(page 48)*; Cocoa
Gingerbread Cookies *(page 35)*; Cut-Out Sugar Cookies *(page 38)*; Double
Mint Chocolate Cookies *(page 46)*; Hidden Treasures *(page 22)*; Lemon
Blossom Cookies *(page 7)*; Merry Cherry Macaroons *(page 20)*; Pinwheel
Cookies *(page 88)*; Rich Lemon Bars *(page 64)*; Spritz *(page 11)*; Triple
Chocolate Cookies *(page 50)*.

8 7 6 5 4 3 2 1

Manufactured in the U.S.A.

Microwave ovens vary in wattage and power output; cooking times
given with microwave directions in this publication may need to be
adjusted. Consult manufacturer's instructions for suitable microwave-
safe cooking dishes.

CHRISTMAS COOKIES

Holiday Favorites

These cookies are sure to bring back delightful holiday memories. Make a batch and start a holiday tradition for your family.

CHOCO-COCO PECAN CRISPS

½ cup butter or margarine, softened
1 cup packed light brown sugar
1 egg
1 teaspoon vanilla

1½ cups all-purpose flour
1 cup chopped pecans
⅓ cup unsweetened cocoa
½ teaspoon baking soda
1 cup flaked coconut

Cream butter and sugar in large bowl until light and fluffy. Beat in egg and vanilla. Combine flour, pecans, cocoa and baking soda in small bowl until well blended. Add to creamed mixture, blending until stiff dough is formed. Sprinkle coconut on work surface. Divide dough into 4 parts. Shape each part into a roll, about 1½ inches in diameter; roll in coconut until thickly coated. Wrap in plastic wrap; chill until firm, at least 1 hour or up to 2 weeks. (For longer storage, freeze up to 6 weeks.)

Preheat oven to 350°F. Line cookie sheets with parchment paper or leave ungreased. Cut rolls into ⅛-inch-thick slices. Place 2 inches apart on cookie sheets.

Bake 10 to 13 minutes or until firm, but not overly browned. Remove to wire racks to cool. *Makes about 6 dozen cookies*

Left: Choco-Coco Pecan Crisps
Right: Holiday Fruit Drops (page 6)

4

HOLIDAY FRUIT DROPS

½ cup butter, softened
¾ cup packed brown sugar
1 egg
1¼ cups all-purpose flour
1 teaspoon vanilla
½ teaspoon baking soda
½ teaspoon ground cinnamon
    Pinch salt
1 cup (8 ounces) diced
    candied pineapple

1 cup (8 ounces) red and
    green candied cherries
8 ounces chopped pitted
    dates
1 cup (6 ounces) semisweet
    chocolate chips
½ cup whole hazelnuts
½ cup pecan halves
½ cup coarsely chopped
    walnuts

Preheat oven to 325°F. Lightly grease cookie sheets or line with parchment paper. Cream butter and sugar in large bowl. Beat in egg until light. Mix in flour, vanilla, baking soda, cinnamon and salt. Stir in pineapple, cherries, dates, chocolate chips, hazelnuts, pecans and walnuts. Drop dough by rounded teaspoonfuls 2 inches apart onto prepared cookie sheets.

Bake 15 to 20 minutes or until firm and lightly browned around edges. Remove to wire racks to cool completely.

Makes about 8 dozen cookies

Note: The cherries, hazelnuts and pecan halves are not chopped, but left whole.

CHOCOLATE-DIPPED OAT COOKIES

2 cups uncooked rolled oats
¾ cup packed brown sugar
½ cup vegetable oil
½ cup finely chopped walnuts
1 egg

2 teaspoons grated orange
    peel
¼ teaspoon salt
1 package (11½ ounces) milk
    chocolate chips

Combine oats, sugar, oil, walnuts, egg, orange peel and salt in large bowl until blended. Cover; refrigerate overnight.

Preheat oven to 350°F. Lightly grease cookie sheets or line with parchment paper. Melt chocolate chips in top of double boiler over hot, not boiling, water; set aside. Shape oat mixture into large marble-sized balls. Place 2 inches apart on prepared cookie sheets.

Bake 10 to 12 minutes or until golden and crisp. Cool 10 minutes on wire racks. Dip tops of cookies, one at a time, into melted chocolate. Place on waxed paper; cool until chocolate is set.

Makes about 6 dozen cookies

LEMON BLOSSOM COOKIES

2 cups margarine or butter, softened
1½ cups confectioners' sugar
¼ cup REALEMON® Lemon Juice from Concentrate
4 cups unsifted all-purpose flour

Finely chopped nuts (optional)
Assorted fruit preserves and jams or pecan halves

In large mixer bowl, beat margarine and sugar until fluffy. Add ReaLemon® brand; beat well. Gradually add flour; mix well. Cover and chill 2 hours.

Preheat oven to 350°F. Grease cookie sheets. Shape dough into 1-inch balls; roll in nuts, if desired. Place 1 inch apart on prepared cookie sheets. Press thumb in center of each ball; fill with preserves or pecan half.

Bake 14 to 16 minutes or until lightly browned. Remove to wire rack to cool completely. *Makes about 6 dozen cookies*

EUROPEAN KOLACKY

1 cup butter or margarine, softened
1 package (8 ounces) cream cheese, softened
1 tablespoon milk
1 tablespoon sugar

1 egg yolk
1½ cups all-purpose flour
½ teaspoon baking powder
1 can SOLO® or 1 jar BAKER® Filling (any flavor)
Confectioners' sugar

Beat butter, cream cheese, milk and sugar in medium bowl with electric mixer until thoroughly blended. Beat in egg yolk. Sift together flour and baking powder; stir into butter mixture to make stiff dough. Cover and refrigerate several hours or overnight.

Preheat oven to 400°F. Roll out dough on lightly floured surface to ¼-inch thickness. Cut dough with floured 2-inch cookie cutter. Place cookies on ungreased cookie sheets about 1 inch apart. Make depression in centers of cookies with thumb or back of spoon. Spoon 1 teaspoon filling into centers of cookies.

Bake 10 to 12 minutes or until lightly browned. Remove from baking sheets and cool completely on wire racks. Sprinkle with confectioners' sugar just before serving. *Makes about 3 dozen cookies*

APRICOT-PECAN TASSIES

BASE
- 1 cup all-purpose flour
- 1/2 cup butter, cut into pieces
- 6 tablespoons reduced-calorie cream cheese

FILLING
- 3/4 cup firmly packed light brown sugar
- 1 egg, lightly beaten
- 1 tablespoon butter, softened
- 1/2 teaspoon vanilla
- 1/4 teaspoon salt
- 2/3 cup California dried apricot halves, diced (about 4 ounces)
- 1/3 cup chopped pecans

For base, in food processor, combine flour, 1/2 cup butter and cream cheese; process until mixture forms large ball. Wrap dough in plastic wrap and chill 15 minutes.

For filling, combine brown sugar, egg, 1 tablespoon butter, vanilla and salt in bowl until smooth. Stir in apricots and nuts.

Preheat oven to 325°F. Shape dough into 2 dozen 1-inch balls and place in paper-lined or greased miniature muffin cups. Press dough on bottom and up side of each cup; fill each with 1 teaspoon apricot-pecan filling. Bake 25 minutes or until golden and filling sets. Cool and remove from cups. Cookies can be wrapped tightly in plastic and frozen up to six weeks. *Makes 2 dozen cookies*

Favorite recipe from California Apricot Advisory Board

SNOWBALLS

- 1/2 cup DOMINO® Confectioners 10-X Sugar
- 1/4 teaspoon salt
- 1 cup butter or margarine, softened
- 1 teaspoon vanilla extract
- 2 1/4 cups all-purpose flour
- 1/2 cup chopped pecans
- Additional DOMINO® Confectioners 10-X Sugar

In large bowl, combine 1/2 cup sugar, salt and butter; mix well. Add vanilla. Gradually stir in flour. Work nuts into dough. Cover and chill until firm.

Preheat oven to 400°F. Form dough into 1-inch balls. Place 1 inch apart on ungreased cookie sheets. Bake 8 to 10 minutes or until set, but not brown. Roll in additional sugar immediately. Cool on wire racks. Roll in sugar again. Store in airtight container. *Makes about 5 dozen cookies*

Apricot-Pecan Tassies

Chocolate-Dipped Almond Horns

CHOCOLATE-DIPPED ALMOND HORNS

1 can SOLO® Almond Paste
3 egg whites
½ cup superfine sugar
½ teaspoon almond extract
**¼ cup plus 2 tablespoons
    all-purpose flour**

½ cup sliced almonds
**5 squares (1 ounce each)
    semisweet chocolate,
    melted and cooled**

Preheat oven to 350°F. Grease 2 cookie sheets; set aside. Break almond paste into small pieces and place in medium bowl or container of food processor. Add egg whites, sugar and almond extract. Beat with electric mixer or process until mixture is very smooth. Add flour and beat or process until blended.

Spoon almond mixture into pastry bag fitted with ½-inch (#8) plain tip. Pipe mixture into 5- or 6-inch crescent shapes on prepared cookie sheets about 1½ inches apart. Sprinkle with sliced almonds.

Bake 13 to 15 minutes or until edges are golden. Cool on cookie sheets on wire racks 2 minutes. Remove from cookie sheets and cool completely on wire racks. Dip ends of cookies in melted chocolate and place on sheet of foil. Let stand until chocolate is set.   *Makes about 16 cookies*

SPRITZ

1 cup BUTTER FLAVOR CRISCO®	¾ teaspoon salt
½ cup sugar	¾ teaspoon vanilla
1 egg	½ teaspoon almond extract
	2¼ cups all-purpose flour

1. Preheat oven to 400°F. Combine Butter Flavor Crisco® and sugar in large bowl. Beat at medium speed of electric mixer until well blended. Beat in egg, salt, vanilla and almond extract. Stir in flour. If dough is too stiff, add a little water. If too soft, add a little extra flour.

2. Place dough in cookie press. Press into desired shapes 2 inches apart on cooled, ungreased baking sheet.

3. Bake 5 to 7 minutes or until set, but not brown. Cool 1 minute. Remove to wire racks to cool completely.   *Makes about 4 dozen cookies*

Note: Dough may be tinted using a few drops of food color. Cookies may be iced and decorated, if desired.

ALMOND RASPBERRY MACAROONS

Macaroons are a classic favorite. Here, the deliciously intense flavor of almond paste is punctuated by a dot of raspberry jam.

2 cups BLUE DIAMOND® Blanched Almond Paste	Powdered sugar
1 cup granulated sugar	Seedless raspberry jam, stirred until smooth
6 large egg whites	

Preheat oven to 350°F. Line cookie sheets with parchment paper or waxed paper. Beat almond paste and granulated sugar until mixture resembles coarse cornmeal. Beat in egg whites, a little at a time, until thoroughly combined.

Place heaping teaspoonfuls 2 inches apart onto prepared cookie sheets. Coat finger with powdered sugar and make an indentation in middle of each cookie. (Coat finger with powdered sugar each time.)

Bake 15 to 20 minutes or until lightly browned. Remove from oven and fill each indentation with about ¼ teaspoon raspberry jam. Cool. If using waxed paper, carefully peel paper off cookies when cooled.

Makes about 2½ dozen cookies

LEMONY SPRITZ STICKS

1 cup margarine or butter, softened

1 cup confectioners' sugar

¼ cup REALEMON® Lemon Juice from Concentrate

2½ cups unsifted all-purpose flour

¼ teaspoon salt

Chocolate Glaze (recipe follows)

Finely chopped nuts

Preheat oven to 375°F. Grease cookie sheets. In large bowl, beat margarine and sugar until fluffy. Add ReaLemon® brand; beat well. Stir in flour and salt; mix well.

Place dough in cookie press with star-shaped plate. Press dough into 3-inch strips onto prepared cookie sheets. Bake 5 to 6 minutes or until lightly browned on ends. Cool 1 to 2 minutes on cookie sheets. Remove to wire rack to cool completely. Dip ends of cookies in Chocolate Glaze, then nuts.   *Makes about 8½ dozen cookies*

Tip: When using electric cookie gun, use decorator tip. Press dough into ½ × 3-inch strips onto greased cookie sheets. Bake 8 to 10 minutes or until lightly browned on ends.

Chocolate Glaze: In small saucepan, melt 3 ounces sweet cooking chocolate and 2 tablespoons margarine or butter.   *Makes about ⅓ cup*

SLICE 'N' BAKE PUMPKIN COOKIES

3 cups all-purpose flour

1 tablespoon pumpkin pie spice

2 teaspoons ground ginger

½ teaspoon salt

1 cup butter, softened

2 cups granulated sugar

1 cup LIBBY'S® Solid Pack Pumpkin

1 egg yolk

In medium bowl, combine flour, pumpkin pie spice, ginger and salt; set aside. In large mixer bowl, cream butter and sugar, beating until light and fluffy. Add pumpkin and egg yolk; mix well. Blend in dry ingredients; mix well. Cover and chill until firm. Divide into 4 parts. Place each part on 14×10-inch sheet of plastic wrap. Wrap loosely around dough. Shape into 1½-inch-diameter roll; wrap securely. Freeze 4 hours or until firm.

Preheat oven to 350°F. Grease cookie sheets. Cut rolls into ¼-inch slices. Place 2 inches apart on prepared cookie sheets; pat to spread slightly. Reserve some slices to make pumpkin stems; cut into fourths. Shape and press onto tops of cookie slices to form stems.

Continued

12

Bake 16 to 18 minutes or until lightly browned. Remove to wire racks to cool completely. Decorate in pumpkin design with orange and green frosting, if desired. *Makes about 5 dozen cookies*

Hint: Spread orange frosting with small spatula. Pipe leaves using leaf frosting tip, then vines with smallest frosting tip.

BAVARIAN COOKIE WREATHS

Use various decorations for special holidays—or serve plain.

3½ cups all-purpose flour
  1 cup sugar, divided
  3 teaspoons grated orange
    peel, divided
  ¼ teaspoon salt
1⅓ cups butter or margarine
  ¼ cup Florida orange juice

⅓ cup finely chopped
    blanched almonds
  1 egg white beaten *with*
    1 teaspoon water
  Tinted Frosting
    (recipe follows)

Preheat oven to 400°F. Lightly grease cookie sheets. In large bowl, mix flour, ¾ cup sugar, 2 teaspoons orange peel and salt. Using pastry blender, cut in butter until mixture resembles coarse crumbs; add orange juice, stirring until mixture holds together. Knead a few times and press into a ball.

Shape dough into ¾-inch balls; lightly roll each on floured surface into 6-inch-long strip. Using two strips, twist together to make rope. Pinch ends of rope together to make wreath; place on prepared cookie sheet.

In shallow dish, mix almonds, remaining ¼ cup sugar and 1 teaspoon orange peel. Brush top of wreaths with egg white mixture and sprinkle with almond-sugar mixture. Bake 8 to 10 minutes or until lightly browned. Remove to wire racks to cool completely. Frost, if desired.
Makes about 5 dozen cookies

TINTED FROSTING

  1 cup confectioners' sugar
  2 tablespoons butter or
    margarine, softened
  1 to 2 teaspoons milk

Few drops green food color
Red cinnamon candies

In small bowl, mix sugar, butter, 1 teaspoon milk and few drops green food color. Add more milk if necessary to make frosting spreadable. Fill pastry bag fitted with small leaf tip (#67). Decorate each wreath with 3 or 4 leaves and red-cinnamon-candy berries.

Favorite recipe from Florida Department of Citrus

PEANUT BUTTER CHOCOLATE BARS

½ cup (1 stick) margarine, softened

⅓ cup sugar

½ cup QUAKER® or AUNT JEMIMA® Enriched Corn Meal

½ cup all-purpose flour

½ cup chopped almonds

½ cup peanut butter

¼ cup semi-sweet chocolate pieces

1 teaspoon shortening

Preheat oven to 375°F. Beat margarine and sugar until fluffy. Stir in corn meal, flour and almonds. Press onto bottom of ungreased 9-inch square baking pan.

Bake 25 to 30 minutes or until edges are light golden brown. Cool about 10 minutes; spread with peanut butter. In saucepan over low heat, melt chocolate pieces and shortening, stirring until smooth.* Drizzle over peanut butter. Cool completely in pan on wire rack. Cut into bars. Store tightly covered.   *Makes 16 bars*

*Microwave directions: Place chocolate pieces and shortening in microwaveable bowl. Microwave at HIGH 1 to 1½ minutes, stirring after 1 minute and then every 15 seconds until smooth.

OLD-FASHIONED BUTTER COOKIES

¾ cup sugar

1 cup LAND O LAKES® Butter, softened

2 egg yolks

1 teaspoon vanilla

2 cups all-purpose flour

¼ teaspoon salt

Pecan halves

Preheat oven to 350°F. In large mixer bowl, combine sugar, butter, egg yolks and vanilla. Beat at medium speed, scraping bowl often, until well mixed, 1 to 2 minutes. Add flour and salt; beat at low speed, scraping bowl often, until well mixed, 2 to 3 minutes.

Shape rounded teaspoonfuls of dough into 1-inch balls. Place 2 inches apart on ungreased cookie sheets. Flatten cookies to ¼-inch thickness with bottom of buttered glass dipped in sugar. Place pecan half in center of each cookie.

Bake 10 to 12 minutes or until edges are lightly browned. Cool 1 minute; remove from cookie sheets.   *Makes about 2½ dozen cookies*

CRISPY NUT SHORTBREAD

6 tablespoons margarine, softened
⅓ cup sugar
1 egg
1 teaspoon vanilla
½ cup QUAKER® or AUNT JEMIMA® Enriched Corn Meal
½ cup all-purpose flour

½ cup finely chopped, husked, toasted hazelnuts or walnuts
½ cup semi-sweet chocolate pieces
1 tablespoon vegetable shortening
Coarsely chopped nuts (optional)

Preheat oven to 300°F. Grease 13×9-inch baking pan. Beat margarine and sugar until fluffy. Blend in egg and vanilla. Add combined corn meal, flour and nuts; mix well. Spread onto bottom of prepared pan. Bake 40 to 45 minutes or until edges are golden brown.

In saucepan over low heat, melt chocolate pieces and shortening, stirring until smooth.* Spread over shortbread. Sprinkle with coarsely chopped nuts, if desired. Cool completely. Cut into 48 squares; cut diagonally into triangles. Store tightly covered. *Makes 4 dozen cookies*

*Microwave directions: Place chocolate pieces and shortening in microwaveable bowl. Microwave at HIGH 1 to 2 minutes, stirring after 1 minute and then every 30 seconds until smooth.

Crispy Nut Shortbread;
Peanut Butter Chocolate Bars (page 14)

PEANUT BUTTER CRACKLES

1½ cups all-purpose flour
1 teaspoon baking soda
⅛ teaspoon salt
½ cup MAZOLA® Margarine, softened
½ cup SKIPPY® Creamy or Super Chunk Peanut Butter

½ cup granulated sugar
½ cup packed brown sugar
1 egg
1 teaspoon vanilla
Granulated sugar
Chocolate candy stars

Preheat oven to 375°F. In small bowl, combine flour, baking soda and salt. In large bowl, beat margarine and peanut butter until well blended. Beat in granulated sugar and brown sugar until blended. Beat in egg and vanilla. Gradually beat in flour mixture until well mixed.

Shape dough into 1-inch balls. Roll in granulated sugar. Place 2 inches apart on ungreased cookie sheets.

Bake 10 minutes or until lightly browned. Remove from oven and quickly press chocolate star firmly into top of each cookie (cookie will crack around edges). Remove to wire racks to cool completely.
Makes about 5 dozen cookies

JINGLE JUMBLES

¾ cup butter or margarine, softened
1 cup packed brown sugar
¼ cup molasses
1 egg
2¼ cups unsifted all-purpose flour

2 teaspoons baking soda
1 teaspoon ground ginger
1 teaspoon ground cinnamon
½ teaspoon salt
½ teaspoon ground cloves
1¼ cups SUN-MAID® Raisins
Granulated sugar

In large bowl, cream butter and sugar. Add molasses and egg; beat until fluffy. In medium bowl, sift together flour, baking soda, ginger, cinnamon, salt and cloves. Stir into molasses mixture. Stir in raisins. Cover and chill about 30 minutes.

Preheat oven to 375°F. Grease cookie sheets. Form dough into 1½-inch balls; roll in granulated sugar, coating generously. Place 2 inches apart on prepared cookie sheets.

Bake 12 to 14 minutes or until edges are firm and centers are still slightly soft. Remove to wire rack to cool. *Makes about 2 dozen cookies*

Holiday Citrus Logs

HOLIDAY CITRUS LOGS

1 (12-ounce) package vanilla
   wafers, crushed
   (about 3 cups)
1 (8-ounce) package candied
   cherries, coarsely
   chopped
1 (8-ounce) package chopped
   dates (1¾ cups)
1 cup chopped pecans or
   almonds
¼ cup REALEMON® Lemon
   Juice from Concentrate

2 tablespoons orange-
   flavored liqueur
1 tablespoon white corn
   syrup
  Additional white corn
   syrup, heated
  Additional finely chopped
   pecans or sliced almonds,
   toasted

In large bowl, combine all ingredients except additional corn syrup and
finely chopped nuts. Shape into two 10-inch logs. Brush with additional
corn syrup; roll in finely chopped nuts. Wrap tightly; refrigerate 3 to 4
days to blend flavors. To serve, cut into ¼-inch slices.

Makes two 10-inch logs

17

ALMOND BRICKLE SUGAR COOKIES

*These tender butter cookies can be made with
almond brickle bits or mini chocolate chips.*

2¼ cups all-purpose flour
1 cup sugar
1 cup LAND O LAKES® Butter,
   softened
1 egg

1 teaspoon baking soda
1 teaspoon vanilla
1 package (6 ounces) almond
   brickle bits*

Preheat oven to 350°F. Grease cookie sheets. In large mixer bowl, combine flour, sugar, butter, egg, baking soda and vanilla. Beat at medium speed, scraping bowl often, until well mixed, 2 to 3 minutes. Stir in almond brickle bits.

Shape rounded teaspoonfuls of dough into 1-inch balls. Place 2 inches apart on prepared cookie sheets. Flatten cookies to ¼-inch thickness with bottom of buttered glass dipped in sugar.

Bake 8 to 11 minutes or until edges are very lightly browned. Remove immediately. *Makes about 4 dozen cookies*

*Substitute 1 cup mini semisweet chocolate chips for the almond brickle bits.

"M&M'S"® CHOCOLATE CANDIES PARTY COOKIES

1 cup butter or margarine,
   softened
1 cup packed light brown
   sugar
½ cup granulated sugar
2 eggs
2 teaspoons vanilla

2¼ cups all-purpose flour
1 teaspoon salt
1 teaspoon baking soda
1½ cups "M&M'S"® Plain
   Chocolate Candies,
   divided

Preheat oven to 375°F. Beat together butter, brown sugar and granulated sugar in large bowl until light and fluffy. Blend in eggs and vanilla. Combine flour, salt and baking soda in small bowl. Add to butter mixture; mix well. Stir in ½ cup of the candies. Drop dough by rounded teaspoonfuls 2 inches apart onto ungreased cookie sheets. Press additional candies into each cookie. Bake 10 to 12 minutes or until golden brown. Remove to wire racks to cool completely.

Makes about 6 dozen cookies

Almond Brickle Sugar Cookies

18

MERRY CHERRY MACAROONS

3 egg whites
¼ teaspoon cream of tartar
½ cup sugar
½ teaspoon vanilla
½ teaspoon almond extract
1⅓ cups (3½ ounces) flaked
  coconut

½ cup chopped red glacé
  cherries
Red glacé cherry halves
  (optional)

Preheat oven to 325°F. Grease cookie sheets or line (foil, waxed paper or parchment paper). In small bowl, beat egg whites and cream of tartar at high speed until foamy. Add sugar, 1 tablespoon at a time, beating constantly until sugar is dissolved* and whites are glossy and stand in soft peaks. Beat in flavorings. Stir together coconut and chopped cherries. Gently, but thoroughly, fold into beaten whites. Drop by rounded tablespoonfuls 2 inches apart onto prepared cookie sheet. Top each cookie with cherry half, if desired.

Bake 18 to 20 minutes until lightly browned. Remove to wire racks to cool completely. Store in airtight container between sheets of foil or waxed paper. *Makes 3½ to 4 dozen cookies*

*Rub a bit of meringue between fingers to feel if sugar has dissolved.

Favorite recipe from American Egg Board

LEMON WAFERS

¾ cup (1½ sticks) margarine,
  softened
½ cup sugar
1 egg
1 tablespoon grated lemon
  peel (about 1 medium
  lemon)

2 cups QUAKER® or AUNT
  JEMIMA® Enriched Corn
  Meal
1½ cups all-purpose flour
½ teaspoon salt (optional)
¼ cup milk

Preheat oven to 375°F. Beat margarine and sugar until fluffy. Blend in egg and lemon peel. Add combined dry ingredients alternately with milk, mixing well after each addition.

Shape into 1-inch balls. Place 2 inches apart on ungreased cookie sheet. Using bottom of greased glass dipped in sugar, press into ⅛-inch-thick circles. Bake 13 to 15 minutes or until bottoms are lightly browned. Cool 2 minutes on cookie sheet; remove to wire rack. Cool completely. Store tightly covered. *Makes about 3 dozen cookies*

ISLAND TREASURE COOKIES

1²/₃ cups all-purpose flour
¾ teaspoon baking powder
½ teaspoon baking soda
½ teaspoon salt
14 tablespoons (1¾ sticks) butter, softened
¾ cup firmly packed brown sugar
⅓ cup sugar

1 teaspoon vanilla extract
1 egg
¾ cup coconut, toasted if desired
¾ cup macadamia nuts or walnuts, chopped
2 cups NESTLÉ® Toll House® milk chocolate morsels

Preheat oven to 375°F. In small bowl, combine flour, baking powder, baking soda and salt; set aside.

In large mixer bowl, beat butter, brown sugar, sugar and vanilla extract until creamy. Beat in egg. Gradually blend in flour mixture. Stir in coconut, nuts and Nestlé® Toll House® milk chocolate morsels. Drop by slightly rounded measuring tablespoonfuls onto ungreased cookie sheets.

Bake 10 to 12 minutes until edges are lightly browned. Let stand 2 minutes. Remove from cookie sheets; cool.

Makes about 2 dozen cookies

DOUBLE ALMOND BUTTER COOKIES

2 cups butter or margarine, softened
2½ cups powdered sugar, sifted and divided
4 cups all-purpose flour
2¼ teaspoons vanilla, divided

⅔ cup BLUE DIAMOND® Blanched Almond Paste
½ cup BLUE DIAMOND® Chopped Natural Almonds, toasted
¼ cup firmly packed light brown sugar

Cream butter with 1 cup of the powdered sugar in large bowl until light and fluffy. Gradually beat in flour. Beat in 2 teaspoons of the vanilla. Cover and chill 30 minutes.

Preheat oven to 350°F. Combine almond paste, almonds, brown sugar and remaining ¼ teaspoon vanilla. Shape dough around ½ teaspoon almond paste mixture; form into 1-inch balls. Place on ungreased cookie sheets.

Bake 15 minutes or until set. Remove to wire racks to cool. Roll in remaining 1½ cups powdered sugar or sift the powdered sugar over cookies.

Makes about 8 dozen cookies

HOLIDAY CHOCOLATE CHIP COOKIES

2¼ cups all-purpose flour
1¼ teaspoons baking powder
¼ teaspoon salt
1 cup (2 sticks) butter, softened
1¼ cups sugar
1 egg
1 teaspoon vanilla extract
One 12-ounce package (2 cups) NESTLE® Toll House® semi-sweet chocolate morsels

1 cup chopped nuts
Three 6-ounce jars (30) maraschino cherries, drained, patted dry
8 small candy spearmint leaves, cut into quarters lengthwise and halved

Preheat oven to 350°F. In small bowl, combine flour, baking powder and salt; set aside.

In large mixer bowl, beat butter and sugar until creamy. Beat in egg and vanilla extract. Gradually blend in flour mixture. Stir in Nestlé® Toll House® semi-sweet chocolate morsels and nuts. Spread in greased 13×9-inch baking pan. Press 30 maraschino cherries into dough, spacing them to form six rows, five cherries per row. Place 2 spearmint "leaves" at base of each cherry; press into dough.

Bake 25 to 30 minutes. Cool completely. Cut into 2-inch squares.

Makes 30 cookies

HIDDEN TREASURES

⅔ cup BUTTER FLAVOR CRISCO®
¾ cup sugar
1 egg
1 tablespoon milk
1 teaspoon vanilla
1¾ cups all-purpose flour
1 teaspoon baking powder
½ teaspoon salt
½ teaspoon baking soda
48 maraschino cherries, well drained on paper towels

WHITE DIPPING CHOCOLATE
1 cup white melting chocolate, cut in small pieces
2 tablespoons BUTTER FLAVOR CRISCO®

DARK DIPPING CHOCOLATE
1 cup semisweet chocolate chips
2 tablespoons BUTTER FLAVOR CRISCO®

Finely chopped pecans
Slivered white chocolate

Continued

1. Preheat oven to 350°F. Cream Butter Flavor Crisco®, sugar, egg, milk and vanilla in large bowl at medium speed of electric mixer until well blended.

2. Combine flour, baking powder, salt and baking soda. Beat into creamed mixture at low speed. Divide into 48 equal pieces.

3. Press dough into very thin layer around well-drained cherries. Place 2 inches apart on ungreased baking sheet.

4. Bake 10 minutes. Cool 1 minute on baking sheet. Remove to wire rack to cool completely.

5. For dipping chocolate, place chocolate of choice and Butter Flavor Crisco® in glass measuring cup. Microwave at 50% (MEDIUM). Stir after 1 minute. Repeat until smooth (or melt on range top in small saucepan on very low heat).

6. Drop one cookie at a time into chocolate. Use fork to turn. Cover completely with chocolate.* Lift cookie out of chocolate with fork. Allow excess to drip off. Place on waxed paper-lined baking sheet.

7. Sprinkle chopped pecans on top of white chocolate cookies before chocolate sets. Sprinkle white chocolate on dark chocolate cookies before chocolate sets. Chill in refrigerator to set chocolate.

Makes about 4 dozen cookies

*If chocolate becomes too firm, reheat in microwave or on range top.

Hidden Treasures

Walnut Christmas Balls

WALNUT CHRISTMAS BALLS

1 cup California walnuts
2/3 cup powdered sugar,
   divided
1 cup butter or margarine,
   softened

1 teaspoon vanilla
1¾ cups all-purpose flour
   Chocolate Filling
   (recipe follows)

Preheat oven to 350°F. In food processor or blender, process walnuts with 2 tablespoons of the sugar until finely ground; set aside. In large bowl, cream butter and remaining sugar. Beat in vanilla. Add flour and ¾ cup of the ground walnuts; mix until blended. Roll dough into about 3 dozen walnut-size balls. Place 2 inches apart on ungreased cookie sheets.

Bake 10 to 12 minutes or until just golden around edges. Remove to wire racks to cool completely.

Prepare Chocolate Filling. Place generous teaspoonful of filling on flat side of half of the cookies. Top with remaining cookies, flat side down, forming sandwiches. Roll chocolate edges of cookies in remaining ground walnuts.   *Makes about 1½ dozen sandwich cookies*

Continued

24

Chocolate Filling: Chop 3 squares (1 ounce each) semisweet chocolate into small pieces; place in food processor or blender with ½ teaspoon vanilla. In small saucepan, heat 2 tablespoons *each* butter or margarine and whipping cream over medium heat until hot; pour over chocolate. Process until chocolate is melted, turning machine off and scraping side as needed. With machine running, gradually add 1 cup powdered sugar; process until smooth.

Favorite recipe from Walnut Marketing Board

CARAMEL PECAN COOKIES

COOKIE
½ cup BUTTER FLAVOR
   CRISCO®, melted
1 package DUNCAN HINES®
   Moist Deluxe Yellow Cake
   Mix
1 cup JIF® Extra Crunchy
   Peanut Butter
2 eggs
2 tablespoons orange juice or
   water

CARAMEL AND CHOCOLATE TOPPING
28 caramels
2 tablespoons milk
2 cups pecan halves
1 package (6 ounces)
   semisweet chocolate
   chips

1. Preheat oven to 350°F. For cookie, combine Butter Flavor Crisco®, Duncan Hines® Yellow Cake Mix, Jif® Extra Crunchy Peanut Butter, eggs and juice in large bowl. Beat at medium speed of electric mixer until well blended.

2. Drop rounded tablespoonfuls of dough, 3 inches apart, onto ungreased cookie sheet.

3. Bake 10 to 12 minutes or until set. Cool 1 minute on cookie sheet. Remove to wire rack to cool completely.

4. For topping, combine caramels and milk in microwave-safe bowl. Cover with waxed paper. Microwave at 50% (MEDIUM). Stir after 1 minute. Repeat until smooth (or melt on range top in small saucepan on very low heat). Drop rounded teaspoonfuls on top of each cookie. Place 3 pecan halves around edge of caramel to resemble turtles.

5. Place chocolate chips in microwave-safe cup. Microwave at 50% (MEDIUM). Stir after 1 minute. Repeat until smooth (or melt on range top in small saucepan on very low heat). Spread rounded teaspoonfuls over top of caramel. Do not cover the pecans. Cool completely.

Makes about 4 dozen cookies

Cookie Cutter Cutouts

Decorating cutout cookies is great fun for the family. Use frostings, colored sugars, candied fruit, chopped nuts, small candies and your imagination.

STAR CHRISTMAS TREE COOKIES

COOKIES
- ½ cup CRISCO® Shortening
- ⅓ cup butter or margarine, softened
- 2 egg yolks
- 1 teaspoon vanilla extract
- 1 package DUNCAN HINES® Moist Deluxe Yellow or Devil's Food Cake Mix
- 1 tablespoon water

FROSTING
- 1 container (16 ounces) DUNCAN HINES® Vanilla Frosting
- Green food coloring
- Red and green sugar crystals for garnish
- Assorted colored candies and decors for garnish

1. Preheat oven to 375°F. For cookies, combine shortening, butter, egg yolks and vanilla extract. Blend in cake mix gradually. Add 1 teaspoonful water at a time until dough is rolling consistency. Divide dough into 4 balls. Flatten one ball with hand; roll to ⅛-inch thickness on lightly floured surface. Cut with graduated star cookie cutters. Repeat using remaining dough. Bake large cookies together on ungreased baking sheet. Bake 6 to 8 minutes or until edges are light golden brown. Cool cookies 1 minute. Remove from baking sheet. Repeat with smaller cookies, testing for doneness at minimum baking time.

2. For frosting, tint vanilla frosting with green food coloring. Frost cookies and stack beginning with largest cookies on bottom and ending with smallest cookies on top. Rotate cookies when stacking to alternate corners. Decorate as desired with colored sugar crystals and assorted colored candies and decors. *Makes 2 to 3 dozen cookies*

Tip: You may use your favorite assorted cookie cutters. Use 3 to 5 cookies to stack into smaller "trees."

Star Christmas Tree Cookies

Cream Cheese Cutout Cookies

CREAM CHEESE CUTOUT COOKIES

1 cup butter, softened
1 package (8 ounces) cream
   cheese, softened
1½ cups sugar
1 egg
1 teaspoon vanilla
½ teaspoon almond extract

3½ cups all-purpose flour
1 teaspoon baking powder
Almond Frosting
   (recipe follows)
Assorted candies for
   decoration (optional)

In large bowl, beat butter and cream cheese until well combined. Add sugar; beat until fluffy. Add egg, vanilla and almond extract; beat well. In small bowl, combine flour and baking powder. Add dry ingredients to cream cheese mixture; beat until well mixed. Divide dough in half. Wrap each portion in plastic wrap; refrigerate about 1½ hours.

Continued

Preheat oven to 375°F. Roll out dough, half at a time, to ⅛-inch thickness on lightly floured surface. Cut out with cookie cutters. Place 2 inches apart on ungreased cookie sheets.

Bake 8 to 10 minutes or until edges are lightly browned. Remove to wire racks to cool completely. Frost cookies with Almond Frosting; decorate with assorted candies, if desired.   *Makes about 7 dozen cookies*

Almond Frosting: In small bowl, beat 2 cups sifted powdered sugar, 2 tablespoons softened butter and ¼ teaspoon almond extract until smooth. For piping consistency, beat in 4 to 5 teaspoons milk. For spreading consistency, add a little more milk. If desired, tint with food coloring.

Favorite recipe from Wisconsin Milk Marketing Board

PEANUT BUTTER GINGERBREAD MEN

5 cups all-purpose flour
1½ teaspoons ground
  cinnamon
1 teaspoon baking soda
½ teaspoon ground ginger
¼ teaspoon salt
¾ cup MAZOLA® Margarine,
  softened

¾ cup SKIPPY® Creamy
  Peanut Butter
1 cup packed brown sugar
1 cup KARO® Dark Corn
  Syrup
2 eggs
  Frosting for decorating
  (optional)

In large bowl, combine flour, cinnamon, baking soda, ginger and salt. In another large bowl, beat margarine and peanut butter until well blended. Add brown sugar, corn syrup and eggs; beat until smooth. Gradually beat in 2 cups of the dry ingredients. With wooden spoon, beat in remaining dry ingredients, 1 cup at a time, until well blended. Divide dough into thirds. Wrap in plastic wrap; chill until firm, at least 1 hour.

Preheat oven to 300°F. Roll out dough, one third at a time, to ⅛-inch thickness on lightly floured surface. Cut out with 5½-inch gingerbread cutter. Place 2 inches apart on ungreased cookie sheets.

Bake 10 to 12 minutes or until lightly browned. Remove to wire racks to cool completely. Pipe frosting on cookies to make eyes and buttons, if desired.   *Makes about 2½ dozen cookies*

DUTCH ST. NICHOLAS COOKIES

¾ cup butter or margarine, softened

½ cup packed brown sugar

2 tablespoons milk

1½ teaspoons ground cinnamon

¼ teaspoon ground nutmeg

¼ teaspoon ground ginger

¼ teaspoon ground cloves

2 cups sifted all-purpose flour

1½ teaspoons baking powder

½ teaspoon salt

½ cup toasted chopped almonds

¼ cup coarsely chopped citron

In large bowl, cream butter, sugar, milk and spices. In small bowl, combine flour, baking powder and salt. Add flour mixture to creamed mixture; blend well. Stir in almonds and citron. Knead dough slightly to make ball. Cover; chill until firm.

Preheat oven to 375°F. Grease cookie sheets. Roll out dough to ¼-inch thickness on lightly floured surface. Cut out with cookie cutters. Place 2 inches apart on prepared cookie sheets. Bake 7 to 10 minutes or until lightly browned. Remove to wire racks to cool.

Makes about 3½ dozen cookies

Favorite recipe from Almond Board of California

COUNTRY SOUR CREAM COOKIES

4 cups all-purpose flour, divided

2 cups sugar

1 cup LAND O LAKES® Butter, softened

½ cup dairy sour cream

2 eggs

1 tablespoon baking powder

1 teaspoon baking soda

½ teaspoon salt

½ teaspoon ground nutmeg

1 teaspoon vanilla

½ teaspoon lemon extract

Sugar for sprinkling

In large mixer bowl, combine 2 cups of the flour, 2 cups sugar, butter, sour cream, eggs, baking powder, baking soda, salt, nutmeg, vanilla and lemon extract. Beat at low speed, scraping bowl often, until well mixed, 2 to 3 minutes. Stir in remaining 2 cups flour. Divide dough into 4 equal portions. Wrap in waxed paper. Refrigerate until firm, 2 hours.

Preheat oven to 350°F. Roll out dough to ⅛-inch thickness on well-floured surface. Cut out with cookie cutters. Place 1 inch apart on ungreased cookie sheets. Sprinkle sugar over tops. Bake 8 to 12 minutes or until edges are lightly browned. *Makes about 6 dozen cookies*

Note: Dough may be tinted with food coloring before refrigerating.

PEANUT BUTTER CUTOUT COOKIES

1 cup REESE'S® Peanut Butter
    Chips
½ cup butter or margarine
⅔ cup packed light brown
    sugar
1 egg

¾ teaspoon vanilla extract
1⅓ cups all-purpose flour
¾ teaspoon baking soda
½ cup finely chopped pecans
    Chocolate Chip Glaze
    (recipe follows)

Melt peanut butter chips and butter in medium saucepan over low heat, stirring constantly. Pour into large mixer bowl; add brown sugar, egg and vanilla, beating until well blended. Stir in flour, baking soda and pecans; blend well. Cover and chill 15 to 20 minutes or until firm enough to roll.

Preheat oven to 350°F. Roll out dough, a small portion at a time, to ¼-inch thickness on lightly floured surface. (Keep remaining dough in refrigerator.) With cookie cutters, cut into desired shapes. Place 2 inches apart on ungreased cookie sheets.

Bake 7 to 8 minutes or until almost set (do not overbake). Cool 1 minute. Remove to wire racks to cool completely. Drizzle Chocolate Chip Glaze onto each cookie; allow to set. *Makes about 3 dozen cookies*

Chocolate Chip Glaze: Melt 1 cup HERSHEY'S Semi-Sweet Chocolate Chips with 1 tablespoon shortening in top of double boiler over hot, not boiling, water; stir until smooth. Remove from heat; cool slightly, stirring occasionally.

Peanut Butter Cutout Cookies

PHILLY CREAM CHEESE COOKIE DOUGH

1 (8-ounce) package
   PHILADELPHIA BRAND®
   Cream Cheese, softened
¾ cup butter, softened

1 cup powdered sugar
2¼ cups all-purpose flour
½ teaspoon baking soda

Beat cream cheese, butter and sugar in large mixing bowl at medium speed with electric mixer until well blended.

Add flour and soda; mix well.
Makes 3 cups dough

CHOCOLATE MINT CUTOUTS

Preheat oven to 325°F.

Add ¼ teaspoon mint extract and few drops green food coloring to 1½ cups Cookie Dough; mix well. Chill 30 minutes.

On lightly floured surface, roll dough to ⅛-inch thickness; cut with assorted 3-inch cookie cutters. Place on ungreased cookie sheet.

Bake 10 to 12 minutes or until edges begin to brown. Cool on wire rack.

Melt ¼ cup mint flavored semi-sweet chocolate chips in small saucepan over low heat, stirring until smooth. Drizzle over cookies.
Makes about 3 dozen cookies

SNOWMEN

Preheat oven to 325°F.

Add ¼ teaspoon vanilla to 1½ cups Cookie Dough; mix well. Chill 30 minutes.

For each snowman, shape dough into two small balls, one slightly larger than the other. Place balls, slightly overlapping, on ungreased cookie sheet; flatten with bottom of glass. Repeat with remaining dough.

Bake 18 to 20 minutes or until light golden brown. Cool on wire rack.

Sprinkle each snowman with sifted powdered sugar. Decorate with icing as desired. Cut miniature peanut butter cups in half for hats.
Makes about 2 dozen cookies

Continued

Clockwise from top left: Preserve Thumbprints (page 34); Snowmen; Choco-Orange Slices (page 34); Chocolate Mint Cutouts

CHOCO-ORANGE SLICES

Preheat oven to 325°F.

Add 1½ teaspoons grated orange peel to 1½ cups Cookie Dough (page 33); mix well. Shape into 8×1½-inch log. Chill 30 minutes.

Cut log into ¼-inch slices. Place on ungreased cookie sheet.

Bake 15 to 18 minutes or until edges begin to brown. Cool on wire rack.

Melt ⅓ cup BAKER'S® Semi-Sweet Real Chocolate Chips with 1 tablespoon orange juice and 1 tablespoon orange flavored liqueur in small saucepan over low heat, stirring until smooth. Dip cookies into chocolate mixture.   *Makes about 2½ dozen cookies*

PRESERVE THUMBPRINTS

Preheat oven to 325°F.

Add ½ cup chopped pecans and ½ teaspoon vanilla to 1½ cups Cookie Dough (page 33); mix well. Chill 30 minutes.

Shape dough into 1-inch balls. Place on ungreased cookie sheet. Indent centers; fill each with 1 teaspoon KRAFT® Preserves.

Bake 14 to 16 minutes or until light golden brown. Cool on wire rack.
             Makes about 3⅓ dozen cookies

CHOCOLATE CANDY THUMBPRINTS

Preheat oven to 325°F.

Add ½ cup chopped pecans and ½ teaspoon vanilla to 1½ cups Cookie Dough (page 33); mix well. Chill 30 minutes.

Shape dough into 1-inch balls. Place on ungreased cookie sheet. Indent centers.

Bake 14 to 16 minutes or until light golden brown.

Immediately place milk chocolate candy kiss in center of each cookie. Let stand 1 to 2 minutes or until chocolate is slightly softened; spread over top of cookies. Cool on wire rack.   *Makes about 3½ dozen cookies*

COCOA GINGERBREAD COOKIES

¼ cup butter or margarine,
  softened
2 tablespoons shortening
⅓ cup packed brown sugar
¼ cup dark molasses
1 egg
1½ cups all-purpose flour
¼ cup unsweetened cocoa

½ teaspoon baking soda
½ teaspoon ground ginger
½ teaspoon ground cinnamon
¼ teaspoon salt
¼ teaspoon ground nutmeg
⅛ teaspoon ground cloves
  Decorator Icing
    (recipe follows)

Preheat oven to 400°F. Lightly grease cookie sheets or line with parchment paper. Cream butter, shortening, brown sugar and molasses in large bowl. Add egg; beat until light. Combine flour, cocoa, baking soda, ginger, cinnamon, salt, nutmeg and cloves in small bowl. Blend into creamed mixture until smooth. (If dough is too soft to handle, cover and refrigerate until firm.)

Roll out dough to ¼-inch thickness on lightly floured surface. Cut out with cookie cutters. Place 2 inches apart on prepared cookie sheets.

Bake 8 to 10 minutes or until firm. Remove to wire racks to cool completely.

Prepare Decorator Icing. Spoon into pastry bag fitted with small tip. Decorate cookies with icing.   *Makes about 6 dozen cookies*

Decorator Icing: Beat 1 egg white* in large bowl until frothy. Gradually beat in 3½ cups powdered sugar until blended. Add 1 teaspoon almond or lemon extract and enough water (2 to 3 tablespoons) to moisten. Beat until smooth and glossy.

*Use clean, uncracked egg.

Lemon Cut-Out Cookies

LEMON CUT-OUT COOKIES

2¾ cups unsifted all-purpose
    flour
  1 teaspoon baking powder
  ½ teaspoon baking soda
  ¼ teaspoon salt
1½ cups sugar
  ½ cup margarine or butter,
    softened

  1 egg
  ⅓ cup REALEMON® Lemon
    Juice from Concentrate
  Lemon Icing (recipe follows)
    (optional)

Sift together flour, baking powder, baking soda and salt; set aside. In large mixer bowl, beat sugar and margarine until fluffy; beat in egg. Gradually add dry ingredients alternately with ReaLemon® brand; mix well (dough will be soft). Cover and chill overnight in refrigerator or 2 hours in freezer.

Continued

Preheat oven to 375°F. Grease cookie sheets. On well-floured surface, roll out dough, one third at a time, to ⅛-inch thickness; cut with floured cookie cutters. Place 1 inch apart on prepared cookie sheets.

Bake 8 to 10 minutes. Remove to wire racks to cool completely. Repeat with remaining dough. Ice and decorate as desired.

Makes 4 to 5 dozen cookies

Lemon Icing: Mix 1¼ cups confectioners' sugar and 2 tablespoons ReaLemon® brand until smooth. Add food coloring, if desired.

Makes about ½ cup

CONFETTI CUTOUTS

COOKIES
1½ cups sugar
⅔ cup butter or margarine, softened
2 eggs
1 tablespoon milk
1½ teaspoons almond extract
3½ cups all-purpose flour

2½ teaspoons baking powder
½ teaspoon salt

FILLING
¼ cup vegetable shortening
1½ cups "M&M'S"® Plain Chocolate Candies

For cookies, in large bowl beat together sugar and butter until light and fluffy; blend in eggs, milk and extract. In bowl combine flour, baking powder and salt. Gradually add dry ingredients, mixing well after each addition. Cover and chill dough several hours.

Preheat oven to 400°F. Roll out dough, one fourth at a time, to ⅛-inch thickness on floured surface. Cut with floured 2½-inch cookie cutters. Cut out small designs in centers of half the cookies with smaller cutter or sharp knife. Place 2 inches apart on ungreased cookie sheets.

Bake 7 to 9 minutes or until edges are very light golden brown. Remove to wire racks to cool completely.

For filling, melt shortening in 2-quart heavy saucepan; add candies. Cook over very low heat, stirring constantly with metal spoon and pressing candies with back of spoon to break up. (Chocolate will be almost melted and pieces of color coating will remain.) Cool slightly or until of spreading consistency. Spread solid cookies with warm filling; top with cutout cookies, pressing lightly to secure. Chill about 30 minutes to set chocolate. Store at room temperature. *Makes about 3 dozen cookies*

CUT-OUT SUGAR COOKIES

²/₃ cup BUTTER FLAVOR
    CRISCO®
¾ cup sugar
  1 tablespoon plus 1 teaspoon
    milk
  1 teaspoon vanilla

1 egg
2 cups all-purpose flour
1½ teaspoons baking powder
  ¼ teaspoon salt
    Colored sugars and decors
      for garnish

1. Cream Butter Flavor Crisco®, sugar, milk and vanilla in large bowl at medium speed of electric mixer until well blended. Beat in egg.

2. Combine flour, baking powder and salt. Mix into creamed mixture at low speed until well blended. Cover and refrigerate several hours or overnight.

3. Preheat oven to 375°F. Roll out dough, half at a time, on floured surface to ⅛-inch thickness. Cut into desired shapes. Place 2 inches apart on ungreased baking sheet. Sprinkle with colored sugars and decors or leave plain to frost* when cool.

4. Bake 7 to 9 minutes or until set. Remove immediately to wire racks to cool completely.

        Makes about 3 dozen cookies (depending on size and shape)

Hint: Floured pastry cloth and rolling pin cover make rolling out dough easier.

Variations
***Creamy Vanilla Frosting:** Combine ½ cup Butter Flavor Crisco®, 1 pound (4 cups) powdered sugar, ⅓ cup milk and 1 teaspoon vanilla in medium bowl. Beat at low speed of electric mixer until well blended. Scrape bowl. Beat at high speed for 2 minutes or until smooth and creamy. One or two drops food color can be used to tint each cup of frosting, if desired. Frost cooled cookies. This frosting works well in decorating tube.

Chocolate Dipped Sugar Cookies: Bake and cool cookies. Combine 1 cup semi-sweet chocolate chips and 1 teaspoon Butter Flavor Crisco® in microwave-safe measuring cup. Microwave at 50% power (MEDIUM). Stir after 1 minute. Repeat until smooth (or melt on range top in small saucepan on very low heat). Dip one end of cooled cookie halfway up in chocolate. Place on waxed paper until chocolate is firm.

Chocolate Nut Sugar Cookies: Dip in melted chocolate as directed for Chocolate Dipped Sugar Cookies. Spread with finely chopped nuts before chocolate hardens.

                                    Cut-Out Sugar Cookies

Buttery Butterscotch Cutouts

BUTTERY BUTTERSCOTCH CUTOUTS

*This buttery cookie has melted butterscotch
stirred in for that special flavor.*

3 cups all-purpose flour
1 cup butterscotch chips,
   melted
½ cup granulated sugar
½ cup firmly packed brown
   sugar
1 cup LAND O LAKES® Butter,
   softened

1 egg
2 tablespoons milk
2 teaspoons vanilla
   Powdered sugar for
   garnish

Continued

40

In large mixer bowl, combine flour, melted butterscotch chips, granulated sugar, brown sugar, butter, egg, milk and vanilla. Beat at low speed, scraping bowl often, until well mixed, 1 to 2 minutes. Divide dough into halves. Wrap in waxed paper; refrigerate until firm, 1 to 2 hours.

Preheat oven to 375°F. Roll out dough to 1/8-inch thickness on well-floured surface. Cut out with 2 1/2-inch cookie cutters. Place 1 inch apart on ungreased cookie sheets.

Bake 5 to 8 minutes or until edges are lightly browned. Remove to wire racks to cool completely. Sprinkle with powdered sugar or decorate as desired.   *Makes about 4 dozen cookies*

CHOCOLATE KAHLÚA® BEARS

1/4 cup KAHLÚA®
2 squares (1 ounce each) unsweetened chocolate
1 2/3 cups sugar
2/3 cup shortening
2 eggs
2 teaspoons vanilla

2 cups sifted all-purpose flour
2 teaspoons baking powder
3/4 teaspoon salt
1/2 teaspoon ground cinnamon
Chocolate Icing (recipe follows)

To Kahlúa® in measuring cup, add enough water to make 1/3 cup liquid. In small saucepan over low heat, melt chocolate; cool. In large bowl, beat sugar, shortening, eggs and vanilla until light and fluffy. Stir in chocolate. In small bowl, combine flour, baking powder, salt and cinnamon. Add dry ingredients to egg mixture alternately with 1/3 cup liquid. Cover; chill until firm.

Preheat oven to 350°F. Roll out dough, one fourth at a time, to 1/4-inch thickness on well-floured surface. Cut out with bear-shaped cookie cutters. Place 2 inches apart on ungreased cookie sheets.

Bake 8 to 10 minutes. Remove to wire racks to cool completely. Spread Chocolate Icing in thin, even layer on cookies. Let stand until set; decorate as desired.   *Makes about 2 1/2 dozen cookies*

Chocolate Icing: In medium saucepan, combine 6 squares (1 ounce each) semisweet chocolate, 1/3 cup butter or margarine, 1/4 cup Kahlúa® and 1 tablespoon light corn syrup. Cook over low heat until chocolate melts, stirring to blend. Add 3/4 cup sifted powdered sugar; beat until smooth. If necessary, beat in additional Kahlúa® to make spreading consistency.

Heavenly Chocolate

Chocolate lovers, look no further! All the cookies in this chapter are chocolatey-good—some are even drizzled with or dipped into luscious chocolate!

CHOCOLATE CHERRY COOKIES

2 squares (1 ounce each)
  unsweetened chocolate
½ cup butter or margarine,
  softened
½ cup sugar
1 egg
2 cups cake flour

1 teaspoon vanilla
¼ teaspoon salt
  Maraschino cherries, well
  drained (about 48)
1 cup (6 ounces) semisweet
  or milk chocolate chips

Melt unsweetened chocolate in top of double boiler over hot, not boiling, water. Remove from heat; cool. Cream butter and sugar in large bowl until light. Add egg and melted chocolate; beat until fluffy. Stir in flour, vanilla and salt until well blended. Cover; refrigerate until firm, about 1 hour.

Preheat oven to 400°F. Lightly grease cookie sheets or line with parchment paper. Shape dough into 1-inch balls. Place 2 inches apart on prepared cookie sheets. With knuckle of finger, make a deep indentation in center of each ball. Place a cherry into each indentation.

Bake 8 minutes or just until set. Meanwhile, melt chocolate chips in small bowl over hot water. Stir until melted. Remove cookies to wire racks to cool. Drizzle melted chocolate over tops while still warm. Refrigerate until chocolate is set. *Makes about 4 dozen cookies*

*Top: Chocolate Spritz (page 45)
and Chocolate Cherry Cookies
Bottom: Triple Chocolate Pretzels (page 44)*

TRIPLE CHOCOLATE PRETZELS

*Buttery pretzel-shaped chocolate cookies are glazed
with dark chocolate, then decorated
with white chocolate for a triple chocolate treat.*

**2 squares (1 ounce each)
   unsweetened chocolate**
**½ cup butter or margarine,
   softened**
½ cup granulated sugar
1 egg
2 cups cake flour

1 teaspoon vanilla
¼ teaspoon salt
**Mocha Glaze
   (recipe follows)**
**2 ounces white chocolate,
   chopped**

Melt unsweetened chocolate in top of double boiler over hot, not boiling, water. Remove from heat; cool. Cream butter and granulated sugar in large bowl until light and fluffy. Add egg and melted chocolate; beat until fluffy. Stir in cake flour, vanilla and salt until well blended. Cover; chill until firm, about 1 hour.

Preheat oven to 400°F. Lightly grease cookie sheets or line with parchment paper. Divide dough into 4 equal parts. Divide each part into 12 pieces. To form pretzels, knead each piece briefly to soften dough. Roll into a rope about 6 inches long. Form each rope on prepared cookie sheet into a pretzel shape. Repeat with all pieces of dough, spacing cookies 2 inches apart.

Bake 7 to 9 minutes or until firm. Remove to wire racks to cool. Prepare Mocha Glaze. Dip pretzels, one at a time, into glaze to coat completely. Place on waxed paper, right side up. Let stand until glaze is set. Melt white chocolate in small bowl over hot water. Squeeze melted chocolate through pastry bag or drizzle over pretzels to decorate. Let stand until chocolate is completely set.
Makes 4 dozen cookies

MOCHA GLAZE

**1 cup (6 ounces) semisweet
   chocolate chips**
1 teaspoon light corn syrup
1 teaspoon shortening

1 cup powdered sugar
**3 to 5 tablespoons hot coffee
   or water**

Combine chocolate chips, corn syrup and shortening in small heavy saucepan. Stir over low heat until chocolate is melted. Stir in powdered sugar and enough coffee to make a smooth glaze.

CHOCOLATE SPRITZ

2 squares (1 ounce each)
   unsweetened chocolate
1 cup butter, softened
½ cup granulated sugar
1 egg

1 teaspoon vanilla
¼ teaspoon salt
2¼ cups all-purpose flour
Powdered sugar

Preheat oven to 400°F. Line cookie sheets with parchment paper or leave ungreased. Melt chocolate in top of double boiler over hot, not boiling, water. Remove from heat; cool. Cream butter, granulated sugar, egg, vanilla and salt in large bowl until light and fluffy. Blend in melted chocolate and flour until stiff. Fit cookie press with your choice of plate. Load press with dough. Press cookies out 2 inches apart onto prepared cookie sheets.

Bake 5 to 7 minutes or just until very slightly browned around edges. Remove to wire rack to cool. Dust with powdered sugar.

Makes about 5 dozen cookies

CHOCOLATE COOKIE SANDWICHES

½ cup shortening
1 cup sugar
1 egg
1 teaspoon vanilla extract
1½ cups all-purpose flour
⅓ cup HERSHEY'S Cocoa

½ teaspoon baking soda
½ teaspoon salt
¼ cup milk
Creme Filling
  (recipe follows)

Preheat oven to 375°F. In large bowl, cream shortening, sugar, egg and vanilla until light and fluffy. Combine flour, cocoa, baking soda and salt; add alternately with milk to creamed mixture until ingredients are combined. Drop by teaspoonfuls onto ungreased cookie sheets.

Bake 11 to 12 minutes or just until soft-set *(do not overbake)*. Cool 1 minute. Remove from cookie sheets; cool completely on wire rack. Prepare Creme Filling. Spread bottom of one cookie with about 1 tablespoon filling; cover with another cookie. Repeat with remaining cookies and filling. *Makes about 2 dozen sandwich cookies*

Creme Filling: In small bowl, cream 2 tablespoons softened butter or margarine and 2 tablespoons shortening; gradually beat in ½ cup marshmallow creme. Blend in ¾ teaspoon vanilla extract and ⅔ cup powdered sugar; beat to spreading consistency.

Double Mint Chocolate Cookies

DOUBLE MINT CHOCOLATE COOKIES

*These puffy chocolate cookies are topped with
a refreshing butter-mint frosting.*

COOKIES
- 2 cups granulated sugar
- 1 cup unsweetened cocoa
- 1 cup LAND O LAKES® Butter, softened
- 1 cup buttermilk or sour milk
- 1 cup water
- 2 eggs
- 2 teaspoons baking soda
- 1 teaspoon baking powder
- 1/2 teaspoon salt
- 1 teaspoon vanilla
- 4 cups all-purpose flour

FROSTING
- 4 cups powdered sugar
- 1 cup LAND O LAKES® Butter, softened
- 1 teaspoon salt
- 2 tablespoons milk
- 2 teaspoons vanilla
- 1/2 teaspoon mint extract
- 1/2 cup crushed starlight peppermint candy

Continued

46

Preheat oven to 400°F. Grease cookie sheets. For cookies, in large bowl, combine granulated sugar, cocoa, 1 cup butter, buttermilk, water, eggs, baking soda, baking powder, ½ teaspoon salt and 1 teaspoon vanilla. Beat at low speed, scraping bowl often, until well mixed, 1 to 2 minutes. Stir in flour until well mixed, 3 to 4 minutes. Drop rounded teaspoonfuls of dough 2 inches apart onto prepared cookie sheets.

Bake 7 to 9 minutes or until top of cookie springs back when touched lightly in center. Remove to wire rack to cool.

For frosting, in small bowl, combine powdered sugar, 1 cup butter, 1 teaspoon salt, milk, 2 teaspoons vanilla and mint extract. Beat at medium speed, scraping bowl often, until light and fluffy, 2 to 3 minutes. Spread ½ tablespoonful of frosting on the top of each cookie. Sprinkle with candy. *Makes about 8 dozen cookies*

BURIED CHERRY COOKIES

Chocolate Frosting
(recipe follows)
½ cup butter or margarine,
   softened
1 cup sugar
1 egg
1½ teaspoons vanilla extract
1½ cups all-purpose flour

⅓ cup HERSHEY'S Cocoa
¼ teaspoon baking powder
¼ teaspoon baking soda
¼ teaspoon salt
1 jar (10 ounces) small
   maraschino cherries
   (about 44)

Prepare Chocolate Frosting; set aside. Preheat oven to 350°F. In large bowl, cream butter, sugar, egg and vanilla until light and fluffy. Combine flour, cocoa, baking powder, baking soda and salt; gradually add to creamed mixture until well blended.

Shape dough into 1-inch balls. Place about 2 inches apart on ungreased cookie sheet. Press thumb gently in center of each cookie. Drain cherries; place one cherry in center of each cookie.

Bake 10 minutes or until edges are set; remove from cookie sheet to wire rack. Spoon scant teaspoonful frosting over cherry, spreading to cover cherry. *Makes about 3½ dozen cookies*

Chocolate Frosting: In small saucepan, combine ⅔ cup sweetened condensed milk and ½ cup HERSHEY'S Semi-Sweet Chocolate Chips. Stir constantly over low heat until chips are melted and mixture is smooth, about 5 minutes. Remove from heat; cool thoroughly.

HONEY-GINGER BOURBON BALLS

1 cup gingersnap cookie
　crumbs
1¼ cups powdered sugar,
　divided
1 cup finely chopped pecans
　or walnuts

1 square (1 ounce)
　unsweetened chocolate,
　chopped
1½ tablespoons honey
¼ cup bourbon

Combine crumbs, 1 cup of the sugar and nuts in large bowl. Combine chocolate and honey in small bowl over hot water; stir until chocolate is melted. Blend in bourbon. Stir bourbon mixture into crumb mixture until well blended. Shape into 1-inch balls. Sprinkle remaining powdered sugar over balls. Refrigerate until firm. *Makes about 4 dozen balls*

Note: These improve with aging; store in airtight container in refrigerator. They will keep several weeks, but are best after 2 to 3 days.

CHOCOLATE TASSIES

Tassies are old-fashioned cookies that resemble miniature pecan tarts. Here, the pecan filling is enriched with chocolate.

PASTRY
2 cups all-purpose flour
1 cup butter or margarine,
　cold, cut into chunks
2 packages (3 ounces each)
　cream cheese, cold, cut
　into chunks

FILLING
2 tablespoons butter or
　margarine
2 squares (1 ounce each)
　unsweetened chocolate
1½ cups packed brown sugar
2 teaspoons vanilla
2 eggs, beaten
　Dash salt
1½ cups chopped pecans

For pastry, place flour in large bowl. Cut in butter and cream cheese. Continue to mix until dough can be shaped into a ball. Wrap dough in plastic wrap; refrigerate 1 hour. Shape dough into 1-inch balls. Press each ball into ungreased miniature (1¾-inch) muffin pan cup, covering bottom and side of cup with dough.

Preheat oven to 350°F. For filling, melt butter and chocolate in medium-sized heavy saucepan over low heat. Remove from heat. Blend in sugar, vanilla, eggs and salt; beat until thick. Stir in pecans. Spoon about 1 teaspoon filling into each unbaked pastry shell. Bake 20 to 25 minutes or until lightly browned and filling is set. Cool in pans on wire racks. Remove from pans; store in airtight containers.

Makes about 5 dozen cookies

DOUBLE CHOCOLATE TREASURES

1 package (12 ounces) semi-
    sweet chocolate pieces
    (2 cups), divided
3/4 cup granulated sugar
1/2 cup margarine, softened
2 eggs
1 teaspoon vanilla

2 cups QUAKER® Oats (Quick
    or Old Fashioned,
    uncooked)
1 1/2 cups all-purpose flour
2 teaspoons baking powder
1/4 teaspoon salt (optional)
1/2 cup powdered sugar

Preheat oven to 350°F. In saucepan over low heat, melt 1 cup chocolate pieces, stirring constantly until smooth; cool slightly.* Beat sugar and margarine until light and fluffy. Blend in eggs, vanilla and melted chocolate. Combine oats, flour, baking powder and salt. Stir into chocolate mixture; mix well. Stir in remaining 1 cup chocolate pieces. Shape into 1-inch balls. Roll in powdered sugar, coating heavily. Place on ungreased cookie sheet.

Bake 10 to 12 minutes. Cool 2 minutes on cookie sheet; remove to wire rack. Cool completely. Store tightly covered.

Makes about 5 dozen cookies

*Microwave Directions: Place chocolate pieces in microwaveable bowl. Microwave at HIGH 1 to 1 1/2 minutes, stirring after 1 minute. Stir until smooth.

DOUBLE CHOCOLATE BLACK-EYED SUSANS

1 package (18.25 or 19.75
    ounces) fudge marble
    cake mix
1 egg

1/3 cup vegetable oil
4 tablespoons water, divided
1 cup HERSHEY'S MINI CHIPS
    Semi-Sweet Chocolate

Preheat oven to 350°F. Lightly grease cookie sheets. In bowl, combine cake mix, egg, oil and 3 tablespoons water; mix with spoon until thoroughly blended. Stir in Mini Chips chocolate. In separate bowl, combine 2/3 cup batter, chocolate packet from cake mix and remaining 1 tablespoon water; mix well.

Drop vanilla batter by rounded teaspoonfuls onto prepared cookie sheet; gently press down centers with thumb or back of spoon. Drop chocolate batter by rounded half teaspoonfuls onto top of each cookie.

Bake 10 to 12 minutes or until very lightly browned. Cool 1 minute. Remove to wire racks to cool completely.

Makes about 3 dozen cookies

CHOCOLATE MADELEINES

1¼ cups all-purpose flour	3 eggs
1 cup sugar	2 egg yolks
⅛ teaspoon salt	½ teaspoon vanilla extract
¾ cup butter, melted	Chocolate Frosting
⅓ cup HERSHEY'S Cocoa	(recipe follows)

Preheat oven to 350°F. Lightly grease indentations of madeleine mold pan (each shell is 3×2 inches). In medium saucepan, stir together flour, sugar and salt. Combine melted butter and cocoa; stir into dry ingredients. In small bowl, lightly beat eggs, egg yolks and vanilla with fork until well blended; stir into chocolate mixture, blending well. Cook over very low heat, stirring constantly, until mixture is warm; *do not simmer or boil.* Remove from heat. Fill each mold half full with batter (do not overfill).

Bake 8 to 10 minutes or until wooden pick inserted in center comes out clean. Invert onto wire rack; cool completely. Prepare Chocolate Frosting; frost flat sides of cookies. Press frosted sides together, forming shells.
Makes about 1½ dozen filled cookies

Chocolate Frosting: In small bowl, stir together 1¼ cups powdered sugar and 2 tablespoons HERSHEY'S Cocoa. In small bowl, beat 2 tablespoons softened butter and ¼ cup of the cocoa mixture until light and fluffy. Gradually add remaining cocoa mixture and 2 to 2½ tablespoons milk, beating to spreading consistency. Stir in ½ teaspoon vanilla extract.

TRIPLE CHOCOLATE COOKIES

1 package DUNCAN HINES® Moist Deluxe Swiss Chocolate Cake Mix	½ cup semisweet chocolate chips
½ cup butter or margarine, melted	½ cup milk chocolate chips
1 egg	½ cup coarsely chopped white chocolate
	½ cup chopped pecans

1. Preheat oven to 375°F. Combine cake mix, melted butter and egg in large bowl. Stir in all 3 chocolates and pecans.

2. Drop by rounded tablespoonfuls 2 inches apart onto ungreased cookie sheets. Bake 9 to 11 minutes. Cool 1 minute on cookie sheet. Remove to wire racks to cool completely.
Makes 3½ to 4 dozen cookies

Chocolate Madeleines

Chocolate Nut Slices

CHOCOLATE NUT SLICES

COOKIES
¾ cup BUTTER FLAVOR
   CRISCO®
½ cup granulated sugar
⅓ cup firmly packed brown
   sugar
2 tablespoons milk
1½ teaspoons vanilla
1 egg
1¼ cups all-purpose flour
⅓ cup unsweetened cocoa
   powder
½ teaspoon baking soda

½ teaspoon salt
¾ cup coarsely chopped
   pecans
½ cup semisweet chocolate
   chips

DRIZZLE
½ teaspoon BUTTER FLAVOR
   CRISCO®
½ cup white melting
   chocolate, cut into small
   pieces
Chopped Pecans (optional)

Continued

52

1. Preheat oven to 350°F. For cookie, combine Butter Flavor Crisco®, granulated sugar, brown sugar, milk and vanilla in large bowl. Beat at medium speed of electric mixer until well blended. Beat in egg.

2. Combine flour, cocoa, baking soda and salt. Mix into creamed mixture at low speed until blended. Stir in nuts and chocolate chips.

3. Divide dough into 4 equal portions. Form each into 1×8-inch roll on waxed paper. Pick up ends of waxed paper and roll dough back and forth to get a nicely shaped roll. Place 3 inches apart on ungreased baking sheet.

4. Bake 10 minutes or until set. Cool on baking sheets.

5. For drizzle, combine Butter Flavor Crisco® and white chocolate in microwave-safe cup. Microwave at 50% (MEDIUM). Stir after 1 minute. Repeat until smooth (or melt on range top in small saucepan on very low heat). Drizzle back and forth over cooled cookie. Sprinkle with nuts before chocolate hardens, if desired.

6. Cut diagonally into 1-inch slices.   *Makes about 3 dozen cookies*

BROWNIE COOKIE BITES

1½ cups (9 ounces) NESTLÉ® Toll House® semi-sweet chocolate morsels, divided
1 tablespoon butter
¼ cup all-purpose flour
¼ teaspoon baking powder
1 egg
⅓ cup sugar
½ teaspoon vanilla extract

Over hot (not boiling) water, melt ½ cup Nestlé® Toll House® semi-sweet chocolate morsels and butter, stirring until smooth.* In small bowl, combine flour and baking powder; set aside.

Preheat oven to 350°F. Grease cookie sheets. In small mixer bowl, beat egg and sugar at high speed until mixture is thick, about 3 minutes. Stir in vanilla and melted chocolate mixture. Gradually blend in flour mixture; stir in remaining 1 cup Nestlé® Toll House® semi-sweet chocolate morsels. Drop by level measuring tablespoonfuls onto prepared cookie sheets.

Bake 8 to 10 minutes until cookies are puffed and tops are cracked and moist. (Cookies will look slightly underbaked.) Let stand on cookie sheets 5 minutes; cool.   *Makes about 1½ dozen cookies*

*Or, place ½ cup Nestlé® Toll House® semi-sweet chocolate morsels and butter in microwave-safe bowl. Microwave on HIGH power 1 minute; stir. Microwave on HIGH power 30 seconds longer; stir until smooth.

Bevy of Bars

Easy-to-make bars are always a favorite. Choose from buttery shortbreads, fruit-topped bars, spice bars and fudgy brownies.

PECAN DATE BARS

CRUST
- 1/3 cup cold butter or margarine
- 1 package DUNCAN HINES® Moist Deluxe White Cake Mix
- 1 egg

TOPPING
- 1 package (8 ounces) chopped dates
- 1 1/4 cups chopped pecans
- 1 cup water
- 1/2 teaspoon vanilla extract
- Confectioners' sugar

1. Preheat oven to 350°F. Grease and flour 13×9-inch pan.

2. For crust, cut butter into cake mix with a pastry blender or 2 knives until mixture is crumbly. Add egg; stir well (mixture will be crumbly). Pat mixture into bottom of pan.

3. For topping, combine dates, pecans and water in medium saucepan. Bring to a boil. Reduce heat and simmer until mixture thickens, stirring constantly. Remove from heat. Stir in vanilla extract. Spread date mixture evenly over crust. Bake 25 to 30 minutes. Cool completely in pan on wire rack. Dust with confectioners' sugar.   *Makes 32 bars*

Tip: Pecan Date Bars are moist and store well in airtight containers. Dust with confectioners' sugar to freshen before serving.

Pecan Date Bars

Almond Toffee Triangles

ALMOND TOFFEE TRIANGLES

**Bar Cookie Crust
(see page 72)**
1/3 cup packed brown sugar
1/3 cup **KARO® Light or Dark
Corn Syrup**

1/4 cup **MAZOLA® Margarine**
1/4 cup heavy cream
1 1/2 cups sliced almonds
1 teaspoon vanilla

Preheat oven to 350°F. Prepare Bar Cookie Crust. In medium saucepan combine brown sugar, corn syrup, margarine and cream. Bring to boil over medium heat; remove from heat. Stir in almonds and vanilla. Pour over hot crust; spread evenly.

Bake 15 to 20 minutes or until set and golden. Cool completely on wire rack. Cut into 2 1/2-inch squares; cut each in half diagonally to create triangles.   *Makes 4 dozen triangles*

DELUXE TOLL HOUSE® MUD BARS

1 cup plus 2 tablespoons
  all-purpose flour
½ teaspoon baking soda
½ teaspoon salt
¾ cup firmly packed brown
  sugar
½ cup (1 stick) butter,
  softened

1 teaspoon vanilla extract
1 egg
One 12-ounce package (2 cups)
  NESTLÉ® Toll House®
  semi-sweet chocolate
  morsels, divided
½ cup chopped walnuts

Preheat oven to 375°F. Grease 9-inch square baking pan. In small bowl, combine flour, baking soda and salt; set aside. In large mixer bowl, beat brown sugar, butter and vanilla extract until creamy. Beat in egg. Gradually add flour mixture. Stir in 1⅓ cups Nestlé® Toll House® semi-sweet chocolate morsels and walnuts. Spread into prepared pan. Bake 23 to 25 minutes.

Immediately sprinkle remaining ⅔ cup Nestlé® Toll House® semi-sweet chocolate morsels over top. Let stand until morsels become shiny and soft. Spread chocolate with spatula. When cool, chill 5 to 10 minutes to set chocolate. Cut into 2×1½-inch square bars. *Makes 2 dozen bars*

PECAN CARAMEL BARS

1½ cups all-purpose flour
1½ cups packed brown sugar,
  divided
½ cup butter, softened

1 cup pecan halves
⅔ cup butter
1 cup milk chocolate pieces

Preheat oven to 350°F. In large mixer bowl, combine flour, 1 cup brown sugar and ½ cup butter. Beat 2 to 3 minutes or until mixture resembles fine crumbs. Pat mixture evenly onto bottom of ungreased 13×9-inch baking pan. Sprinkle nuts evenly over crumb mixture.

In small saucepan, combine ⅔ cup butter and remaining ½ cup brown sugar. Cook and stir over medium heat until entire surface is bubbly. Cook and stir up to 1 minute more. Pour over crust, spreading evenly.

Bake 18 to 20 minutes or until entire surface is bubbly. Remove from oven; immediately sprinkle with chocolate pieces. Let stand 2 to 3 minutes to allow chocolate to melt; use knife to swirl chocolate slightly. Cool completely on wire rack. Cut into bars. *Makes 4 dozen bars*

Favorite recipe from Wisconsin Milk Marketing Board

PEANUT BUTTER BARS

1 package DUNCAN HINES®
   Peanut Butter Cookie
   Mix
2 egg whites

½ cup chopped peanuts
1 cup confectioners' sugar
2 tablespoons water
½ teaspoon vanilla extract

1. Preheat oven to 350°F.

2. Combine cookie mix, peanut butter packet from Mix and egg whites in large bowl. Stir until thoroughly blended. Press into ungreased 13 × 9-inch pan. Sprinkle peanuts over dough. Press lightly. Bake 16 to 18 minutes or until golden brown. Cool completely in pan on wire rack. Combine confectioners' sugar, water and vanilla extract in small bowl. Stir until blended. Drizzle glaze over top. Cut into bars.   *Makes 24 bars*

ENGLISH TOFFEE BARS

2 cups all-purpose flour
1 cup packed light brown
   sugar
½ cup butter
1 cup pecan halves

Toffee Topping
   (recipe follows)
1 cup HERSHEY'S Milk
   Chocolate Chips

Preheat oven to 350°F. In large mixer bowl, combine flour, brown sugar and butter; mix until fine crumbs form. (A few large crumbs may remain.) Press into ungreased 13×9-inch baking pan. Sprinkle pecans over crust. Prepare Toffee Topping and immediately drizzle over pecans and crust.

Bake 20 to 22 minutes or until topping is bubbly and golden. Remove from oven. Immediately sprinkle milk chocolate chips over top; press gently onto surface. Cool completely in pan on wire rack. Cut into bars.   *Makes about 3 dozen bars*

Toffee Topping: In small saucepan, over medium heat, combine ⅔ cup butter and ⅓ cup packed light brown sugar. Cook, stirring constantly, until mixture comes to a boil. Continue boiling and stirring 30 seconds; use immediately.

Peanut Butter Bars

CHOCOLATE CHERRY BROWNIES

1 jar (16 ounces) maraschino
  cherries
²⁄₃ cup (1 stick plus 3
  tablespoons) margarine
1 package (6 ounces) semi-
  sweet chocolate pieces
  (1 cup), divided
1 cup sugar
1 teaspoon vanilla
2 eggs

1¼ cups all-purpose flour
¾ cup QUAKER® Oats (Quick
  or Old Fashioned,
  uncooked)
1 teaspoon baking powder
¼ teaspoon salt (optional)
½ cup chopped nuts
  (optional)
2 teaspoons vegetable
  shortening

Preheat oven to 350°F. Lightly grease 13×9-inch baking pan. Drain
cherries; reserve 12 and chop remainder. In large saucepan over low heat,
melt margarine and ½ cup chocolate pieces, stirring until smooth.
Remove from heat; cool slightly. Add sugar and vanilla. Beat in eggs, one
at a time. Add combined flour, oats, baking powder and salt. Stir in
chopped cherries and nuts. Spread into prepared pan.

Bake about 25 minutes or until brownies pull away from sides of pan.
Cool completely in pan on wire rack.

Cut reserved cherries in half; place evenly on top of brownies. In
saucepan over low heat, melt remaining ½ cup chocolate pieces and
vegetable shortening, stirring constantly until smooth.* Drizzle over
brownies; cut into about 2½-inch squares. Store tightly covered.

Makes about 2 dozen bars

*Microwave Directions: Place chocolate pieces and shortening in
microwaveable bowl. Microwave at HIGH 1 to 1½ minutes, stirring after
1 minute.

PECAN MINCE BARS

1½ cups plus 3 tablespoons
  unsifted all-purpose
  flour, divided
⅓ cup confectioners' sugar
¾ cup cold margarine or
  butter
4 eggs, beaten
1 (9-ounce) package NONE
  SUCH® Condensed
  Mincemeat, crumbled

1 cup chopped pecans
⅓ cup firmly packed light
  brown sugar
1 teaspoon grated lemon rind
½ teaspoon baking powder
  Pecan halves (optional)

Continued

Preheat oven to 350°F. Lightly grease 13×9-inch baking pan. In small mixer bowl, combine *1½ cups* flour, confectioners' sugar and margarine; mix until crumbly. Press onto bottom of prepared pan. Bake 20 minutes.

Meanwhile, in large bowl, combine remaining *3 tablespoons* flour, eggs, mincemeat, chopped pecans, brown sugar, lemon rind and baking powder; beat well. Spread evenly over baked crust. Bake 20 to 25 minutes more or until set. Cool in pan on wire rack. Garnish with pecan halves, if desired. Cut into bars. Store loosely covered at room temperature.

Makes 2 to 3 dozen bars

ORANGE PUMPKIN BARS

BARS
1½ cups all-purpose flour
  1 teaspoon baking powder
  1 teaspoon pumpkin pie spice
  ½ teaspoon baking soda
  ½ teaspoon salt
  1 cup canned solid-packed
      pumpkin (not pumpkin
      pie filling)
  ¾ cup granulated sugar
  ⅔ cup CRISCO® Oil
  2 eggs
  ¼ cup firmly packed light
      brown sugar

  2 tablespoons orange juice
  ½ cup chopped nuts
  ½ cup raisins

ICING
1½ cups powdered sugar
  2 tablespoons orange juice
  2 tablespoons butter or
      margarine, softened
  ½ teaspoon grated orange
      peel

1. Preheat oven to 350°F. Grease and flour 12×8-inch baking dish.

2. For bars, combine flour, baking powder, pumpkin pie spice, baking soda and salt in medium mixing bowl. Combine pumpkin, granulated sugar, Crisco® Oil, eggs, brown sugar and orange juice in large mixing bowl. Beat at low speed of electric mixer until blended, scraping bowl constantly. Add flour mixture. Beat at medium speed until smooth, scraping bowl frequently. Stir in nuts and raisins. Pour into prepared pan.

3. Bake about 35 minutes or until center springs back when touched lightly. Cool completely on wire rack.

4. For icing, combine powdered sugar, orange juice, butter and orange peel. Beat at medium speed of electric mixer until smooth. Spread over cooled bars.

Makes 24 bars

Almond Apricot Bars

ALMOND APRICOT BARS

²/₃ cup dried apricots
1¹/₃ cups all-purpose flour,
    divided
¹/₄ cup granulated sugar
¹/₃ cup cold butter
  1 cup sliced natural almonds,
    toasted and divided

  2 eggs
  1 cup packed brown sugar
¹/₂ teaspoon vanilla extract
¹/₄ teaspoon almond extract
¹/₄ teaspoon grated lemon peel
  1 tablespoon lemon juice
¹/₂ teaspoon baking powder

Continued

Preheat oven to 350°F. Place apricots in small saucepan; cover with water and bring to a boil. Simmer apricots 10 minutes; drain, chop and set aside. Blend 1 cup flour with granulated sugar. Cut in butter until mixture resembles cornmeal. Stir in ½ cup almonds. Pat into ungreased 9-inch square pan.

Bake 20 minutes. Beat eggs and brown sugar until sugar is dissolved. Blend in vanilla and almond extracts, lemon peel and lemon juice. Blend remaining ⅓ cup flour with baking powder. Fold into egg mixture. Stir in chopped apricots. Pour over base. Sprinkle with remaining ½ cup almonds. Return to oven; bake 25 minutes. Cool in pan on wire rack. Cut into bars. *Makes 2 dozen bars*

Favorite recipe from Almond Board of California

PUMPKIN PECAN PIE BARS

1 cup firmly packed brown sugar
½ cup margarine or butter, softened
1½ cups unsifted all-purpose flour
1 cup rolled oats
1 teaspoon baking powder
1 teaspoon salt
1 (16-ounce) can pumpkin (about 2 cups)

1 (14-ounce) can EAGLE® Brand Sweetened Condensed Milk (NOT evaporated milk)
2 eggs, beaten
2 teaspoons pumpkin pie spice
1½ teaspoons vanilla extract
1 cup chopped pecans
Confectioners' sugar (optional)

Preheat oven to 350°F. In large mixer bowl, beat sugar and margarine until fluffy; add flour, oats, baking powder and ½ *teaspoon* salt. Mix until crumbly. Reserve ½ cup crumb mixture. Press remaining crumb mixture on bottom of ungreased 15×10-inch baking pan. Bake 20 minutes.

Meanwhile, in medium bowl, combine pumpkin, sweetened condensed milk, eggs, pumpkin pie spice, vanilla and remaining ½ *teaspoon* salt. Spread over crust. In small bowl, combine reserved crumb mixture with pecans; sprinkle over pumpkin mixture. Bake 30 to 35 minutes or until set. Cool in pan on wire rack. Sprinkle with confectioners' sugar, if desired. Cut into bars. Store covered in refrigerator. *Makes 3 to 4 dozen bars*

ALMOND SHORTBREAD BARS

These tender almond bars are perfect with fruit or after dinner coffee.

2 cups all-purpose flour
1 cup sugar
1 cup LAND O LAKES® Butter, softened

1 egg, separated
¼ teaspoon almond extract
1 tablespoon water
½ cup chopped almonds

Preheat oven to 350°F. Grease 15×10×1-inch jelly-roll pan. In large mixer bowl, combine flour, sugar, butter, egg yolk and almond extract. Beat at low speed of electric mixer, scraping bowl often, until particles are fine, 2 to 3 minutes. Press on bottom of prepared pan. In small bowl, beat egg white and water until frothy; brush on dough. Sprinkle nuts over top. Bake for 15 to 20 minutes or until very lightly browned. Cool completely in pan on wire rack. Cut into bars. *Makes about 2½ dozen bars*

RICH LEMON BARS

1½ cups plus 3 tablespoons unsifted all-purpose flour
½ cup confectioners' sugar
¾ cup cold margarine or butter
4 eggs, slightly beaten

1½ cups granulated sugar
1 teaspoon baking powder
½ cup REALEMON® Lemon Juice from Concentrate
Additional confectioners' sugar

Preheat oven to 350°F. Lightly grease 13×9-inch baking pan. In medium bowl, combine *1½ cups* flour and confectioners' sugar; cut in margarine until crumbly. Press onto bottom of prepared pan. Bake 15 minutes.

Meanwhile, in large bowl, combine eggs, granulated sugar, baking powder, ReaLemon® brand and remaining *3 tablespoons* flour; mix well. Pour over baked crust; bake 20 to 25 minutes or until golden brown. Cool. Cut into bars. Sprinkle with additional confectioners' sugar. Store covered in refrigerator; serve at room temperature.

Makes 2 to 3 dozen bars

Lemon Pecan Bars: Omit 3 tablespoons flour in lemon mixture. Sprinkle ¾ cup finely chopped pecans over top of lemon mixture. Bake as directed.

Coconut Lemon Bars: Omit 3 tablespoons flour in lemon mixture. Sprinkle ¾ cup flaked coconut over top of lemon mixture. Bake as directed.

Almond Shortbread Bars

APPLESAUCE FRUITCAKE BARS

1 (14-ounce) can EAGLE®
    Brand Sweetened
    Condensed Milk
    (NOT evaporated milk)
2 eggs
¼ cup margarine or butter,
    melted
2 teaspoons vanilla extract
3 cups biscuit baking mix
1 (15-ounce) jar applesauce

1 cup chopped dates
1 (6-ounce) container green
    candied cherries,
    chopped
1 (6-ounce) container red
    candied cherries,
    chopped
1 cup chopped nuts
1 cup raisins
    Confectioners' sugar

Preheat oven to 325°F. Grease well and flour 15×10-inch baking pan. In large mixer bowl, beat sweetened condensed milk, eggs, margarine and vanilla. Stir in remaining ingredients except confectioners' sugar; mix well. Spread evenly into prepared pan.

Bake 35 to 40 minutes or until wooden pick inserted in center comes out clean. Cool in pan on wire rack. Sprinkle with confectioners' sugar. Cut into bars. Store tightly covered at room temperature.

Makes 3 to 4 dozen bars

Applesauce Fruitcake Bars

ALMOND DREAM BARS

18 graham crackers, divided
¾ cup firmly packed brown
  sugar
½ cup butter or margarine
½ cup *undiluted* CARNATION®
  Evaporated Milk

1 cup graham cracker crumbs
1 cup sliced almonds, divided
1 cup flaked coconut
½ cup chopped dried apricots
  Almond Icing
  (recipe follows)

Butter 8-inch square dish. Line bottom with 9 of the graham crackers. In medium saucepan, combine brown sugar, butter and evaporated milk. Cook over medium heat, stirring constantly, until mixture comes to a full boil. Remove from heat. Immediately stir in graham cracker crumbs, *¾ cup* almonds, coconut and apricots. Spread apricot mixture evenly over graham crackers in dish. Top with remaining 9 graham crackers. Press down firmly. Spread with Almond Icing. Sprinkle with remaining ¼ cup almonds. Chill until firm. Cut into bars.   *Makes 32 bars*

Almond Icing: In medium bowl, blend 1½ cups sifted powdered sugar with 2 tablespoons softened butter or margarine. Add 2 tablespoons *undiluted* CARNATION® Evaporated Milk and ½ teaspoon almond extract. Beat until smooth.

BANANA-DATE BARS

3 ripe, medium DOLE®
  Bananas, peeled
½ cup margarine, softened
1 cup brown sugar, packed
2 eggs
2 cups all-purpose flour
1 teaspoon baking soda

1 teaspoon ground cinnamon
½ teaspoon baking powder
½ teaspoon ground nutmeg
¼ teaspoon salt
1 cup DOLE® Chopped Dates
1 cup chopped walnuts
  Powdered sugar

Preheat oven to 350°F. Grease 13×9-inch pan. Purée 1 banana in blender or food processor, making ½ cup purée. Dice remaining 2 bananas. Cream margarine and brown sugar until light and fluffy. Beat in eggs. Beat in puréed banana. Combine dry ingredients; beat into creamed mixture until well blended. Fold in dates, nuts and diced bananas. Turn batter into prepared pan.

Bake 25 minutes. Cool in pan on wire rack. Sprinkle with powdered sugar. Cut into bars.   *Makes 2 dozen bars*

BLONDE BRICKLE BROWNIES

1⅓ cups all-purpose flour
½ teaspoon baking powder
¼ teaspoon salt
2 eggs, room temperature
½ cup granulated sugar
½ cup packed brown sugar
⅓ cup butter or margarine, melted

1 teaspoon vanilla
¼ teaspoon almond extract
1 package (6 ounces) BITS 'O BRICKLE®, divided
½ cup chopped pecans (optional)

Preheat oven to 350°F. Grease 8-inch square baking pan. Combine flour, baking powder and salt; set aside. Beat eggs well. Gradually add granulated and brown sugar; beat until thick and creamy. Add melted butter, vanilla and almond extract. Gently stir in flour mixture until moistened. Fold in ⅔ cup of the Bits 'O Brickle® and nuts. Pour into prepared pan.

Bake 30 minutes. Remove from oven and immediately sprinkle remaining Bits 'O Brickle® over top. Cool completely in pan on wire rack before cutting.   *Makes 16 generous bars*

HERSHEY'S PREMIUM DOUBLE CHOCOLATE BROWNIES

¾ cup HERSHEY'S Cocoa
½ teaspoon baking soda
⅔ cup butter or margarine, melted and divided
½ cup boiling water
2 cups sugar
2 eggs, slightly beaten
1⅓ cups all-purpose flour

1 teaspoon vanilla extract
¼ teaspoon salt
2 cups (12-ounce package) HERSHEY'S Semi-Sweet Chocolate Chips
½ cup coarsely chopped nuts (optional)

Preheat oven to 350°F. Grease 13×9-inch baking pan. In bowl, stir together cocoa and baking soda; blend in ⅓ cup melted butter. Add boiling water; stir until mixture thickens. Stir in sugar, eggs and remaining ⅓ cup melted butter; stir until smooth. Add flour, vanilla and salt; blend well. Stir in chocolate chips and nuts, if desired. Pour into prepared pan. Bake 35 to 40 minutes or until brownies begin to pull away from sides of pan. Cool completely in pan on wire rack. Cut into squares.
Makes about 3 dozen bars

Blonde Brickle Brownies

PRUNE BARS

2 cups all-purpose flour
1 cup sugar
1 teaspoon salt
½ teaspoon baking soda
¾ cup cold butter or
   margarine

1½ cups shredded or flaked
   coconut
1 cup chopped nuts (walnuts,
   pecans or almonds)
1 can SOLO® *or* BAKER®
   Prune or Date Filling

Preheat oven to 400°F. Grease 13×9-inch baking pan. Combine flour, sugar, salt and baking soda in medium bowl and stir until blended. Cut in butter until mixture resembles coarse crumbs. Add coconut and chopped nuts; stir until well mixed. Reserve 2 cups of the flour-coconut mixture. Press remaining mixture into bottom of prepared pan.

Bake 10 minutes. Remove from oven and spread prune filling over baked crust. Sprinkle reserved flour-coconut mixture over filling. Bake 15 minutes more or until top is golden brown. Cool completely in pan on wire rack. Cut into bars. *Makes 3 dozen bars*

Prune Bars

LINZER BARS

*This fancy dessert treat is filled with jam
and crisscrossed with a lattice design.*

¾ cup butter or margarine,
    softened
½ cup sugar
 1 egg
½ teaspoon grated lemon peel
½ teaspoon ground cinnamon
¼ teaspoon salt

⅛ teaspoon ground cloves
2 cups all-purpose flour
1 cup DIAMOND® Walnuts,
    finely chopped or ground
1 cup raspberry or apricot
    jam

Preheat oven to 325°F. Grease 9-inch square pan. In large bowl, cream butter, sugar, egg, lemon peel, cinnamon, salt and cloves. Blend in flour and walnuts. Set aside about ¼ of the dough for lattice top. Pat remaining dough into bottom and about ½ inch up sides of pan. Spread with jam. Make pencil-shaped strips of remaining dough, rolling against floured board with palms of hands. Arrange in lattice pattern over top, pressing ends against dough on sides.

Bake 45 minutes or until lightly browned. Cool in pan on wire rack. Cut into bars. *Makes 2 dozen small bars*

HERSHEY'S CHOCOLATE CHIP BLONDIES

¾ cup packed light brown
    sugar
 6 tablespoons butter or
    margarine, softened
1 egg
1 tablespoon milk
1 teaspoon vanilla extract
1 cup all-purpose flour

½ teaspoon baking soda
⅛ teaspoon salt
 2 cups (12-ounce package)
    HERSHEY'S Semi-Sweet
    Chocolate Chips
½ cup coarsely chopped nuts
    (optional)

Preheat oven to 350°F. Grease 9-inch square baking pan. In large mixer bowl, beat brown sugar and butter until light and fluffy. Add egg, milk and vanilla; beat well. Stir together flour, baking soda and salt; add to butter mixture. Stir in chocolate chips and nuts, if desired; spread in prepared pan. Bake 20 to 25 minutes or until lightly browned. Cool completely in pan on wire rack. Cut into bars.
Makes about 1½ dozen bars

CHOCOLATE PECAN PIE BARS

1⅓ cups all-purpose flour
½ cup plus 2 tablespoons
   packed light brown sugar,
   divided
½ cup butter or margarine
 2 eggs
½ cup light corn syrup

¼ cup HERSHEY'S Cocoa
2 tablespoons butter or
   margarine, melted
1 teaspoon vanilla extract
⅛ teaspoon salt
1 cup coarsely chopped
   pecans

Preheat oven to 350°F. In medium bowl stir together flour and
2 tablespoons brown sugar. Cut in ½ cup butter until mixture resembles
coarse crumbs; press onto bottom and about 1 inch up sides of 9-inch
square baking pan.

Bake 10 to 12 minutes or until set. With back of spoon, lightly press crust
into corners and against sides of pan.

Meanwhile, in small bowl lightly beat eggs, corn syrup, remaining ½ cup
brown sugar, cocoa, melted butter, vanilla and salt. Stir in pecans. Pour
mixture over warm crust.

Return to oven. Bake 25 minutes more or until pecan filling is set. Cool
completely in pan on wire rack. Cut into bars.   *Makes 16 bars*

BAR COOKIE CRUST

MAZOLA® No Stick Cooking
   Spray
2½ cups all-purpose flour
 1 cup cold MAZOLA®
   Margarine, cut in pieces

½ cup confectioners' sugar
¼ teaspoon salt

Preheat oven to 350°F. Spray 15×10×1-inch baking pan with cooking
spray. In large bowl with mixer at medium speed, beat flour, margarine,
sugar and salt until mixture resembles coarse crumbs; press firmly and
evenly into prepared pan.

Bake 20 minutes or until golden brown. Top with desired filling. Finish
baking according to individual recipe directions.

Chocolate-Drizzled Peanut Bars

CHOCOLATE-DRIZZLED PEANUT BARS

Bar Cookie Crust
(see page 72)
½ cup packed brown sugar
⅓ cup KARO® Light Corn
  Syrup
¼ cup MAZOLA® Margarine
¼ cup heavy cream

1 teaspoon vanilla
¼ teaspoon lemon juice
1½ cups coarsely chopped
  roasted peanuts
Chocolate Glaze
  (recipe follows)

Preheat oven to 350°F. Prepare Bar Cookie Crust. In medium saucepan combine brown sugar, corn syrup, margarine and cream. Bring to boil over medium heat; remove from heat. Stir in vanilla and lemon juice, then peanuts. Pour over hot crust; spread evenly.

Bake 15 to 20 minutes or until set. Cool completely on wire rack. Drizzle with Chocolate Glaze; cool before cutting.   *Makes about 5 dozen bars*

Chocolate Glaze: In small heavy saucepan over low heat, combine ⅔ cup semisweet chocolate chips and 1 tablespoon MAZOLA® Margarine; stir until melted and smooth.

CHOCOLATE CREAM CHEESE SUGAR COOKIE BARS

1 box (15 ounces) golden
    sugar cookie mix
1 package (8 ounces) cream
    cheese, softened
¼ cup butter or margarine,
    softened

¼ cup HERSHEY'S Cocoa
½ cup granulated sugar
1 egg
1 teaspoon vanilla extract
    Powdered sugar (optional)

Preheat oven to 350°F. Mix cookie dough according to package directions; spread in 9-inch square baking pan. In small mixer bowl, beat cream cheese and butter until light and fluffy. Stir together cocoa and granulated sugar; add to butter mixture. Add egg and vanilla; beat until smooth. Spread cream cheese mixture over cookie batter.

Bake 40 minutes or until no imprint remains when touched lightly. Cool completely in pan on wire rack. Sprinkle powdered sugar over top, if desired. Cut into bars. Cover; refrigerate. *Makes about 16 bars*

ALMOND SHORTBREAD

Rich, delicate shortbread dough is laced with crisp, toasted chips of sliced almonds to add new flavor and texture to a popular classic.

1 cup all-purpose flour
½ cup sifted powdered sugar
¼ cup cornstarch
½ cup butter, softened
¼ teaspoon vanilla extract

¼ teaspoon almond extract
½ cup BLUE DIAMOND®
    Sliced Natural Almonds,
    toasted and lightly
    crushed

Preheat oven to 350°F. In food processor, combine flour, sugar and cornstarch. With on-off bursts, add butter, vanilla and almond extracts and almonds until mixture just forms a ball. (To prepare without a food processor, combine flour, powdered sugar and cornstarch. With fingertips, work butter into flour mixture until mixture resembles coarse cornmeal. Add vanilla and almond extracts and almonds and form dough into ball.)

Pat dough into ungreased 8-inch round pie pan; smooth top. Prick top with fork. With knife, score into eight wedges. Decorate edge by indenting with tines of fork. Bake 25 minutes or until firm. Cut into wedges. *Makes 8 wedges*

Chocolate Cream Cheese Sugar Cookie Bars

MINT CHOCOLATE TRUFFLE BARS

BASE
¾ cup (1½ sticks) butter,
    softened
1½ cups all-purpose flour
½ cup sugar
    2 tablespoons NESTLÉ® cocoa

4 eggs
¼ cup sugar
2 tablespoons all-purpose
    flour
1 teaspoon vanilla extract
Confectioners' sugar

TOPPING
One 10-ounce package (1½ cups)
    NESTLÉ® Toll House® mint
    flavored semi-sweet
    chocolate morsels
½ cup (1 stick) butter

Base: Preheat oven to 350°F. In small mixer bowl, beat ingredients for base until a soft dough forms; spread dough in ungreased 13×9-inch baking pan. Bake 8 to 9 minutes or until crust is barely set.

Topping: In small saucepan over very low heat, melt Nestlé® Toll House® mint flavored semi-sweet chocolate morsels and butter, stirring constantly; remove from heat.

In small mixer bowl, beat eggs and sugar until light and fluffy, about 3 minutes. At low speed, beat in flour, vanilla extract and melted chocolate. Pour over crust.

Bake 18 minutes or *just* until toothpick inserted in center comes out clean. (Topping may puff and crack, but will flatten as it cools.) Cool in pan on wire rack. Sprinkle with confectioners' sugar. Cut into 1½-inch squares.
Makes about 4 dozen bars

CRANBERRY WALNUT BARS

Bar Cookie Crust
    (see page 72)
4 eggs
1⅓ cups KARO® Light or Dark
    Corn Syrup
1 cup sugar

3 tablespoons MAZOLA®
    Margarine, melted
2 cups coarsely chopped
    fresh or frozen
    cranberries
1 cup chopped walnuts

Preheat oven to 350°F. Prepare Bar Cookie Crust. In large bowl beat eggs, corn syrup, sugar and margarine until well blended. Stir in cranberries and walnuts. Pour over hot crust; spread evenly. Bake 25 to 30 minutes or until set. Cool completely on wire rack before cutting.
Makes 4 dozen bars

CHOCOLATE PEANUT BUTTER SQUARES

1½ cups chocolate-covered
   graham cracker crumbs
   (about 17 crackers)
3 tablespoons PARKAY®
   Margarine, melted
1 (8-ounce) package
   PHILADELPHIA BRAND®
   Cream Cheese, softened

½ cup chunk style peanut
   butter
1 cup powdered sugar
¼ cup BAKER'S® Semi-Sweet
   Real Chocolate Chips
1 teaspoon shortening

Preheat oven to 350°F.

Stir together crumbs and margarine in small bowl. Press onto bottom of 9-inch square baking pan. Bake 10 minutes. Cool.

Beat cream cheese, peanut butter and sugar in small mixing bowl at medium speed with electric mixer until well blended. Spread over crust.

Melt chocolate chips with shortening in small saucepan over low heat, stirring until smooth. Drizzle over cream cheese mixture. Chill 6 hours or overnight. Cut into squares.   *Makes about 1 dozen bars*

Microwave Tip: Microwave chocolate chips and shortening in small microwave-safe bowl on HIGH 1 to 2 minutes or until chocolate begins to melt, stirring every minute. Stir until chocolate is melted.

Chocolate Peanut Butter Squares

Fancy Cookies

These eye-catching cookies are as delectable as they look! The sensational results are worth the extra time it takes to make them.

BRANDY LACE COOKIES

Reserve these crisp, intriguing cookies for a special occasion. If time is limited, curling the cookies is optional.

¼ cup sugar
¼ cup MAZOLA® Margarine
¼ cup KARO® Light or Dark Corn Syrup
½ cup all-purpose flour
¼ cup very finely chopped pecans or walnuts

2 tablespoons brandy
Melted white and/or semisweet chocolate (optional)

Preheat oven to 350°F. Lightly grease and flour cookie sheets. In small saucepan combine sugar, margarine and corn syrup. Bring to boil over medium heat, stirring constantly. Remove from heat. Stir in flour, pecans and brandy. Drop 12 evenly spaced half teaspoonfuls of batter onto prepared cookie sheets.

Bake 6 minutes or until golden. Cool 1 to 2 minutes or until cookies can be lifted but are still warm and pliable; remove with spatula. Curl around handle of wooden spoon; slide off when crisp. If cookies harden before curling, return to oven to soften. Drizzle with melted chocolate, if desired.   *Makes 4 to 5 dozen cookies*

Top: Brandy Lace Cookies
Bottom: Kentucky Bourbon Pecan Tarts (page 85)

Top: Honey-Ginger Bourbon Balls (page 48)
Bottom: Chocolate-Frosted Lebkuchen

CHOCOLATE-FROSTED LEBKUCHEN

Lebkuchen are holiday favorites in Germany.

  4 eggs
  1 cup sugar
1½ cups all-purpose flour
  1 cup (6 ounces) pulverized almonds*
  ⅓ cup candied lemon peel, finely chopped
  ⅓ cup candied orange peel, finely chopped

1½ teaspoons ground cinnamon
  1 teaspoon grated lemon peel
  ½ teaspoon ground cardamom
  ½ teaspoon ground nutmeg
  ¼ teaspoon ground cloves
  Bittersweet Glaze (recipe follows)

Continued

In large bowl of electric mixer, combine eggs and sugar. Beat at high speed for 10 minutes. Meanwhile, in separate bowl, combine flour, almonds, candied lemon and orange peels, cinnamon, lemon peel, cardamom, nutmeg and cloves. Blend in egg mixture, stirring until evenly mixed. Cover; refrigerate 12 hours or overnight.

Preheat oven to 350°F. Grease cookie sheets and dust with flour or line with parchment paper. Drop dough by rounded teaspoonfuls 2 inches apart onto prepared cookie sheets.

Bake 8 to 10 minutes or until just barely browned. Do not overbake. Remove to wire racks. While cookies bake, prepare Bittersweet Glaze. Spread over tops of warm cookies using pastry brush. Cool until glaze is set. Store in airtight container. *Makes about 5 dozen cookies*

*To pulverize almonds, place in food processor or blender. Process until thoroughly ground with a dry, not pasty, texture.

Bittersweet Glaze: Melt 3 chopped squares (1 ounce each) bittersweet or semisweet chocolate and 1 tablespoon butter or margarine in small bowl over hot water. Stir until smooth.

WHITE BROWNIE BITES

One 8-ounce package
    (4 bars) NESTLÉ®
    semi-sweet chocolate
    baking bars, broken up
2 tablespoons butter or
    margarine
½ cup all-purpose flour
½ teaspoon baking powder

2 eggs
⅔ cup sugar
1 teaspoon vanilla extract
Two 6-ounce packages (6 bars)
    NESTLÉ® Premier White
    baking bars, coarsely
    chopped

Preheat oven to 350°F. Over hot (not boiling) water, melt Nestlé® semi-sweet chocolate baking bars and butter, stirring until smooth. In small bowl, combine flour and baking powder; set aside.

In small mixer bowl, beat eggs and sugar at high speed until mixture is thick, about 5 minutes. Stir in vanilla extract and melted chocolate mixture. Gradually blend in flour mixture. Stir in Nestlé® Toll House® Premier White baking bars. Drop by level measuring tablespoonfuls onto greased cookie sheets.

Bake 8 to 10 minutes until cookies are puffed and tops are cracked and moist. (Cookies will look slightly underbaked.) Let stand on cookie sheets 5 minutes; cool. *Makes about 3 dozen cookies*

ALMOND RICE MADELEINES

Vegetable oil cooking spray
1 cup whole blanched
    almonds, lightly toasted
1½ cups sugar
¾ cup flaked coconut
3 cups cooked rice, chilled
3 egg whites

Fresh raspberries
    (optional)
Frozen nondairy whipped
    topping, thawed
    (optional)
Powdered sugar (optional)

Preheat oven to 350°F. Coat madeleine pans* with vegetable oil cooking spray. Place almonds in food processor fitted with knife blade; process until finely ground. Add sugar and coconut to processor; process until coconut is finely minced. Add rice; pulse to blend. Add egg whites; pulse to blend. Spoon mixture evenly into madeleine pans, filling to tops.

Bake 25 to 30 minutes or until lightly browned. Cool completely in pans on wire rack. Cover and refrigerate 2 hours or until serving time. Run a sharp knife around each madeleine shell and gently remove from pan. Invert onto serving plates; serve with raspberries and whipped topping, if desired. Sprinkle with powdered sugar, if desired.

Makes about 3 dozen madeleines

*You may substitute miniature muffin pans for madeleine pans, if desired.

Favorite recipe from USA Rice Council

MINI MORSEL MERINGUE WREATHS

2 egg whites
¼ teaspoon cream of tartar
⅓ cup sugar

½ cup (¼ of 12-ounce
    package) NESTLÉ® Toll
    House® semi-sweet
    chocolate mini morsels
One 3-ounce package candied
    cherries, quartered

Preheat oven to 275°F. In small mixer bowl, beat egg whites and cream of tartar until soft peaks form. Gradually add sugar; beat until stiff peaks form. Fold in Nestlé® Toll House® semi-sweet chocolate mini morsels. Spoon into pastry bag fitted with plain #7 pastry tip. Pipe 2-inch circles onto parchment paper-lined cookie sheets. Top each wreath with two candied cherry pieces. Bake 20 minutes. Turn oven off; let stand in oven 30 minutes with door ajar. Cool; peel off paper. Store in airtight container.

Makes 2½ dozen cookies

Almond Rice Madeleines

CHOCOLATE PISTACHIO FINGERS

*Both ends of these buttery, finger-shaped cookies are dipped into
melted chocolate. Then, for an elegant finish, the chocolate ends are
covered with chopped pistachios.*

¾ cup butter or margarine,
   softened
⅓ cup sugar
3 ounces (about ⅓ cup)
   almond paste
1 egg yolk

1⅔ cups all-purpose flour
1 cup (6 ounces) semisweet
   chocolate chips
½ cup finely chopped natural
   pistachios

Preheat oven to 350°F. Line cookie sheets with parchment paper or
lightly grease and dust with flour. Cream butter and sugar in large bowl
until blended. Add almond paste and egg yolk; beat until light. Blend in
flour to make a smooth dough. (If dough is too soft to handle, cover and
refrigerate until firm.)

Turn out onto lightly floured board. Divide into 8 equal pieces; divide
each piece in half. Roll each half into a 12-inch rope; cut each rope into
2-inch lengths. Place 2 inches apart on prepared cookie sheets.

Bake 10 to 12 minutes or until edges just begin to brown. Remove to wire
racks to cool.

Melt chocolate chips in small bowl over hot water. Stir until smooth. Dip
both ends of cookies about ½ inch into melted chocolate, then dip the
chocolate ends into pistachios. Place on waxed paper; let stand until
chocolate is set.   *Makes about 8 dozen cookies*

***Chocolate Pistachio Fingers;
Chocolate-Dipped Oat Cookies (page 6)***

KENTUCKY BOURBON PECAN TARTS

These bite-size Southern favorites are ideal for a dessert buffet.
For added convenience, prepare ahead and keep frozen
for up to two weeks.

**Cream Cheese Pastry
(recipe follows)**
2 eggs
½ cup granulated sugar
**½ cup KARO® Light or Dark
Corn Syrup**
2 tablespoons bourbon

**1 tablespoon MAZOLA®
Margarine, melted**
½ teaspoon vanilla
**1 cup chopped pecans
Confectioners' sugar
(optional)**

Preheat oven to 350°F. Prepare Cream Cheese Pastry. Divide dough in half; set aside one half. On floured surface roll out pastry to ⅛-inch thickness. *If necessary, add small amount of flour to keep pastry from sticking.* Cut into 12 (2¼-inch) rounds. Press evenly into bottoms and up sides of 1¾-inch muffin pan cups. Repeat with remaining pastry. Refrigerate.

In medium bowl, slightly beat eggs. Stir in granulated sugar, corn syrup, bourbon, margarine and vanilla until well blended. Spoon 1 heaping teaspoon pecans into each pastry-lined cup; top with 1 tablespoon corn syrup mixture.

Bake 20 to 25 minutes or until lightly browned and toothpick inserted into center comes out clean. Cool in pans 5 minutes. Remove; cool completely on wire rack. If desired, sprinkle with confectioners' sugar.

Makes about 2 dozen tarts

CREAM CHEESE PASTRY

1 cup all-purpose flour
**¾ teaspoon baking powder
Pinch salt**
**½ cup MAZOLA® Margarine,
softened**

**1 package (3 ounces) cream
cheese, softened**
2 teaspoons sugar

In small bowl combine flour, baking powder and salt. In large bowl mix margarine, cream cheese and sugar until well combined. Stir in flour mixture until well blended. Press firmly into ball with hands.

DOUBLE-DIPPED HAZELNUT CRISPS

³/₄ cup semisweet chocolate
    chips
1¹/₄ cups all-purpose flour
³/₄ cup powdered sugar
²/₃ cup whole hazelnuts,
    toasted, hulled and
    pulverized*
¹/₄ teaspoon instant espresso
    coffee powder
    Dash salt

¹/₂ cup butter or margarine,
    softened
2 teaspoons vanilla
4 squares (1 ounce each)
    bittersweet or semisweet
    chocolate
4 ounces white chocolate
2 teaspoons shortening,
    divided

Preheat oven to 350°F. Lightly grease cookie sheets or line with parchment paper. Melt chocolate chips in top of double boiler over hot, not boiling, water. Remove from heat; cool. Blend flour, sugar, hazelnuts, coffee powder and salt in large bowl. Blend in butter, melted chocolate and vanilla until dough is stiff but smooth. (If dough is too soft to handle, cover and refrigerate until firm.)

Roll out dough, one fourth at a time, to ¹/₈-inch thickness on lightly floured surface. Cut out with 2-inch scalloped round cutter. Place 2 inches apart on prepared cookie sheets.

Bake 8 minutes or until not quite firm. (Cookies should not brown. They will puff up during baking and then fall again.) Remove to wire racks to cool.

Place bittersweet and white chocolates in separate small bowls. Add 1 teaspoon shortening to each bowl. Place bowls over hot water; stir until chocolates are melted and smooth. Dip cookies, one at a time, halfway into bittersweet chocolate. Place on waxed paper; refrigerate until chocolate is set. Dip other halves of cookies into white chocolate; refrigerate until set. Store cookies in airtight container in cool place. (If cookies are frozen, chocolate may discolor.)

Makes about 4 dozen cookies

*To pulverize hazelnuts, place in food processor or blender. Process until thoroughly ground with a dry, not pasty, texture.

Double-Dipped Hazelnut Crisps;
Pecan Florentines (page 88)

PECAN FLORENTINES

Florentines are lacy confections that require a bit more skill to prepare than the average drop cookie. When baked on foil as directed, they are much easier to handle.

3/4 **cup pecan halves, pulverized***

1/2 **cup all-purpose flour**

1/3 **cup packed brown sugar**

1/4 **cup light corn syrup**

1/4 **cup butter or margarine**

2 **tablespoons milk**

1/3 **cup semisweet chocolate chips**

Preheat oven to 350°F. Line cookie sheets with foil; lightly grease foil. Combine pecans and flour in small bowl. Combine brown sugar, syrup, butter and milk in medium saucepan. Stir over medium heat until mixture comes to a boil. Remove from heat; stir in flour mixture. Drop batter by teaspoonfuls about 3 inches apart onto prepared cookie sheets.

Bake 10 to 12 minutes or until lacy and golden brown. (Cookies are soft when hot, but become crisp as they cool.) Remove cookies by lifting foil from cookie sheet; set foil on flat, heat-proof surface. Cool cookies completely on foil.

Place chocolate chips in small heavy-duty plastic bag; close securely. Set bag in bowl of hot water until chips are melted, being careful not to let any water into bag. (Knead bag lightly to check that chips are completely melted.) Pat bag dry. With scissors, snip off a small corner from one side of bag. Squeeze melted chocolate over cookies to decorate. Let stand until chocolate is set. Peel cookies off foil.   *Makes about 3 dozen cookies*

*To pulverize pecans, place in food processor or blender. Process until thoroughly ground with a dry, not pasty, texture.

PINWHEEL COOKIES

1/2 **cup BUTTER FLAVOR CRISCO®**

1/3 **cup plus 1 tablespoon butter, softened and divided**

2 **egg yolks**

1/2 **teaspoon vanilla**

1 **package DUNCAN HINES® Moist Deluxe Fudge Marble Cake Mix**

1. Combine Butter Flavor Crisco®, 1/3 cup butter, egg yolks and vanilla in large bowl. Mix at low speed of electric mixer until blended. Set aside cocoa packet from cake mix. Gradually add cake mix. Blend well.

Continued

2. Divide dough in half. Add cocoa packet and remaining 1 tablespoon butter to *half* the dough. Knead until well blended and chocolate colored.

3. Roll out yellow dough between two pieces of waxed paper into 18×12×⅛-inch rectangle. Repeat for chocolate dough. Remove top pieces of waxed paper from chocolate and yellow dough. Lay yellow dough directly on top of chocolate. Remove remaining waxed paper. Roll up jelly-roll fashion, beginning at wide side. Cover and refrigerate 2 hours.

4. Preheat oven to 350°F. Grease baking sheets. Cut dough into ⅛-inch slices. Bake 9 to 11 minutes or until lightly browned. Cool 5 minutes on baking sheets. Remove to wire racks to cool completely.

Makes about 3½ dozen cookies

Tip: You can use DUNCAN HINES® Moist Deluxe White Cake Mix in place of Fudge Marble Cake Mix. Divide dough as directed, then color one portion of dough with red or green food coloring.

BISCOTTI

1 (8-ounce) package PHILADELPHIA BRAND® Cream Cheese, softened	½ teaspoon anise extract
	4 eggs
¾ cup PARKAY® Margarine, softened	3¼ cups all-purpose flour
	1 teaspoon CALUMET® Baking Powder
¾ cup sugar	⅛ teaspoon salt
1 teaspoon vanilla	½ cup sliced almonds, toasted

Preheat oven to 400°F.

Beat cream cheese, margarine, sugar, vanilla and anise extract in large mixing bowl at medium speed with electric mixer until well blended. Blend in eggs.

Gradually add combined dry ingredients; mix well. Stir in almonds.

On well-floured surface with floured hands, shape dough into three 12×1½-inch logs. Place logs, 2 inches apart, on greased and floured cookie sheet.

Bake 15 to 20 minutes or until light golden brown. (Dough will spread and flatten slightly during baking.) Cool slightly.

Diagonally cut each log into ¾-inch slices. Place on cookie sheet.

Continue baking 5 to 10 minutes or until light golden brown. Cool on wire rack.

Makes about 3 dozen cookies

CHOCO-CARAMEL DELIGHTS

⅔ cup sugar
½ cup butter or margarine,
  softened
1 egg, separated
2 tablespoons milk
1 teaspoon vanilla extract
1 cup all-purpose flour
⅓ cup HERSHEY'S Cocoa
¼ teaspoon salt

1 cup finely chopped pecans
Caramel Filling
  (recipe follows)
½ cup HERSHEY'S Semi-Sweet
  Chocolate Chips or
  Premium Semi-Sweet
  Chocolate Chunks
1 teaspoon shortening

In small mixer bowl, beat sugar, butter, egg yolk, milk and vanilla until blended. Stir together flour, cocoa and salt; blend into butter mixture. Chill dough at least 1 hour or until firm enough to handle.

Preheat oven to 350°F. Lightly grease cookie sheets. Beat egg white slightly. Shape dough into 1-inch balls. Dip each ball into egg white; roll in pecans to coat. Place 1 inch apart on prepared cookie sheet. Press thumb gently in center of each ball.

Bake 10 to 12 minutes or until set. While cookies bake, prepare Caramel Filling. Press center of each cookie again with thumb to make indentation. Immediately spoon about ½ teaspoon Caramel Filling in center of each cookie. Carefully remove to wire racks to cool completely.

In small microwave-safe bowl combine chocolate chips and shortening. Microwave at HIGH (100%) 1 minute or until softened; stir. Allow to stand several minutes to finish melting; stir until smooth. Place waxed paper under wire racks with cookies. Drizzle chocolate mixture over top of cookies. *Makes about 2 dozen cookies*

Caramel Filling: In small saucepan, combine 14 unwrapped light caramels and 3 tablespoons whipping cream. Cook over low heat, stirring frequently, until caramels are melted and mixture is smooth.

Choco-Caramel Delights

OATS 'N' PUMPKIN PINWHEELS

1½ cups sugar, divided
½ cup (1 stick) margarine, softened
2 egg whites
1½ cups all-purpose flour
1 cup QUAKER® Oats (Quick or Old Fashioned, uncooked)

¼ teaspoon baking soda
1 cup canned pumpkin
½ teaspoon pumpkin pie spice
¼ cup sesame seeds

Beat 1 cup sugar and margarine until fluffy; mix in egg whites. Stir in combined flour, oats and baking soda. On waxed paper, press into 16×12-inch rectangle. Spread combined pumpkin, remaining ½ cup sugar and spice over dough to ½ inch from edge. From narrow end, roll up dough. Sprinkle sesame seeds around roll, pressing gently. Wrap in waxed paper; freeze overnight or until firm.

Preheat oven to 400°F. Spray cookie sheet with no-stick cooking spray. Cut frozen dough into ¼-inch slices; place 1 inch apart on prepared cookie sheet.

Bake 9 to 11 minutes or until golden brown. Remove to wire rack; cool completely.   *Makes about 4 dozen cookies*

CHOCOLATE-DIPPED ALMOND CRESCENTS

One end of these crescent-shaped cookies is dipped into melted chocolate—a decorative touch that makes them look special.

1 cup butter or margarine, softened
1 cup powdered sugar
2 egg yolks

2½ cups all-purpose flour
1½ teaspoons almond extract
1 cup (6 ounces) semisweet chocolate chips

Preheat oven to 375°F. Line cookie sheets with parchment paper or leave ungreased. Cream butter, sugar and egg yolks in large bowl. Beat in flour and almond extract until well mixed. Shape dough into 1-inch balls. (If dough is too soft to handle, cover and refrigerate until firm.) Roll balls into 2-inch long ropes, tapering both ends. Curve ropes into crescent shapes. Place 2 inches apart on prepared cookie sheets.

Bake 8 to 10 minutes or until set, but not browned. Remove to wire racks to cool. Melt chocolate chips in top of double boiler over hot, not boiling, water. Dip one end of each crescent in melted chocolate. Place on waxed paper; cool until chocolate is set.   *Makes about 5 dozen cookies*

Caramel Lace Chocolate Chip Cookies

CARAMEL LACE
CHOCOLATE CHIP COOKIES

¼ cup BUTTER FLAVOR
   CRISCO®
½ cup light corn syrup
1 tablespoon brown sugar
½ teaspoon vanilla
1½ teaspoons grated orange
   peel (optional)

½ cup all-purpose flour
¼ teaspoon salt
⅓ cup semi-sweet chocolate
   chips
⅓ cup coarsely chopped
   pecans

1. Preheat oven to 375°F. Grease baking sheet with Butter Flavor Crisco®.

2. Combine Butter Flavor Crisco®, corn syrup, brown sugar, vanilla and orange peel in large bowl. Beat at medium speed of electric mixer until well blended.

3. Combine flour and salt. Mix into creamed mixture at low speed until blended. Stir in chocolate chips and nuts. Drop teaspoonfuls of dough 4 inches apart onto baking sheet.

4. Bake 5 minutes or until edges are golden brown. (Chips and nuts will remain in center while dough spreads out.) *Do not overbake.* Cool 2 minutes on baking sheet. Lift cookie edge with edge of spatula. Grasp cookie edge gently and lightly pinch or flute the edge, bringing it up to the chips and nuts in center. Work around each cookie until completely fluted. Remove to cooling rack. *Makes about 3 dozen cookies*

Acknowledgments

FAVORITE BRAND NAME RECIPES MAGAZINE would like to thank the companies and organizations listed below for the use of their recipes in this magazine.

Almond Board of California
American Egg Board
Amstar Sugar Corporation
Best Foods, a Division of CPC
  International
Blue Diamond Growers
Borden, Inc.
California Apricot Advisory Board
Carnation Company
Diamond Walnut Growers, Inc.
Dole Food Company
Florida Department of Citrus
Hershey Chocolate U.S.A.
Kahlúa Liqueur

Kraft General Foods, Inc.
Land O'Lakes, Inc.
Leaf, Inc.
Libby's, Nestlé Food Company
M&M/Mars
Nestlé Chocolate and Confection
  Company
The Procter & Gamble
  Company, Inc.
The Quaker Oats Company
Sokol and Company
Sun·Maid Growers of California
USA Rice Council
Walnut Marketing Board
Wisconsin Milk Marketing Board

Photo Credits

FAVORITE BRAND NAME RECIPES MAGAZINE would like to thank the companies and organizations listed below for the use of their photographs in this magazine.

Almond Board of California
Best Foods, a Division of CPC
  International
Borden, Inc.
California Apricot Advisory Board
Hershey Chocolate U.S.A.
Kraft General Foods, Inc.
Land O'Lakes, Inc.

Leaf, Inc.
The Procter & Gamble
  Company, Inc.
The Quaker Oats Company
Sokol and Company
USA Rice Council
Walnut Marketing Board
Wisconsin Milk Marketing Board

Index

96

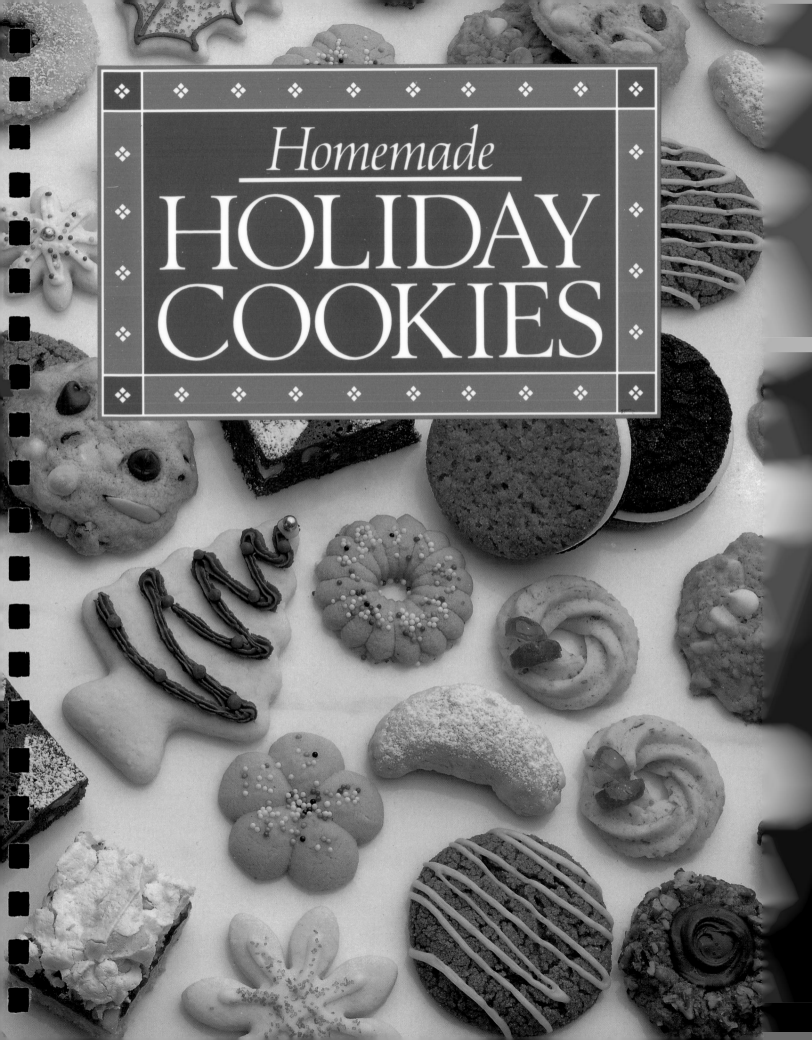

FAVORITE ALL TIME RECIPES™

Homemade
HOLIDAY COOKIES

PUBLICATIONS INTERNATIONAL, LTD.

MICROWAVE COOKING
Microwave ovens vary in wattage. The cooking times given in this publication are approximate. Use the cooking times as guidelines and check for
doneness before adding more time.

Homemade
HOLIDAY COOKIES

Homespun Holiday Favorites

Baking a batch of these delightful cookies will fill your home with holiday cheer.

GLAZED SUGAR COOKIES

COOKIES
1 package DUNCAN HINES®
   Golden Sugar Cookie Mix

1 egg

GLAZE
1 cup sifted confectioners
   sugar
1 to 2 tablespoons water or
   milk
½ teaspoon vanilla extract

Food coloring (optional)
Red and green sugar
   crystals, nonpareils or
   cinnamon candies

1. Preheat oven to 375°F.

2. **For cookies,** combine cookie mix, contents of buttery flavor packet from Mix and egg in large bowl. Stir until thoroughly blended. Roll dough to ⅛-inch thickness on lightly floured surface. Cut dough into desired shapes using floured cookie cutters. Place cookies 2 inches apart on ungreased baking sheets. Bake at 375°F for 5 to 6 minutes or until edges are light golden brown. Cool 1 minute on baking sheets. Remove to cooling racks. Cool completely.

3. **For glaze,** combine confectioners sugar, water and vanilla extract in small bowl. Beat until smooth. Tint glaze with food coloring, if desired. Brush glaze on each cookie with clean pastry brush. Sprinkle cookies with sugar crystals, nonpareils or cinnamon candies before glaze sets. Allow glaze to set before storing between layers of waxed paper in airtight container. *Makes 2½ to 3 dozen cookies*

Glazed Sugar Cookies

SUGAR COOKIE WREATHS

1 package DUNCAN HINES®
Golden Sugar Cookie Mix
1 egg

Green food coloring
Candied or maraschino
cherry pieces

1. Preheat oven to 375°F. Combine cookie mix, contents of buttery flavor packet from Mix and egg in large bowl. Stir until thoroughly blended.

2. Tint dough with green food coloring. Stir until desired color. Form into balls the size of miniature marshmallows. For each wreath, arrange 9 or 10 balls with sides touching into a ring, 2 inches apart, on ungreased baking sheets. Flatten slightly with fingers. Place small piece of candied cherry on each ball.

3. Bake at 375°F for 5 to 7 minutes or until set but not browned. Cool 1 minute on baking sheets. Remove to cooling racks. Cool completely. Store in airtight container.

Makes 2 dozen cookies

STAINED GLASS COOKIES

½ cup BLUE BONNET®
Margarine, softened
½ cup sugar
½ cup honey
1 egg
1 teaspoon vanilla extract
3 cups all-purpose flour

1 teaspoon DAVIS® Baking
Powder
½ teaspoon baking soda
½ teaspoon salt
5 rolls LIFE SAVERS® Fancy
Fruits Candy

In large bowl with electric mixer at medium speed, beat margarine, sugar, honey, egg and vanilla extract until thoroughly blended. Blend in flour, baking powder, baking soda and salt. Cover; chill at least 2 hours.

On lightly floured surface, roll out dough to ¼-inch thickness. Cut dough with cookie cutters into desired shapes. Trace smaller version of cookie shape on dough leaving a ½- to ¾-inch border of dough. Cut out and remove dough from center of cookies. Place cookie outlines on baking sheets lined with foil.

Crush each color of candy separately between two layers of waxed paper with mallet. Spoon crushed candy inside centers of cookies.

Bake at 350°F for 6 to 8 minutes or until candy is melted and cookie is lightly browned. Cool cookies completely before removing from foil.

Makes 3½ dozen cookies

Sugar Cookie Wreaths

MERRY SPRITZ COOKIES

1 foil-wrapped bar
    (2 ounces) NESTLÉ®
    Premier White®
    baking bar
¾ cup (1½ sticks) butter or
    margarine, softened
½ cup sugar
½ teaspoon salt

1 egg
2 teaspoons vanilla extract
2½ cups all-purpose flour
One 9-ounce package (1½ cups)
    NESTLÉ® Toll House®
    semi-sweet chocolate
    Rainbow™ Morsels

Preheat oven to 350°F. In small saucepan over low heat, melt Nestlé Premier White baking bar; set aside.

In large mixer bowl, beat butter, sugar and salt until creamy. Blend in egg and vanilla extract. Blend in melted baking bar. Gradually beat in flour. Place dough in cookie press fitted with desired plate. Press dough onto ungreased cookie sheets; decorate with Nestlé Toll House semi-sweet chocolate Rainbow Morsels.

Bake 7 to 9 minutes until set. Let stand 1 minute. Remove from cookie sheets; cool completely. *Makes about 6 dozen cookies*

CHOCOLATE-RASPBERRY SPRITZ

1½ foil-wrapped bars
    (3 ounces) NESTLÉ®
    unsweetened chocolate
    baking bars
¾ cup (1½ sticks) butter or
    margarine, softened
1 cup sugar
½ teaspoon salt

1 egg
½ cup raspberry preserves
1 teaspoon vanilla extract
3 cups all-purpose flour
One 9-ounce package (1½ cups)
    NESTLÉ® Toll House®
    semi-sweet chocolate
    Rainbow™ Morsels

Preheat oven to 350°F. In small saucepan over low heat, melt Nestlé unsweetened chocolate baking bars; set aside.

In large mixer bowl, beat butter, sugar and salt until creamy. Blend in egg, preserves and vanilla extract. Blend in melted chocolate. Gradually beat in flour. Place dough in cookie press fitted with desired plate. Press dough onto ungreased cookie sheets; decorate with Nestlé Toll House semi-sweet chocolate Rainbow Morsels.

Bake 8 to 10 minutes until set. Let stand 1 minute. Remove from cookie sheets; cool completely. *Makes 8 dozen cookies*

LINZER TARTS

1 cup BLUE BONNET®
    Margarine, softened
1 cup granulated sugar
2 cups all-purpose flour
1 cup PLANTERS® Slivered
    Almonds, chopped

1 teaspoon grated lemon
    peel
¼ teaspoon ground
    cinnamon
⅓ cup raspberry preserves
    Confectioner's sugar

In large bowl with electric mixer at high speed, beat margarine and granulated sugar until light and fluffy. Stir in flour, almonds, lemon peel and cinnamon until blended. Cover; chill 2 hours.

Divide dough in half. On floured surface, roll out one half of dough to ⅛-inch thickness. Using 2½-inch round cookie cutter, cut circles from dough. Reroll scraps to make additional rounds. Cut out ½-inch circles from centers of half the rounds. Repeat with remaining dough. Place on ungreased baking sheets. Bake at 325°F for 12 to 15 minutes or until lightly browned. Remove from sheets; cool on wire racks. Spread preserves on top of whole cookies. Top with cut-out cookies to make sandwiches. Dust with confectioner's sugar. *Makes 2 dozen cookies*

YULETIDE GINGER COOKIES

¾ cup firmly packed brown
    sugar
½ cup light corn syrup
½ cup (1 stick) margarine,
    softened
2 egg whites, slightly beaten
3 cups QUAKER® Oat Bran
    Hot Cereal, uncooked

¾ cup all-purpose flour
2 teaspoons ground ginger
1 teaspoon baking soda
1 teaspoon ground
    cinnamon
¼ cup red or green colored
    sugar crystals

Heat oven to 350°F. Beat brown sugar, corn syrup and margarine in large bowl until fluffy. Blend in egg whites. Gradually add combined oat bran, flour, ginger, baking soda and cinnamon; mix well. Shape into 1-inch balls; roll in colored sugar crystals to coat. Place 2 inches apart on ungreased cookie sheet. Gently press balls into 2-inch circles. Bake 11 to 13 minutes or until light golden brown. Cool 2 minutes on cookie sheet; remove to wire rack. Cool completely. Store tightly covered.

Makes about 3½ dozen cookies

Milk Chocolate Florentine Cookies

MILK CHOCOLATE FLORENTINE COOKIES

⅔ cup butter or margarine
2 cups quick oats, uncooked
1 cup sugar
⅔ cup all-purpose flour
¼ cup corn syrup
¼ cup milk

1 teaspoon vanilla extract
¼ teaspoon salt
One 11½-ounce package
   (2 cups) NESTLÉ® Toll
   House® milk chocolate
   morsels

Preheat oven to 375°F.

Melt butter in medium saucepan over low heat. Remove from heat. Stir in oats, sugar, flour, corn syrup, milk, vanilla extract and salt; mix well. Drop by measuring teaspoonfuls, about 3 inches apart, onto foil-lined cookie sheets. Spread thin with rubber spatula.

Bake 5 to 7 minutes. Cool on cookie sheets. Peel foil away from cookies.

Melt Nestlé Toll House milk chocolate morsels over hot (not boiling) water; stir until smooth. Spread chocolate on flat side of half the cookies. Top with remaining cookies.   *Makes 3½ dozen sandwich cookies*

SUGAR COOKIE ORNAMENTS

1 package DUNCAN HINES®
    Golden Sugar Cookie Mix
1 egg
1 teaspoon milk
    Assorted colored sugar
    crystals, cinnamon
    gems, nonpareils or
    decors

DUNCAN HINES® Vanilla
Layer Cake Frosting
(optional)

1. Preheat oven to 375°F.

2. Combine cookie mix, contents of buttery flavor packet from Mix, egg and milk in large bowl. Stir until thoroughly blended. Form dough into 1-inch balls. Place 3 inches apart on ungreased baking sheets. Grease and flour bottom of drinking glass. Press gently to flatten cookies to form 2-inch circles.

3. Press end of drinking straw into top of each cookie to make hole. Decorate cookies as desired or leave plain to frost.

4. Bake at 375°F for 5 to 7 minutes or until set but not browned. Press straw through holes in top of cookies again. Cool 1 minute on baking sheets. Remove to cooling racks. Cool completely. Frost plain cookies, if desired.

5. String ribbon through holes in cookies. Tie at top.

Makes 3½ to 4 dozen cookies

Tip: Frosting can be divided and tinted with a few drops of red and green food coloring. Stir until well blended. Frost patterns on ornaments or frost and sprinkle with decors.

Painted Ornaments: Combine 1 egg yolk and 1 teaspoon water. Stir well. Divide into 3 custard cups. Tint each with 1 drop of different food coloring. Sketch design on unbaked cookie with tip of knife. Use clean watercolor paint brushes to paint designs on cookies before baking. Bake and cool as directed.

PREMIER WHITE® SUGAR COOKIES

Two 6-ounce packages (6 foil-
  wrapped bars) NESTLÉ®
  Premier White® baking
  bars, divided
2¼ cups all-purpose flour
  1 teaspoon baking powder
  ¼ teaspoon salt
  ½ cup (1 stick) butter or
  margarine, softened

⅓ cup sugar
1 egg
1 teaspoon vanilla extract
One 9-ounce package (1½ cups)
  NESTLÉ® Toll House®
  semi-sweet chocolate
  Rainbow™ Morsels

Preheat oven to 350°F. In small saucepan over low heat, melt 3 foil-wrapped bars (6 ounces) Nestlé Premier White baking bars; set aside. In small bowl, combine flour, baking powder and salt; set aside.

In large mixer bowl, beat butter and sugar until creamy. Blend in egg and vanilla extract. Beat in melted baking bars. Gradually beat in flour mixture until soft dough forms. Shape dough into ball; flatten to ¾-inch thickness. Wrap in plastic wrap; refrigerate 15 minutes until firm.

On lightly floured surface, roll out dough to ⅛-inch thickness. With 2½- to 3-inch cookie cutters, cut dough into shapes. Place on ungreased cookie sheets.

Bake 8 to 10 minutes until edges are golden brown. Let stand 2 minutes. Remove from cookie sheets; cool completely.

In small saucepan over low heat, melt remaining 3 foil-wrapped bars (6 ounces) baking bars. Spread or pipe melted baking bars on cookies. Decorate with Nestlé Toll House semi-sweet chocolate Rainbow Morsels, attaching with melted baking bars.   *Makes about 3½ dozen cookies*

Christmas Tree Hanging Cookies: With skewer, make ½-inch hole near top edge of each cut out before baking.

HOLIDAY ALMOND WREATHS

¾ cup FLEISCHMANN'S®
  Margarine, softened
½ cup sugar
¼ cup EGG BEATERS®
  Cholesterol-Free 99%
  Real Egg Product, thawed

1 teaspoon almond extract
2 cups all-purpose flour
½ cup ground PLANTERS®
  Almonds
Green and red candied
  cherries (optional)

In medium bowl with electric mixer at medium speed, beat margarine and sugar until light and fluffy. Add egg product and almond extract; beat well. Stir in flour and ground almonds. Using pastry bag with ½-inch star tip, pipe dough into 1½-inch wreaths, 2 inches apart, on ungreased baking sheets. Decorate wreaths with green and red candied cherries, if desired. Bake at 400°F for 10 to 12 minutes or until golden brown. Cool on wire racks.

Makes 3 dozen cookies

SUGAR COOKIES

1 cup BUTTER FLAVOR
  CRISCO®
1 cup sugar
1 egg
1½ teaspoons vanilla

2 cups all-purpose flour
1 teaspoon baking soda
1 teaspoon cream of tartar
½ teaspoon salt

1. Cream Butter Flavor Crisco and sugar in large bowl at medium speed of electric mixer. Beat in egg and vanilla.

2. Combine flour with baking soda, cream of tartar and salt. Blend into creamed mixture. Cover and chill at least 2 hours.

3. Preheat oven to 375°F.

4. Roll out dough on floured surface to ⅛-inch thickness. Cut into desired shapes with cookie cutters. Place on ungreased baking sheets.

5. Bake at 375°F for 6 to 7 minutes. Cool on baking sheets about 1 minute. Remove to cooling racks.

Makes 5½ to 6 dozen cookies

Note: For holidays, cut dough into desired holiday shapes. Sprinkle with colored sugar crystals before baking.

SPICED BANANA COOKIE WREATHS

2 extra-ripe, medium DOLE®
   Bananas, peeled
2 cups granola
1½ cups all-purpose flour
1 cup brown sugar, packed
1 teaspoon baking powder
1 teaspoon ground
   cinnamon
½ teaspoon ground nutmeg
¼ teaspoon salt
1 egg

½ cup margarine, melted
¼ cup vegetable oil
1 cup DOLE® Raisins
⅓ cup chopped DOLE®
   Almonds
½ cup powdered sugar
1 tablespoon milk
   Candied cherries or
   colored sugar crystals
   (optional)

• Place bananas in blender. Process until puréed; use 1 cup for recipe.

• Combine granola, flour, brown sugar, baking powder, cinnamon, nutmeg and salt in large bowl. Beat in 1 cup banana, egg, margarine and oil. Stir in raisins. For each of 3 wreaths, arrange about 16 generous teaspoonfuls dough with sides touching into a ring on greased cookie sheets. Sprinkle with almonds.

• Bake in 375°F oven 15 to 18 minutes until lightly browned. Cool on baking sheets.

• Combine powdered sugar and milk in small bowl until smooth. Drizzle over cooled wreaths. Decorate with candied cherries if desired. Tie with a bow to give as a gift.   *Makes 3 wreaths (16 cookies per wreath)*

SNOW-COVERED ALMOND CRESCENTS

1 cup (2 sticks) margarine or
   butter, softened
¾ cup powdered sugar
½ teaspoon almond extract
   or 2 teaspoons vanilla
   extract
2 cups all-purpose flour

¼ teaspoon salt (optional)
1 cup QUAKER® Oats (quick
   or old fashioned,
   uncooked)
½ cup finely chopped
   almonds
   Additional powdered sugar

Heat oven to 325°F. Beat margarine, powdered sugar and almond extract until fluffy. Add flour and salt; mix until well blended. Stir in oats and almonds. Using level measuring tablespoonfuls, shape dough into crescents. Bake on ungreased cookie sheet 14 to 17 minutes or until bottoms are light golden brown. Remove to wire rack. Sift additional powdered sugar generously over warm cookies. Cool completely.

Makes about 4 dozen cookies

RICHEST SPRITZ

1¼ cups confectioners' sugar
1 cup butter, softened
2 egg yolks *or* 1 whole egg
1 teaspoon vanilla extract

½ teaspoon almond extract
   (optional)
2½ cups all-purpose flour
½ teaspoon salt
   Food color (optional)

Preheat oven to 400°F. Cream confectioners' sugar and butter in large bowl with electric mixer at medium speed. Beat in egg yolks, vanilla and almond extracts. Combine flour and salt. Add to butter mixture; mix well. Tint dough with food color, if desired. Place dough in cookie press fitted with plate. Load press with dough. Press onto ungreased cookie sheets, about 2 inches apart. Decorate as desired. Bake 6 to 8 minutes or until very slightly browned around edges. Remove to wire racks to cool.

Makes about 6½ dozen cookies

Spiced Banana Cookie Wreath

ANISE PILLOWS
PFEFFERNEUSSE

1⅔ cups all-purpose flour
1½ teaspoons DAVIS® Baking
    Powder
½ teaspoon grated lemon
    peel
¼ teaspoon salt
¼ teaspoon ground
    cinnamon
¼ teaspoon ground nutmeg
⅛ teaspoon ground cloves

⅛ teaspoon white pepper
⅓ cup BLUE BONNET®
    Margarine, softened
½ cup sugar
1 egg
½ cup milk
½ cup PLANTERS® Walnuts,
    finely chopped
½ teaspoon anise seed
    Confectioner's sugar

In small bowl, combine flour, baking powder, lemon peel, salt, spices and pepper; set aside. In large bowl, beat together margarine and sugar until creamy; beat in egg. Add flour mixture alternately with milk, beating well after each addition. Stir in walnuts and anise seed. Drop dough by teaspoonfuls, 2 inches apart, on lightly greased baking sheets.

Bake at 350°F for 15 to 17 minutes. Cool slightly on wire racks. Roll in confectioner's sugar while still warm; cool completely.

Makes 5 dozen cookies

OATMEAL-BANANA LEBKUCHEN

¾ cup margarine, softened
½ cup brown sugar, packed
¼ cup honey
1½ teaspoons ground
    cinnamon
1½ teaspoons ground ginger
1 teaspoon ground
    cardamom
½ teaspoon ground cloves
2 extra-ripe, medium DOLE®
    Bananas, peeled

2 eggs, beaten
1¾ cups all-purpose flour
½ teaspoon baking powder
½ teaspoon baking soda
½ teaspoon salt
¾ cup DOLE® Chopped
    Almonds
½ cup mixed candied fruit,
    finely chopped
2 cups quick oats, uncooked

LEMON GLAZE
¾ cup sifted powdered sugar
    Juice from 1 DOLE® Lemon
    (1 tablespoon)

1 drop almond extract

Continued

• Beat margarine, brown sugar and honey in large bowl. Beat in cinnamon, ginger, cardamom and cloves.

• Mash bananas with fork in small bowl; use 1 cup for recipe. Add 1 cup banana and eggs to margarine mixture; beat until blended.

• Combine flour, baking powder, baking soda and salt in small bowl. Stir in almonds and candied fruit. Add to margarine mixture. Stir until well blended. Stir in oats.

• Drop by heaping teaspoonfuls, 2 inches apart, onto greased cookie sheets. Bake in 400°F oven 8 minutes. Cool completely on wire racks. Spread with Lemon Glaze or dust with powdered sugar. When glaze has set, store cookies in airtight container.   *Makes 4 dozen cookies*

Lemon Glaze: Combine all ingredients until blended.

CHRISTMAS TREASURE NUGGETS

1 cup (2 sticks) margarine or butter, softened
1 cup firmly packed brown sugar
¾ cup granulated sugar
2 eggs
1 teaspoon vanilla
1¾ cups all-purpose flour
1 teaspoon baking soda
½ teaspoon baking powder
½ teaspoon salt (optional)
2 cups QUAKER® Oats (quick or old fashioned, uncooked)
2 cups QUAKER® 100% Natural Cereal, any flavor
Whole blanched almonds

Heat oven to 375°F. Beat margarine and sugars in large bowl until fluffy. Blend in eggs and vanilla. Combine flour, baking soda, baking powder and salt; add to margarine mixture and mix well. Stir in oats and cereal.

Drop by rounded teaspoonfuls, 2 inches apart, onto ungreased cookie sheet. Press 1 almond onto each cookie. Bake 8 to 10 minutes or until golden brown. Cool 2 minutes on cookie sheet; remove to wire rack. Cool completely. Store tightly covered.   *Makes 6 dozen cookies*

PEANUT BUTTER REINDEER

COOKIES

1 package DUNCAN HINES®
Peanut Butter
Cookie Mix

1 egg
2 teaspoons all-purpose
flour

ASSORTED DECORATIONS

Miniature semi-sweet
chocolate chips
Vanilla milk chips

Candy-coated semi-sweet
chocolate chips
Colored sprinkles

1. **For cookies,** combine cookie mix, contents of peanut butter packet from Mix and egg in large bowl. Stir until thoroughly blended. Form dough into ball. Place flour in jumbo (15×13-inch) resealable plastic bag. Place ball of dough in bag. Shake to coat with flour. Place dough in center of bag (do not seal). Roll dough with rolling pin out to edges of bag. Slide bag onto baking sheet. Chill in refrigerator at least 1 hour.

2. Preheat oven to 375°F. Use scissors to cut bag down center and across ends. Turn plastic back to uncover dough. Dip reindeer cookie cutter in flour. Cut dough with reindeer cookie cutter. Dip cookie cutter in flour after each cut. Transfer cut-out cookies to ungreased baking sheets using floured pancake turner. Decorate each reindeer as desired. Bake at 375°F for 5 to 7 minutes or until set but not browned. Cool 2 minutes on baking sheets. Remove to cooling racks. Cool completely. Store between layers of waxed paper in airtight container. *Makes about 2 dozen cookies*

Tip: Reroll dough by folding plastic back over dough.

SANTA'S THUMBPRINTS

1 cup (2 sticks) margarine,
softened
½ cup firmly packed brown
sugar
1 whole egg or egg white
1 teaspoon vanilla

1½ cups QUAKER® Oats (quick
or old fashioned,
uncooked)
1½ cups all-purpose flour
1 cup finely chopped nuts
⅓ cup jelly or preserves

Heat oven to 350°F. Beat margarine and sugar in large bowl until fluffy. Blend in egg and vanilla. Add combined oats and flour; mix well. Shape into 1-inch balls; roll in chopped nuts. Place 2 inches apart on ungreased cookie sheet. Make indentation in center of each ball with thumb. Fill each thumbprint with about ¼ teaspoon jelly. Bake 12 to 15 minutes or until light golden brown. Cool completely on wire rack. Store loosely covered. *Makes about 3 dozen cookies*

Peanut Butter Reindeer

Chips 'n' Chocolate

Chocolate in every flavor and form is evident in this chapter—white, dark and milk chocolate in chips, glazes, fillings and more!

CHOCOLATE CHIPS THUMBPRINT COOKIES

1 cup HERSHEY'S Semi-Sweet
   Chocolate Chips, divided
¼ cup butter or margarine,
   softened
¼ cup shortening
½ cup sugar

1 egg, separated
½ teaspoon vanilla extract
1 cup all-purpose flour
¼ teaspoon salt
1 cup finely chopped nuts

Heat oven to 350°F. In small microwave-safe bowl, place ¼ cup chocolate chips. Microwave at HIGH (100%) 20 to 30 seconds or just until chocolate is melted and smooth when stirred; set aside to cool slightly. In large mixer bowl, combine butter, shortening, sugar, reserved melted chocolate, egg yolk and vanilla; blend well. Stir in flour and salt.
Roll dough into 1-inch balls. With fork, slightly beat egg white. Dip each ball into egg white; roll in chopped nuts. Place balls on ungreased cookie sheet, about 1 inch apart. Press center of each ball with thumb to make indentation. Bake 10 to 12 minutes or until set. Remove from oven; immediately place several of remaining ¾ cup chocolate chips in center of each cookie. Carefully remove from cookie sheet to wire rack. After several minutes, swirl melted chocolate in each thumbprint. Cool completely. *Makes about 2½ dozen cookies*

Chocolate Chips Thumbprint Cookies

White Chocolate Biggies and Peanut Butter Jumbos

WHITE CHOCOLATE BIGGIES

1½ cups butter or margarine,
    softened
1 cup granulated sugar
¾ cup packed light brown
    sugar
2 teaspoons vanilla
2 eggs
2½ cups all-purpose flour

⅔ cup unsweetened cocoa
1 teaspoon baking soda
½ teaspoon salt
1 package (10 ounces) large,
    white chocolate chips
¾ cup pecan halves, coarsely
    chopped
½ cup golden raisins

Preheat oven to 350°F. Lightly grease cookie sheets or line with
parchment paper. Beat butter, sugars, vanilla and eggs in large bowl until
light and fluffy. Combine flour, cocoa, baking soda and salt in medium
bowl; blend into creamed mixture until smooth. Stir in white chocolate
chips, pecans and raisins. Scoop out about ⅓ cup dough for each cookie.
Place on prepared cookie sheets, about 4 inches apart. Flatten each
cookie slightly. Bake 12 to 14 minutes or until firm in center. Cool 5
minutes on cookie sheets; remove to wire racks to cool completely.

Makes about 2 dozen large cookies

PEANUT BUTTER JUMBOS

1½ cups peanut butter
½ cup butter or margarine, softened
1 cup packed brown sugar
1 cup granulated sugar
3 eggs
2 tablespoons baking soda

1 teaspoon vanilla
4½ cups rolled oats, uncooked
1 cup (6 ounces) semisweet chocolate chips
1 cup candy-coated chocolate pieces

Preheat oven to 350°F. Lightly grease cookie sheets or line with parchment paper. Beat peanut butter, butter, sugars and eggs in large bowl until light and fluffy. Blend in baking soda, vanilla and oats until well mixed. Stir in chocolate chips and candy pieces. Scoop out about ⅓ cup dough for each cookie. Place on prepared cookie sheets, about 4 inches apart. Flatten each cookie slightly. Bake 15 to 20 minutes or until firm in center. Remove to wire racks to cool completely.

Makes about 1½ dozen large cookies

ALMOND DOUBLE CHIP COOKIES

¾ cup butter or margarine, softened
¾ cup packed light brown sugar
1 egg
½ teaspoon almond extract
1½ cups all-purpose flour
¼ teaspoon baking soda

Dash salt
1 cup (6 ounces) semisweet chocolate chips
1 cup (6 ounces) vanilla milk chips
½ cup slivered blanched almonds

Preheat oven to 375°F. Line cookie sheets with parchment paper or leave ungreased. Beat butter and brown sugar in large bowl until creamy. Beat in egg and almond extract. Combine flour, baking soda and salt in small bowl. Blend into butter mixture. Stir in semisweet and vanilla milk chips and almonds. Drop dough by rounded tablespoonfuls, 3 inches apart, onto prepared cookie sheets. Bake 8 to 10 minutes or until light brown. *Do not overbake.* Cool 2 minutes on cookie sheets; remove to wire racks to cool completely.

Makes about 3 dozen cookies

ORIGINAL TOLL HOUSE® CHOCOLATE CHIP COOKIES

2¼ cups all-purpose flour
1 teaspoon baking soda
1 teaspoon salt
1 cup (2 sticks) butter, softened
¾ cup granulated sugar
¾ cup firmly packed brown sugar

2 eggs
1 teaspoon vanilla extract
One 12-ounce package (2 cups) NESTLÉ® Toll House® semi-sweet chocolate morsels
1 cup nuts, chopped

Preheat oven to 375°F. In small bowl, combine flour, baking soda and salt; set aside.

In large mixer bowl, beat butter, granulated sugar and brown sugar until creamy. Add eggs, 1 at a time, beating well after each addition. Blend in vanilla extract. Gradually beat in flour mixture. Stir in Nestlé Toll House semi-sweet chocolate morsels and nuts. Drop by rounded measuring tablespoonfuls onto ungreased cookie sheets.

Bake 9 to 11 minutes until edges are golden brown. Let stand 2 minutes. Remove from cookie sheets; cool completely.

Makes about 5 dozen cookies

Toll House Pan Cookies: Preheat oven to 375°F. Prepare dough as directed; spread in greased 15½ × 10½-inch baking pan. Bake 20 to 25 minutes until golden brown. Cool completely. Cut into 2-inch squares. Makes about 3 dozen cookies.

Refrigerator Toll House Cookies: Prepare dough as directed. Divide dough in half; wrap halves separately in waxed paper. Refrigerate 1 hour or until firm. On waxed paper, shape each dough half into 15-inch log; wrap in waxed paper. Refrigerate 30 minutes.*

Preheat oven to 375°F. Cut each log into 30 (½-inch) slices. Place on ungreased cookie sheets. Bake 8 to 10 minutes until edges are golden brown. Makes 5 dozen cookies.

*Dough may be stored up to 1 week in refrigerator or up to 8 weeks in freezer, if foil- or freezer-wrapped.

Original Toll House® Chocolate Chip Cookies

CHOCOLATE CHIP LOLLIPOPS

1 package DUNCAN HINES® Chocolate Chip Cookie Mix	2 teaspoons water
	24 flat ice cream sticks
	Assorted decors
1 egg	

1. Preheat oven to 375°F.

2. Combine cookie mix, buttery flavor packet from Mix, egg and water in large bowl. Stir until thoroughly blended. Shape dough into 24 (1-inch) balls. Place balls 3 inches apart on ungreased baking sheets. Push ice cream stick into center of each ball. Flatten each ball with hand to form round lollipop. Decorate by pressing decors onto dough.

3. Bake at 375°F for 8 to 9 minutes or until light golden brown. Cool 1 minute on baking sheets. Remove to cooling racks. Cool completely. Store in airtight container.   *Makes 2 dozen cookies*

Tip: For best results, use shiny baking sheets for baking cookies. Dark baking sheets cause cookie bottoms to become too brown.

MINT CHOCOLATE CHEWS

½ cup BLUE BONNET® Margarine	1 teaspoon vanilla extract
1 cup sugar	1¾ cups all-purpose flour
2 (1-ounce) squares unsweetened chocolate, melted	½ teaspoon baking soda
	¼ teaspoon salt
	3 (.35-ounce) packages Pep-O-Mint LIFE SAVERS® Holes
1 egg	
⅓ cup buttermilk	½ cup walnuts, chopped

In large bowl with mixer at medium speed, beat margarine, sugar, melted chocolate and egg until creamy. Stir in buttermilk and vanilla until smooth. Mix in flour, baking soda and salt until blended; stir in holes and walnuts. Cover and chill dough at least 1 hour.

Drop dough by level tablespoonfuls, 2 inches apart, onto ungreased baking sheets. Bake at 400°F for 8 to 10 minutes or until set. Remove from sheets; cool on wire racks.   *Makes 3 dozen cookies*

Chocolate Chip Lollipops

CHOCOLATE MINT PINWHEELS

One 10-ounce package
(1½ cups) NESTLÉ® Toll
House® mint flavored
semi-sweet chocolate
morsels, divided
¾ cup (1½ sticks) butter,
softened

⅓ cup sugar
½ teaspoon salt
1 egg
1 teaspoon vanilla extract
2¼ cups all-purpose flour

Over hot (not boiling) water, melt ½ cup Nestlé Toll House mint flavored semi-sweet chocolate morsels, stirring until smooth. Cool to room temperature; set aside.

In large mixer bowl, beat butter, sugar and salt until creamy. Beat in egg and vanilla extract.* Gradually add flour.

Place 1 cup dough in medium bowl; blend in reserved melted morsels. Shape each dough into a ball; flatten and cover with plastic wrap. Refrigerate until firm, about 1½ hours.

Preheat oven to 375°F. Between sheets of waxed paper, roll each ball of dough into a 13×9-inch rectangle. Remove top layers of waxed paper. Invert chocolate dough onto plain dough. Peel off remaining waxed paper. Starting with a long side, roll up, jelly-roll style. Cut into ¼-inch slices; place on ungreased cookie sheets.

Bake 7 to 10 minutes. Let stand on cookie sheets 2 minutes. Remove from cookie sheets; cool completely.

Over hot (not boiling) water, melt remaining 1 cup mint flavored semi-sweet chocolate morsels, stirring until smooth. Spread flat side of each cookie with slightly rounded ½ teaspoonful melted chocolate. Refrigerate 10 minutes to set chocolate.   *Makes 3½ dozen cookies*

*Mixture may look curdled.

Clockwise from top right: Chocolate Mint Pinwheels; Chocolate Raspberry Linzer Cookies (page 30); New Wave Chocolate Spritz Cookies (page 30)

CHOCOLATE RASPBERRY LINZER COOKIES

2⅓ cups all-purpose flour
1 teaspoon baking powder
½ teaspoon cinnamon
½ teaspoon salt
1 cup sugar
¾ cup (1½ sticks) butter, softened
2 eggs

½ teaspoon almond extract
One 12-ounce package (2 cups) NESTLÉ® Toll House® semi-sweet chocolate morsels
6 tablespoons raspberry jam or preserves
Confectioners' sugar

In small bowl, combine flour, baking powder, cinnamon and salt; set aside. In large mixer bowl, beat sugar and butter until creamy. Beat in eggs and almond extract. Gradually add flour mixture. Divide dough in half. Wrap in plastic wrap; refrigerate until firm.

Preheat oven to 350°F. On lightly floured board, roll out half of dough to ⅛-inch thickness. Cut with 2½-inch round cookie cutter. Repeat with remaining dough. Cut 1-inch-round centers from half of unbaked cookies. Place on ungreased cookie sheets. Reroll dough trimmings, if necessary.

Bake 8 to 10 minutes just until set. Let stand on cookie sheets 2 minutes. Remove from cookie sheets; cool completely.

Over hot (not boiling) water, melt Nestlé Toll House semi-sweet chocolate morsels, stirring until smooth. Spread 1 measuring teaspoonful melted chocolate on flat side of each whole cookie. Top with ½ measuring teaspoon raspberry jam. Sprinkle confectioners' sugar on cookies with center holes; place flat side down on top of chocolate-jam cookies to form cookie sandwiches.

Makes about 3 dozen sandwich cookies

NEW WAVE CHOCOLATE SPRITZ COOKIES

One 6-ounce package (1 cup) NESTLÉ® Toll House® semi-sweet chocolate morsels
1 cup (2 sticks) butter, softened

⅔ cup sugar
1 teaspoon vanilla extract
2 eggs
2½ cups all-purpose flour
One 4-ounce jar cinnamon candies

Continued

Over hot (not boiling) water, melt Nestlé Toll House semi-sweet chocolate morsels, stirring until smooth; set aside.

In large mixer bowl, beat butter, sugar and vanilla extract until creamy. Beat in eggs. Stir in melted morsels. Gradually beat in flour. Cover dough; refrigerate 30 to 45 minutes.

Preheat oven to 400°F. Place dough in cookie press fitted with star plate. Press dough into 2-inch circles on ungreased cookie sheets; decorate with cinnamon candies.

Bake 5 minutes or just until set. Let stand on cookie sheets 2 minutes. Remove from cookie sheets; cool completely.

Makes about 7½ dozen cookies

CHOCOLATE MINT SNOW-TOP COOKIES

1½ cups all-purpose flour
1½ teaspoons baking powder
¼ teaspoon salt
One 10-ounce package (1½ cups) NESTLÉ® Toll House® mint flavored semi-sweet chocolate morsels, divided

6 tablespoons (¾ stick) butter, softened
1 cup granulated sugar
1½ teaspoons vanilla extract
2 eggs
Confectioners' sugar

In small bowl, combine flour, baking powder and salt; set aside. Over hot (not boiling) water, melt 1 cup Nestlé Toll House mint flavored semi-sweet chocolate morsels, stirring until smooth; set aside.

In large mixer bowl, beat butter and granulated sugar until creamy. Add melted mint flavored semi-sweet chocolate morsels and vanilla extract. Beat in eggs. Gradually beat in flour mixture. Stir in remaining ½ cup mint flavored semi-sweet chocolate morsels. Wrap dough in plastic wrap and freeze until firm, about 20 minutes.

Preheat oven to 350°F. Shape dough into 1-inch balls; coat with confectioners' sugar. Place on ungreased cookie sheets.

Bake 10 to 12 minutes until tops appear cracked. Let stand on cookie sheets 5 minutes. Remove from cookie sheets; cool completely.

Makes about 3 dozen cookies

CHOCOLATE SUGAR COOKIES

3 squares BAKER'S®
  Unsweetened Chocolate
1 cup (2 sticks) margarine or
  butter
1 cup sugar
1 egg

1 teaspoon vanilla
2 cups all-purpose flour
1 teaspoon baking soda
¼ teaspoon salt
  Additional sugar

Microwave chocolate and margarine in large microwavable bowl on HIGH 2 minutes or until margarine is melted. Stir until chocolate is completely melted.

Stir 1 cup sugar into melted chocolate mixture until well blended. Stir in egg and vanilla until completely blended. Mix in flour, baking soda and salt. Refrigerate 30 minutes.

Heat oven to 375°F. Shape dough into 1-inch balls; roll in additional sugar. Place, 2 inches apart, on ungreased cookie sheets. (If flatter, crisper cookies are desired, flatten balls with bottom of drinking glass.)

Bake 8 to 10 minutes or until set. Remove from cookie sheets to cool on wire racks. *Makes about 3½ dozen cookies*

Prep time: 15 minutes
Chill time: 30 minutes
Baking time: 8 to 10 minutes

Jam-Filled Chocolate Sugar Cookies: Prepare Chocolate Sugar Cookie dough as directed. Roll in finely chopped nuts in place of sugar. Make indentation in each ball; fill center with your favorite jam. Bake as directed.

Chocolate-Caramel Sugar Cookies: Prepare Chocolate Sugar Cookie dough as directed. Roll in finely chopped nuts in place of sugar. Make indentation in each ball; bake as directed. Microwave 1 package (14 ounces) KRAFT Caramels with 2 tablespoons milk in microwavable bowl on HIGH 3 minutes or until melted, stirring after 2 minutes. Fill centers of cookies with caramel mixture. Drizzle with melted BAKER'S Semi-Sweet Chocolate.

Top to bottom: Chocolate Sugar Cookies; Jam-Filled Chocolate Sugar Cookies; Chocolate-Caramel Sugar Cookies

CHOCOLATE MELTING MOMENTS

1 cup butter or margarine,
   softened
$\frac{1}{3}$ cup confectioners sugar
$\frac{1}{4}$ cup unsweetened cocoa

$1\frac{1}{2}$ cups cake flour
Mocha Filling (recipe
   follows)

Preheat oven to 350°F. Lightly grease cookie sheets or line with
parchment paper. Beat 1 cup butter, confectioners sugar and cocoa in
large bowl until fluffy. Blend in cake flour until smooth. Shape dough
into marble-size balls. (If dough is too soft to handle, cover and
refrigerate until firm.) Place 2 inches apart on prepared cookie sheets.
Press center of each ball with knuckle of finger to make indentation.
Bake 10 to 12 minutes or until set. Remove to wire racks. Prepare Mocha
Filling. While cookies are still warm, spoon about $\frac{1}{2}$ teaspoonful filling
into center of each. *Makes about 5 dozen cookies*

MOCHA FILLING

1 tablespoon butter or
   margarine
1 square (1 ounce)
   unsweetened chocolate

1 cup confectioners sugar
1 teaspoon vanilla
1 to 2 tablespoons hot coffee
   or water

Melt 1 tablespoon butter and chocolate in small heavy saucepan over low
heat; stir until melted. Blend in confectioners sugar, vanilla and enough
coffee to make a smooth filling.

ALL-AMERICAN CHOCOLATE CHIP COOKIES

$\frac{2}{3}$ cup butter or margarine,
   softened
$\frac{1}{3}$ cup shortening
1 cup packed brown sugar
$\frac{1}{2}$ cup granulated sugar
1 egg
1 teaspoon vanilla

2 cups all-purpose flour
1 teaspoon baking soda
1 teaspoon salt
1 package (12 ounces)
   semisweet chocolate
   chips
1 cup chopped walnuts

In large bowl, cream butter, shortening and sugars. Beat in egg and
vanilla. Combine flour, baking soda and salt; stir into butter mixture,
mixing well. Stir in chocolate chips and nuts. Drop by teaspoonfuls, 2
inches apart, onto greased baking sheets. Bake in 350°F oven 8 to 10
minutes, just until edges are golden (centers will still be soft). Remove to
wire racks to cool. *Makes about 3 dozen cookies*

Favorite recipe from Walnut Marketing Board

CHOCOLATE MINT SUGAR COOKIE DROPS

2½ cups all-purpose flour
1¼ teaspoons baking powder
¾ teaspoon salt
1 cup granulated sugar
¾ cup vegetable oil
2 eggs
1 teaspoon vanilla extract

One 10-ounce package
(1½ cups) NESTLÉ® Toll
House® mint flavored
semi-sweet chocolate
morsels
Assorted colored sugars or
additional granulated
sugar

Preheat oven to 350°F. In small bowl, combine flour, baking powder and salt; set aside.

In large mixer bowl, combine granulated sugar and oil. Add eggs, 1 at a time, beating well after each addition. Blend in vanilla extract. Gradually beat in flour mixture. Stir in Nestlé Toll House mint flavored semi-sweet chocolate morsels. Shape rounded measuring teaspoonfuls of dough into balls; roll in colored sugar. Place on ungreased cookie sheets.

Bake 8 to 10 minutes until set. Let stand on cookie sheets 2 minutes. Remove from cookie sheets; cool completely.

Makes about 5½ dozen cookies

Chocolate Mint Sugar Cookie Drops

CHOCOLATE LACE CORNUCOPIAS

½ cup firmly packed brown
   sugar
½ cup corn syrup
¼ cup (½ stick) margarine or
   butter
4 squares BAKER'S® Semi-
   Sweet Chocolate

1 cup all-purpose flour
1 cup finely chopped nuts
   Whipped cream or COOL
   WHIP® Whipped
   Topping, thawed

Heat oven to 350°F. Microwave sugar, corn syrup and margarine in large microwavable bowl on HIGH 2 minutes or until boiling. Stir in chocolate until completely melted. Gradually stir in flour and nuts until well blended. Drop by level tablespoonfuls, 4 inches apart, onto foil-lined cookie sheets.

Bake 10 minutes. Lift foil and cookies onto wire racks. Cool 3 to 4 minutes or until cookies can be easily peeled off foil. Remove foil; finish cooling cookies on wire racks that have been covered with paper towels.

Place several cookies, lacy side down, on foil-lined cookie sheet. Heat at 350°F for 2 to 3 minutes or until slightly softened. Remove from foil, 1 at a time, and roll, lacy side out, to form cones. Cool completely. Just before serving, fill with whipped cream.   *Makes about 30 cornucopias*

Prep time: 20 minutes
Baking time: 12 to 13 minutes

Saucepan preparation: Mix sugar, corn syrup and margarine in 2-quart saucepan. Bring to boil over medium heat, stirring constantly. Remove from heat; stir in chocolate until completely melted. Continue as directed.

Chocolate Lace Cornucopias

Peanut Butter and Chocolate Cookie Sandwich Cookies

PEANUT BUTTER AND CHOCOLATE COOKIE SANDWICH COOKIES

½ cup REESE'S Peanut Butter Chips
3 tablespoons plus ½ cup butter or margarine, softened and divided
1¼ cups sugar, divided
¼ cup light corn syrup
1 egg
1 teaspoon vanilla extract
2 cups plus 2 tablespoons all-purpose flour, divided

2 teaspoons baking soda
¼ teaspoon salt
½ cup HERSHEY'S Cocoa
5 tablespoons butter or margarine, melted
Additional sugar
About 2 dozen large marshmallows

Continued

Heat oven to 350°F. In small saucepan over very low heat, melt peanut butter chips and 3 tablespoons softened butter. Remove from heat; cool slightly. In large mixer bowl, beat remaining ½ cup softened butter and 1 cup sugar until light and fluffy. Add corn syrup, egg and vanilla; blend thoroughly. Combine 2 cups flour, baking soda and salt; add to butter mixture, blending well. Remove 1¼ cups batter and place in small bowl; with wooden spoon, stir in remaining 2 tablespoons flour and peanut butter chip mixture. Blend cocoa, remaining ¼ cup sugar and melted butter into remaining batter. Refrigerate both batters 5 to 10 minutes or until firm enough to handle.

Roll both doughs into 1-inch balls; roll in additional sugar. Place on ungreased cookie sheet. Bake 10 to 11 minutes or until set. Cool slightly; remove from cookie sheet to wire rack. Cool completely. Place 1 marshmallow on flat side of 1 chocolate cookie. Microwave at MEDIUM (50%) 10 seconds or until marshmallow is softened; place a peanut butter cookie over marshmallow, pressing down slightly. Repeat with remaining marshmallows and cookies. Serve immediately.

Makes about 2 dozen sandwich cookies

NUTTY CHOCOLATE STARS

¾ cup (1½ sticks) margarine
    or butter, softened
¾ cup firmly packed brown
    sugar
1 egg
1 teaspoon vanilla
3 cups QUAKER® Oats (quick
    or old fashioned,
    uncooked)

1 cup all-purpose flour
½ teaspoon baking soda
⅔ cup finely chopped nuts
One 6- to 7-ounce package milk
    chocolate candy stars or
    kisses

Heat oven to 350°F. Lightly grease cookie sheet. Beat margarine and sugar until fluffy. Blend in egg and vanilla. Add combined oats, flour and baking soda; mix well. Shape into 1-inch balls; roll in nuts. Place on prepared cookie sheet. Bake 10 to 12 minutes or until light golden brown. Remove from oven; gently press chocolate candy into center of each cookie. Cool 2 minutes on cookie sheet; remove to wire rack. Cool completely. Store tightly covered.

Makes 3½ dozen cookies

Notes:
Dough may be covered and stored in the refrigerator for up to two days.

Candied cherries may be substituted for chocolate candy, if desired.

From the Cookie Jar

It won't be easy to keep the cookie jar full with these fabulous favorites.

PEANUT BUTTER SPRITZ SANDWICHES

1 package DUNCAN HINES®
   Peanut Butter
   Cookie Mix

1 egg
3 bars (1.55 ounces each)
   milk chocolate

1. Preheat oven to 375°F.

2. Combine cookie mix, contents of peanut butter packet from Mix and egg in large bowl. Stir until thoroughly blended. Fill cookie press with dough. Press desired shapes 2 inches apart onto ungreased baking sheets. Bake at 375°F for 7 to 9 minutes or until set but not browned. Cool 1 minute on baking sheets.

3. Cut each milk chocolate bar into 12 sections by following division marks on bars.

4. To assemble, carefully remove one cookie from baking sheet. Place one milk chocolate section on bottom of warm cookie; top with second cookie. Press together to make sandwich. Repeat with remaining cookies. Place sandwich cookies on cooling racks until chocolate is set. Store in airtight container.   *Makes 2½ to 3 dozen sandwich cookies*

Tip: For best appearance, use cookie press plates that give solid shapes.

Peanut Butter Spritz Sandwiches

Pineapple-Raisin Jumbles

PINEAPPLE-RAISIN JUMBLES

2 cans (8 ounces each)
   DOLE® Crushed
   Pineapple in Juice
½ cup margarine, softened
½ cup sugar
1 teaspoon vanilla extract
1 cup all-purpose flour

4 teaspoons grated DOLE®
   Orange peel
1 cup DOLE® Blanched
   Slivered Almonds,
   toasted
1 cup DOLE® Raisins

• Drain pineapple well, pressing out excess liquid with back of spoon. Reserve juice for beverage.

• Beat margarine and sugar in large bowl until light and fluffy. Stir in drained pineapple and vanilla. Beat in flour and orange peel. Stir in almonds and raisins.

• Drop by heaping tablespoonfuls, 2 inches apart, onto greased cookie sheets.

• Bake in 350°F oven 20 to 22 minutes until firm. Cool on wire racks.

Makes 2 to 2½ dozen cookies

CHUNKY BUTTER CHRISTMAS COOKIES

1¼ cups butter, softened
1 cup packed brown sugar
½ cup dairy sour cream
1 egg
2 teaspoons vanilla
1½ cups all-purpose flour
1 teaspoon baking soda
1 teaspoon salt

1½ cups old fashioned or
   quick oats, uncooked
1 package (10 ounces)
   vanilla milk chips
1 cup flaked coconut
1 jar (3½ ounces)
   macadamia nuts,
   coarsely chopped

Beat butter and brown sugar in large bowl until light and fluffy. Blend in sour cream, egg and vanilla. Combine flour, baking soda and salt. Add to butter mixture; mix well. Stir in oats, vanilla milk chips, coconut and nuts. Drop rounded teaspoonfuls of dough, 2 inches apart, onto ungreased cookie sheet.

Bake at 375°F for 10 to 12 minutes or until edges are lightly browned. Cool on cookie sheet 1 minute. Remove to cooling rack; cool completely.

Makes 5 dozen cookies

Favorite recipe from Wisconsin Milk Marketing Board

ORANGE SUGAR COOKIES

2 cups all-purpose flour
1½ teaspoons baking soda
½ cup FLEISCHMANN'S®
   Margarine, softened
1 cup sugar

2 teaspoons grated orange
   peel
1 teaspoon vanilla extract
¼ cup EGG BEATERS® 99%
   Real Egg Product
   Additional sugar (optional)

In small bowl, combine flour and baking soda; set aside.

In medium bowl with electric mixer at medium speed, beat margarine, 1 cup sugar, orange peel and vanilla until creamy. Add egg product; beat until smooth. Gradually stir in flour mixture until blended. Cover; chill dough 1 hour.

Shape dough into 42 (¾-inch) balls; roll in additional sugar if desired. Place on lightly greased baking sheets, about 2 inches apart. Bake at 375°F for 8 to 10 minutes or until light golden brown. Remove from sheets; cool on wire racks.

Makes 3½ dozen cookies

MERRY SUGAR COOKIES

2¾ cups all-purpose flour
1 teaspoon baking soda
½ teaspoon baking powder
¼ teaspoon salt
1 cup (2 sticks) butter or
   margarine, softened
1½ cups sugar

1 egg
1 teaspoon vanilla extract
One 9-ounce package
   (1½ cups) NESTLÉ® Toll
   House® semi-sweet
   chocolate Rainbow™
   Morsels, divided

Preheat oven to 375°F. In small bowl, combine flour, baking soda, baking powder and salt; set aside.

In large mixer bowl, beat butter and sugar until creamy. Blend in egg and vanilla extract. Gradually beat in flour mixture. (Batter will be stiff.) Stir in 1 cup Nestlé Toll House semi-sweet chocolate Rainbow Morsels. Shape rounded teaspoonfuls dough into balls; place on ungreased cookie sheets. Gently press 3 or 4 remaining Rainbow Morsels into each ball.

Bake 8 to 10 minutes until edges are lightly browned. Let stand 2 minutes. Remove from cookie sheets; cool.

Makes about 4½ dozen cookies

SNICKERDOODLES

1 cup BUTTER FLAVOR
   CRISCO®
1¾ cups sugar, divided
2 eggs
1 teaspoon vanilla

2¼ cups all-purpose flour
2 teaspoons cream of tartar
1 teaspoon baking soda
¾ teaspoon salt
1 teaspoon cinnamon

1. Preheat oven to 400°F.

2. Cream Butter Flavor Crisco, 1½ cups sugar, eggs and vanilla thoroughly in large bowl at medium speed of electric mixer. Combine flour, cream of tartar, baking soda and salt. Stir into creamed mixture.

3. Shape into 1-inch balls. Combine remaining ¼ cup sugar and cinnamon in small bowl. Roll balls of dough in cinnamon-sugar mixture. Place 2 inches apart on ungreased baking sheets.

4. Bake at 400°F for 7 to 8 minutes. Remove to wire racks to cool completely.

Makes 6 dozen cookies

GINGERBREAD COOKIES

½ cup vegetable shortening
⅓ cup packed light brown
   sugar
¼ cup dark molasses
1 egg white
½ teaspoon vanilla
1½ cups all-purpose flour

½ teaspoon baking soda
¼ teaspoon baking powder
½ teaspoon salt
1 teaspoon ground
   cinnamon
½ teaspoon ground ginger

Beat shortening, brown sugar, molasses, egg white and vanilla in large bowl at high speed of electric mixer until smooth. Combine flour, baking soda, baking powder, salt and spices in small bowl. Add to shortening mixture; mix well. Cover; refrigerate until firm, about 8 hours or overnight.

Preheat oven to 350°F. Grease cookie sheets. Roll out dough on lightly floured surface to ⅛-inch thickness. Cut into desired shapes with cookie cutters. Place on prepared cookie sheets.

Bake 6 to 8 minutes or until edges begin to brown. Remove to wire racks; cool completely. Decorate as desired. *Makes about 2½ dozen cookies*

PEANUT BUTTER JEWELS

1 package DUNCAN HINES®
   Peanut Butter
   Cookie Mix
1 egg
¼ cup sugar

¼ cup cocktail peanuts,
   finely chopped
Strawberry jam or apricot
   preserves

1. Preheat oven to 375°F.

2. Combine cookie mix, peanut butter flavor packet from Mix and egg in large bowl. Stir until thoroughly blended. Shape dough into 36 (1-inch) balls. Roll half the balls in sugar and half in chopped peanuts. Place 2 inches apart on ungreased baking sheets. Make indentation in center of each ball with finger or handle end of wooden spoon. Fill each with ¼ teaspoon strawberry jam. Bake at 375°F for 8 to 10 minutes or until light golden brown. Cool 1 minute on baking sheets. Remove to cooling racks. Cool completely. Store in airtight container. *Makes 3 dozen cookies*

Tip: For a delicious flavor variation, try seedless red raspberry or blackberry jam.

MARVELOUS MACAROONS

1 can (8 ounces) DOLE®
  Crushed Pineapple in
  Juice
1 can (14 ounces) sweetened
  condensed milk
1 package (7 ounces) flaked
  coconut

½ cup DOLE® Chopped
  Almonds, toasted
½ cup margarine, melted
  Grated peel from 1 DOLE®
  Lemon
¼ teaspoon almond extract
1 cup all-purpose flour
1 teaspoon baking powder

• Drain pineapple well. Reserve juice for beverage.

• Combine drained pineapple, sweetened condensed milk, coconut, almonds, margarine, 1 teaspoon lemon peel and almond extract in large bowl; mix well.

• Combine flour and baking powder in small bowl. Beat into pineapple mixture until blended.

• Drop by heaping tablespoonfuls, 1 inch apart, onto greased cookie sheets.

• Bake in 350°F oven 13 to 15 minutes. Cool on wire racks. Store in refrigerator.   *Makes 3½ dozen cookies*

FAVORITE PEANUT BUTTER COOKIES

½ cup peanut butter
¼ cup (½ stick) margarine or
  butter, softened
¾ cup sugar
1 egg, beaten

½ cup all-purpose flour
½ teaspoon baking powder
¼ teaspoon salt (optional)
2 cups Rice CHEX® brand
  cereal, crushed to 1 cup

Preheat oven to 350°F. Lightly grease cookie sheet. In large bowl, cream peanut butter, margarine and sugar. Add egg. Stir in flour and baking powder; add salt, if desired. Stir in cereal; mix well. For each cookie, roll 1 level tablespoon dough into ball. Place on prepared cookie sheet. With fork dipped in sugar, flatten slightly in criss-cross pattern. Bake 8 to 10 minutes or until bottoms are lightly browned. Let stand 1 minute before removing from cookie sheet. Cool on wire rack.

Makes 2½ dozen cookies

Marvelous Macaroons

PINEAPPLE-OATMEAL COOKIES

1 can (20 ounces) DOLE®
    Crushed Pineapple in
    Syrup*
1½ cups brown sugar, packed
1 cup margarine
1 egg
3 cups rolled oats, uncooked
2 cups all-purpose flour

1 teaspoon baking powder
1 teaspoon ground
    cinnamon
½ teaspoon salt
1 cup DOLE® Raisins
1 cup DOLE® Natural
    Almonds, toasted and
    chopped

• Drain pineapple well. Reserve ½ cup syrup.

• Beat sugar and margarine in large bowl until light and fluffy. Beat in egg, drained pineapple and reserved ½ cup syrup. Combine remaining ingredients in medium bowl; blend into pineapple mixture.

• Drop by 2 heaping tablespoonfuls, 2 inches apart, onto greased cookie sheets. Flatten tops with back of spoon.

• Bake in 350°F oven 20 to 25 minutes until golden. Cool on wire racks.

Makes about 2½ dozen cookies

*Use pineapple packed in juice, if desired.

AUNTIE VAN'S CHRISTMAS COOKIES

2 cups granulated sugar
1 cup butter, softened
2 eggs
1 teaspoon vanilla
5 cups all-purpose flour

1 teaspoon baking soda
1 cup sour cream
    Coffee Frosting (page 45)
    or canned vanilla
    frosting

Beat granulated sugar and 1 cup butter in large bowl until light and fluffy. Blend in eggs and 1 teaspoon vanilla. Combine flour and baking soda; add alternately with sour cream, mixing well after each addition. Refrigerate 6 hours or overnight. Divide dough into 4 pieces. Roll out 1 piece on lightly floured surface to ⅛-inch thickness (keep remaining dough refrigerated). Cut into desired shapes; place on ungreased cookie sheets. Bake at 325°F for 10 to 12 minutes or until bottoms are golden brown. Repeat with remaining dough. Cool completely. Frost with Coffee Frosting.

Makes 6 dozen cookies
Continued

COFFEE FROSTING

1 tablespoon instant coffee
   granules
1 tablespoon hot water
6 tablespoons butter,
   softened

1 teaspoon vanilla
3 cups sifted powdered sugar
1/4 to 1/3 cup whipping cream

Dissolve coffee granules in water. Beat 6 tablespoons butter in medium bowl until soft. Stir in coffee mixture and 1 teaspoon vanilla. Add powdered sugar; mix until well combined. Gradually add cream until good spreading consistency.

Favorite recipe from Wisconsin Milk Marketing Board

SESAME-ALMOND COOKIES

1 cup FILIPPO BERIO® Brand
   Olive Oil
1 (2-inch) strip lemon peel
4 teaspoons sesame seeds
1/2 cup dry white wine
1 teaspoon grated lemon
   peel

1 teaspoon grated orange
   peel
1/3 cup sugar
1/2 cup sliced almonds
3½ cups all-purpose flour
1 tablespoon ground
   cinnamon

1. Heat oil, 2-inch strip lemon peel and sesame seeds in large skillet over medium heat until seeds are lightly browned. Remove from heat; cool.

2. Remove lemon peel strip. Pour oil and sesame seeds into large bowl. Add wine, grated lemon and orange peels, sugar and almonds; stir.

3. Combine flour and cinnamon in small bowl. Add to oil mixture gradually, stirring well. Gather dough into ball; knead once or twice until smooth. Set aside to rest for 30 minutes.

4. Preheat oven to 350°F. Divide dough into 18 equal pieces. Roll each into a ball and flatten to about 3 inches across and 1/4 inch thick. Place on lightly greased baking sheet. Bake 20 minutes or until lightly browned and firm. Cool on wire rack. Store in covered container.

Makes 18 cookies

PEANUT BUTTER PIZZA COOKIES

2 packages DUNCAN HINES®
   Peanut Butter
   Cookie Mix
2 eggs
1 tablespoon water
   Sugar
1 container (16 ounces)
   DUNCAN HINES®
   Chocolate Layer Cake
   Frosting

Cashews
Candy-coated chocolate
   pieces
Gumdrops, halved
Flaked coconut
1 bar (2 ounces) white
   chocolate baking bar
1 tablespoon CRISCO®
   Shortening

1. Preheat oven to 375°F.

2. For cookies, place cookie mixes in large bowl. Break up any lumps. Add eggs, contents of peanut butter packets from Mixes and water. Stir until thoroughly blended. Shape into 18 (2-inch) balls (about 3 level tablespoons each). Place 3½ inches apart on ungreased baking sheets. Flatten with bottom of large glass dipped in sugar to make 3-inch circles. Bake at 375°F for 9 to 11 minutes or until set. Cool 1 minute on baking sheets. Remove to cooling racks. Cool completely.

3. Frost cookies with Chocolate frosting. Decorate with cashews, chocolate pieces, gumdrops and coconut. Melt white chocolate and shortening in small saucepan on low heat, stirring constantly until smooth. Drizzle over cookies.

Makes 18 (3-inch) cookies

CAP'N'S COOKIES

1 cup firmly packed brown
   sugar
½ cup (1 stick) margarine or
   butter, softened
2 eggs
1 teaspoon vanilla
1½ cups all-purpose flour

1 teaspoon baking powder
½ teaspoon salt (optional)
2 cups CAP'N CRUNCH®
   Cereal, any flavor,
   coarsely crushed
1 cup raisins or semi-sweet
   chocolate pieces

Heat oven to 375°F. Lightly grease cookie sheet. Beat sugar and margarine until fluffy. Blend in eggs and vanilla. Add combined flour, baking powder and salt; mix well. Stir in cereal and raisins. Drop by rounded teaspoonfuls onto prepared cookie sheet. Bake 10 to 12 minutes or until light golden brown. Cool 2 minutes on cookie sheet; remove to wire rack. Cool completely. Store tightly covered.

Makes about 3 dozen cookies

Peanut Butter Pizza Cookies

Mini Morsel Granola Cookies and Banana Bars (page 63)

MINI MORSEL GRANOLA COOKIES

2½ cups all-purpose flour
2 teaspoons baking powder
1 teaspoon baking soda
1 teaspoon cinnamon
1 cup (2 sticks) butter, softened
1¼ cups firmly packed brown sugar

2 eggs
One 12-ounce package (2 cups) NESTLÉ® Toll House® semi-sweet chocolate mini morsels
2 cups granola cereal
1 cup raisins

Preheat oven to 375°F. In small bowl, combine flour, baking powder, baking soda and cinnamon; set aside.

In large mixer bowl, beat butter and brown sugar until creamy. Beat in eggs. Gradually beat in flour mixture. Stir in Nestlé Toll House semi-sweet chocolate mini morsels, granola and raisins. Drop by rounded measuring tablespoonfuls onto ungreased cookie sheets.

Bake 9 to 11 minutes until edges are golden brown. Let stand on cookie sheets 5 minutes. Remove from cookie sheets; cool.

Makes about 4 dozen cookies

NORWEGIAN MOLASSES COOKIES

2¼ cups all-purpose flour
2 teaspoons baking soda
1 cup firmly packed light
brown sugar
¾ cup FLEISCHMANN'S®
Margarine, softened
¼ cup EGG BEATERS® 99%
Real Egg Product

¼ cup BRER RABBIT® Light
or Dark Molasses
¼ cup granulated sugar
Water
Confectioner's Sugar Glaze
(recipe follows) (optional)
Colored sprinkles
(optional)

In small bowl, combine flour and baking soda; set aside.

In medium bowl with electric mixer at medium speed, cream brown sugar and margarine. Add egg product and molasses; beat until smooth. Stir in flour mixture. Cover; chill dough 1 hour.

Shape dough into 48 (1¼-inch) balls; roll in granulated sugar. Place on greased and floured baking sheets, about 2 inches apart. Lightly sprinkle dough with water. Bake at 350°F for 18 to 20 minutes or until flattened. Remove from sheets; cool on wire racks. Decorate with Confectioner's Sugar Glaze and colored sprinkles if desired.   *Makes 4 dozen cookies*

Confectioner's Sugar Glaze: Combine 1 cup confectioner's sugar and 5 to 6 teaspoons skim milk.

GIANT OATMEAL COOKIES

1 cup firmly packed brown
sugar
¾ cup (1½ sticks) margarine
or butter, softened
2 eggs
1 teaspoon vanilla
1¼ cups all-purpose flour
½ teaspoon baking soda

½ teaspoon salt (optional)
2½ cups QUAKER® Oats (quick
or old fashioned,
uncooked)
One 6-ounce package (1 cup)
semi-sweet chocolate
pieces
½ cup chopped nuts

Heat oven to 350°F. Lightly grease 2 large cookie sheets. Beat sugar and margarine until fluffy. Blend in eggs and vanilla. Add combined flour, baking soda, salt and oats; mix well. Stir in chocolate pieces and nuts. Divide dough in half. Press each half into circle about ¾ inch thick on prepared cookie sheets. Bake 17 to 20 minutes or until lightly browned. Cool 5 minutes on cookie sheets; remove to wire racks. Cool completely. Cut into wedges to serve.   *Makes 2 giant cookies*

Variation: Drop dough by rounded tablespoonfuls onto greased cookie sheets. Bake 10 to 12 minutes. Makes about 3 dozen cookies.

OATMEAL SCOTCHIES

1¼ cups all-purpose flour
1 teaspoon baking soda
½ teaspoon salt
½ teaspoon cinnamon
1 cup (2 sticks) butter, softened
¾ cup granulated sugar
¾ cup firmly packed brown sugar
2 eggs

1 teaspoon vanilla extract *or* grated peel of 1 orange
3 cups quick or old fashioned oats, uncooked
One 12-ounce package (2 cups) NESTLE® Toll House® butterscotch flavored morsels

Preheat oven to 375°F. In small bowl, combine flour, baking soda, salt and cinnamon; set aside.

In large mixer bowl, beat butter, granulated sugar, brown sugar, eggs and vanilla extract until creamy. Gradually beat in flour mixture. Stir in oats and Nestlé Toll House butterscotch flavored morsels. Drop by measuring tablespoonfuls onto ungreased cookie sheets. Bake 7 to 8 minutes for chewier cookies (9 to 10 minutes for crisper cookies). Remove from cookie sheets; cool completely.   *Makes about 4 dozen cookies*

PEANUT BUTTER COOKIES

⅔ cup firmly packed light brown sugar
½ cup chunky or smooth peanut butter
⅓ cup BLUE BONNET® Margarine, softened
1 egg

½ cup Regular, Instant or Quick CREAM OF WHEAT® Cereal
1 teaspoon vanilla extract
1¼ cups all-purpose flour
½ teaspoon baking soda

In medium bowl with electric mixer at medium speed, beat brown sugar, peanut butter, margarine and egg until fluffy; blend in cereal and vanilla. Stir in flour and baking soda to make a stiff dough.

Shape dough into 1-inch balls. Place 2 inches apart on greased baking sheets. Flatten balls with bottom of floured glass; press with fork tines to make criss-cross pattern. Bake at 350°F for 8 to 9 minutes or until lightly browned. Remove from sheets; cool on wire racks.

Makes 4 dozen cookies

Oatmeal Scotchies

Lunch Box Lollipops

FAMOUS OATMEAL COOKIES

¾ cup vegetable shortening
1 cup firmly packed brown
   sugar
½ cup granulated sugar
1 egg
¼ cup water
1 teaspoon vanilla

3 cups QUAKER® Oats (quick
   or old fashioned,
   uncooked)
1 cup all-purpose flour
1 teaspoon salt (optional)
½ teaspoon baking soda

Heat oven to 350°F. Beat shortening, sugars, egg, water and vanilla until creamy. Add combined oats, flour, salt and baking soda; mix well. Drop by rounded teaspoonfuls onto ungreased cookie sheet. Bake 12 to 15 minutes or until light golden brown. Remove to cooling rack; cool completely. Store tightly covered. *Makes about 5 dozen cookies*

My Own Special Cookies: Add 1 cup of any or a combination of the following ingredients to basic cookie dough: raisins, chopped nuts, chocolate chips or coconut. Makes about 5 dozen cookies.

LUNCH BOX LOLLIPOPS

2 extra-ripe, medium DOLE®
   Bananas
¾ cup brown sugar, packed
¾ cup margarine, softened
1 egg
1¾ cups quick-cooking oats
1½ cups all-purpose flour
1 teaspoon ground
   cinnamon

½ teaspoon ground nutmeg
½ teaspoon baking soda
½ teaspoon salt
1½ cups DOLE® Raisins
1 cup DOLE® Chopped
   Almonds
4 dozen wooden popsicle
   sticks (optional)

• Place bananas in blender. Process until puréed; use 1 cup for recipe.

• Beat brown sugar and margarine in large bowl until light and fluffy. Beat in egg, then 1 cup banana.

• Combine oats, flour, cinnamon, nutmeg, baking soda and salt in small bowl; stir into banana mixture just until blended. Stir in raisins and almonds.

• Drop by 2 heaping tablespoonfuls, 2 inches apart, onto lightly greased cookie sheets. Push popsicle stick into center of each, if desired. Flatten tops of cookies with back of spoon.

• Bake in 350°F oven 15 to 18 minutes until lightly browned. Cool on wire racks. *Makes 3½ to 4 dozen cookies*

SOFT RAISIN COOKIES

1 cup butter, softened
¾ cup packed brown sugar
½ cup granulated sugar
2 eggs
1½ teaspoons vanilla
3 cups all-purpose flour
½ cup wheat germ

2 teaspoons baking powder
¾ teaspoon baking soda
½ teaspoon salt
½ teaspoon nutmeg
½ cup milk
1 cup raisins

Beat butter, sugars, eggs and vanilla in large mixer bowl. Combine flour, wheat germ, baking powder, baking soda, salt and nutmeg in medium bowl. Add to butter mixture alternately with milk, mixing well after each addition. Stir in raisins. Drop dough by teaspoonfuls, 2 inches apart, onto ungreased cookie sheets. Bake in 350°F oven 10 to 12 minutes or until light brown. Immediately remove to wire racks to cool.

Makes about 7 dozen cookies

Favorite recipe from Wisconsin Milk Marketing Board

Outrageous Brownies & Bars

Rich brownies and delicious bar cookies are quick to make and will satisfy the cookie monster in your house.

ONE BOWL BROWNIES

4 squares BAKER'S®
  Unsweetened Chocolate
¾ cup (1½ sticks) margarine
  or butter
2 cups sugar

3 eggs
1 teaspoon vanilla
1 cup all-purpose flour
1 cup chopped nuts
  (optional)

Heat oven to 350°F. Microwave chocolate and margarine in large microwavable bowl on HIGH 2 minutes or until margarine is melted. Stir until chocolate is completely melted. Stir sugar into melted chocolate mixture. Mix in eggs and vanilla until well blended. Stir in flour and nuts. Spread in greased 13×9-inch pan.

Bake 30 to 35 minutes or until toothpick inserted into center comes out with fudgy crumbs. *Do not overbake.* Cool in pan; cut into bars.

Makes about 24 brownies

Prep time: 10 minutes
Baking time: 30 to 35 minutes

Tips:
• For cakelike brownies, stir in ½ cup milk with eggs and vanilla. Increase flour to 1½ cups.

• When using a glass baking dish, reduce oven temperature to 325°F.

Continued on page 60

Top to bottom: Peanut Butter Swirl Brownies (page 60); Rocky Road Brownies (page 60)

Rocky Road Brownies: Prepare One Bowl Brownies as directed. Bake at 350°F for 30 minutes. Sprinkle 2 cups KRAFT® Miniature Marshmallows, 1 cup BAKER'S® Semi-Sweet Real Chocolate Chips and 1 cup chopped nuts over brownies immediately. Continue baking 3 to 5 minutes or until topping begins to melt together. Cool in pan; cut into bars. Makes about 24 brownies.

Prep time: 15 minutes
Baking time: 35 minutes

Peanut Butter Swirl Brownies: Prepare One Bowl Brownie batter as directed, reserving 1 tablespoon margarine and 2 tablespoons sugar. Spread batter in greased 13×9-inch pan. Add reserved ingredients to ⅔ cup peanut butter; mix well. Place spoonfuls of peanut butter mixture over brownie batter. Swirl with knife to marbleize. Bake at 350°F for 30 to 35 minutes or until toothpick inserted into center comes out with fudgy crumbs. Cool in pan; cut into bars. Makes about 24 brownies.

Prep time: 15 minutes
Baking time: 30 to 35 minutes

PECAN TURTLE BARS

1½ cups all-purpose flour
1½ cups packed brown sugar,
    divided
½ cup butter, softened

1 cup pecan halves
⅔ cup butter
1 cup milk chocolate pieces

Combine flour, 1 cup brown sugar and softened butter in large mixer bowl. Beat at medium speed of electric mixer 2 to 3 minutes or until mixture resembles fine crumbs. Pat mixture evenly onto bottom of ungreased 13×9-inch baking pan. Sprinkle pecans evenly over crumb mixture.

Combine ⅔ cup butter and remaining ½ cup brown sugar in small saucepan. Cook and stir over medium heat until entire surface is bubbly. Cook and stir ½ to 1 minute more. Pour into pan, spreading evenly over crust. Bake in 350°F oven 18 to 20 minutes or until entire surface is bubbly. Remove from oven; immediately sprinkle with chocolate pieces. Let stand 2 to 3 minutes to allow chocolate to melt; use knife to swirl chocolate slightly. Cool completely in pan on wire rack. Use sharp knife to cut into 48 bars. *Makes 48 bars*

Favorite recipe from Wisconsin Milk Marketing Board

BLACK RUSSIAN BROWNIES

4 squares (1 ounce *each*)
   unsweetened chocolate
1 cup butter
¾ teaspoon black pepper
4 eggs, lightly beaten
1½ cups sugar
1½ teaspoons vanilla
⅓ cup KAHLÚA®

2 tablespoons vodka
1⅓ cups all-purpose flour
½ teaspoon salt
¼ teaspoon baking powder
1 cup chopped walnuts or
   toasted sliced almonds
Powdered sugar (optional)

Line bottom of 13×9-inch baking pan with waxed paper. Melt chocolate and butter with pepper in small saucepan over low heat. Remove from heat.

Combine eggs, sugar and vanilla in large bowl; beat well. Stir in cooled chocolate mixture, Kahlúa and vodka. Combine flour, salt and baking powder; add to chocolate mixture and stir until blended. Add walnuts. Spread in prepared pan.

Bake in 350°F oven just until toothpick inserted into center comes out clean, about 25 minutes. *Do not overbake.* Cool in pan on wire rack. Cut into bars. Sprinkle with powdered sugar, if desired.

Makes about 30 brownies

BAKED S'MORES

1 package DUNCAN HINES®
   Golden Sugar Cookie Mix
1 egg
1 tablespoon water

3 bars (1.55 ounces each)
   milk chocolate
1 jar (7 ounces)
   marshmallow creme

1. Preheat oven to 350°F. Grease 8-inch square pan.

2. Combine cookie mix, contents of buttery flavor packet from Mix, egg and water in large bowl. Stir until thoroughly blended. Divide cookie dough in half. Press half the dough evenly into bottom of pan.

3. Cut each milk chocolate bar into 12 sections by following division marks on bars. Arrange chocolate sections into 4 rows, with 9 sections in each row.

4. Place spoonfuls of marshmallow creme on top of chocolate. Spread to cover chocolate and cookie dough. Drop remaining cookie dough by teaspoonfuls on top of marshmallow creme. Spread slightly with back of spoon. Bake at 350°F for 25 to 30 minutes or until light golden brown. Cool completely. Cut into squares.

Makes 9 squares

FRUIT AND CHOCOLATE DREAM SQUARES

TOPPING

⅔ cup all-purpose flour
½ cup pecans, chopped
⅓ cup firmly packed brown
   sugar

6 tablespoons (¾ stick)
   butter, softened

CRUST

1¼ cups all-purpose flour
½ cup granulated sugar
½ cup (1 stick) butter
½ cup strawberry or
   raspberry jam

One 11½-ounce package
   (2 cups) NESTLÉ® Toll
   House® milk chocolate
   morsels

Topping: In small bowl, combine ⅔ cup flour, pecans and brown sugar. With pastry blender or 2 knives, cut in 6 tablespoons butter until mixture resembles coarse crumbs; set aside.

Crust: Preheat oven to 375°F. Grease 9-inch square baking pan. In small bowl, combine 1¼ cups flour and granulated sugar. With pastry blender or 2 knives, cut in ½ cup butter until mixture resembles fine crumbs. Press into prepared pan.

Bake 20 to 25 minutes until set but not brown. Spread with jam. Top with Nestlé Toll House milk chocolate morsels and Topping.

Bake 15 to 20 minutes longer until top is lightly browned. Cool completely; cut into 2¼-inch squares. *Makes 16 squares*

PEANUT BUTTER-RAISIN BARS

¼ cup firmly packed light
   brown sugar
¼ cup corn syrup
¼ cup chunky peanut butter

2 cups SPOON SIZE®
   Shredded Wheat,
   coarsely crushed
¾ cup seedless raisins

In large saucepan over medium heat, stir together brown sugar and corn syrup until sugar dissolves and mixture is warm. Remove from heat; blend in peanut butter. Stir in cereal and raisins until well coated. Press into lightly greased 8×8-inch baking pan. Cool until firm. Cut into 24 bars. Store in airtight container. *Makes 24 bars*

Fruit and Chocolate Dream Squares

BANANA BARS

1½ cups all-purpose flour
½ cup whole wheat flour
2 teaspoons baking powder
½ teaspoon salt
¾ cup (1½ sticks) butter, softened
⅔ cup granulated sugar
⅔ cup firmly packed light brown sugar

1 teaspoon vanilla extract
2 medium bananas, mashed
1 egg
One 12-ounce package (2 cups) NESTLÉ® Toll House® semi-sweet chocolate mini morsels
Confectioners' sugar

Preheat oven to 350°F. In small bowl, combine flours, baking powder and salt; set aside.

In large mixer bowl, beat butter, granulated sugar, brown sugar and vanilla extract until creamy. Beat in bananas and egg. Gradually beat in flour mixture. Stir in Nestlé Toll House semi-sweet chocolate mini morsels. Spread into greased 15½ × 10½-inch baking pan.

Bake 25 to 30 minutes. Cool completely. Sprinkle with confectioners' sugar. Cut into 2 × 1-inch bars. *Makes about 6½ dozen bars*

Variation: Omit whole wheat flour. Increase all-purpose flour to 2 cups.

PINEAPPLE PECAN BARS

CRUST
2 cups all-purpose flour
²/₃ cup powdered sugar

1 cup margarine

PINEAPPLE TOPPING
1 can (20 ounces) DOLE®
    Crushed Pineapple in
    Syrup or Juice, drained
4 eggs

¾ cup brown sugar, packed
⅓ cup all-purpose flour
2 cups coarsely chopped
    pecans

For crust, combine 2 cups flour and powdered sugar. Cut in margarine until mixture is crumbly. Press into bottom of 13×9-inch baking pan. Bake in 350°F oven 15 minutes. Remove from oven.

For topping, combine drained pineapple, eggs, brown sugar and ⅓ cup flour. Stir in pecans. Pour over partially baked crust. Bake in 350°F oven 30 to 35 minutes or until set. Cool completely. Cut into bars.

Makes 32 bars

MALLOW-GRAHAM BARS

2 tablespoons BLUE
    BONNET® Margarine
3 cups marshmallows
1 stay fresh package HONEY
    MAID® Honey Grahams,
    coarsely chopped

½ cup seedless raisins
½ cup chopped dry roasted
    peanuts

In large saucepan over low heat, melt margarine. Add marshmallows; stir until melted. Remove from heat; stir in graham crackers, raisins and peanuts. Spread mixture into greased 9×9-inch baking pan. Cool 1 hour or until firm. Cut into 18 bars. Store in airtight container.

Makes 18 bars

Pineapple Pecan Bars

CHOCOLATE PECAN PIE BARS

CRUST
1½ cups all-purpose flour
½ cup (1 stick) butter,
    softened

¼ cup firmly packed brown
    sugar

FILLING
3 eggs
¾ cup dark or light corn
    syrup
¾ cup granulated sugar
2 tablespoons (¼ stick)
    butter, melted
1 teaspoon vanilla extract

1½ cups coarsely chopped
    pecans
One 12-ounce package (2 cups)
    NESTLÉ® Toll House®
    semi-sweet chocolate
    morsels

Crust: Preheat oven to 350°F. In small mixer bowl, beat flour, ½ cup butter and brown sugar until crumbly. Press into greased 13×9-inch baking pan. Bake 12 to 15 minutes until lightly browned.

Filling: In medium bowl with wire whisk, beat eggs, corn syrup, granulated sugar, melted butter and vanilla extract. Stir in pecans and Nestlé Toll House semi-sweet chocolate morsels. Pour evenly over baked crust.

Bake 25 to 30 minutes until set. Cool; cut into 2×1½-inch bars.

Makes about 3 dozen bars

FUDGY CHEESECAKE SWIRL BROWNIES

CREAM CHEESE BATTER
One 8-ounce package cream
    cheese, softened
½ cup sugar

1 egg
1 teaspoon vanilla extract

CHOCOLATE BATTER
¾ cup (1½ sticks) butter
2 foil-wrapped bars
    (4 ounces) NESTLÉ®
    unsweetened chocolate
    baking bars

1¾ cups sugar
3 eggs, well beaten
1¾ cups all-purpose flour

Continued

Fudgy Cheesecake Swirl Brownies

Cream Cheese Batter: Preheat oven to 350°F. In small mixer bowl, beat cream cheese and ½ cup sugar until smooth. Beat in 1 egg and vanilla extract; set aside.

Chocolate Batter: In heavy-gauge, medium saucepan over low heat, melt butter and Nestlé unsweetened chocolate baking bars, stirring until smooth. Stir in 1¾ cups sugar. Blend in 3 eggs. Stir in flour.

Spread Chocolate Batter into greased 13 × 9-inch baking pan. Spoon Cream Cheese Batter over top. Swirl metal spatula through batters to marbleize.

Bake 30 to 35 minutes until edges begin to pull away from sides of pan. Cool completely; cut into 2-inch bars.

Makes about 2 dozen brownies

Chocolate Apple Crisp

CHOCOLATE APPLE CRISP

1½ cups all-purpose flour
1 cup firmly packed brown sugar
½ teaspoon baking soda
¼ teaspoon salt
¾ cup (1½ sticks) butter
1½ cups quick oats, uncooked

One 12-ounce package (2 cups) NESTLE® Toll House® semi-sweet chocolate mini morsels, divided
3 apples, unpeeled if desired, chopped
1 cup pecans or walnuts, chopped

Preheat oven to 375°F. In large bowl, combine flour, brown sugar, baking soda and salt. With pastry blender or 2 knives, cut in butter until mixture resembles fine crumbs. Stir in oats; press half of oat mixture into greased 13×9-inch baking pan.

To remaining oat mixture, add Nestlé Toll House semi-sweet chocolate mini morsels, apples and pecans; stir to combine. Sprinkle over base.

Bake 35 to 40 minutes until lightly browned. Cool slightly; cut into squares. *Makes about 15 servings*

MOCHA BROWNIES

1¼ cups all-purpose flour
1 teaspoon baking powder
½ teaspoon salt
4 (1-ounce) squares
    semisweet chocolate
¾ cup BLUE BONNET®
    Margarine
1 tablespoon instant coffee
    granules

1 cup granulated sugar
4 eggs
1 teaspoon vanilla extract
1¼ cups PLANTERS® Walnuts,
    chopped and divided
Creamy Coffee Frosting
    (recipe follows)

In small bowl, combine flour, baking powder and salt; set aside.

In large saucepan over low heat, stir together chocolate, margarine and 1 tablespoon coffee granules until blended. Remove from heat; stir in granulated sugar. Add eggs, 1 at a time, beating well after each addition. Stir in flour mixture and vanilla until blended. Stir in 1 cup walnuts. Spread in greased 13×9-inch baking pan.

Bake at 350°F for 25 to 30 minutes. Cool in pan on wire rack. Spread with Creamy Coffee Frosting; sprinkle with remaining ¼ cup walnuts. Cut into 2×1½-inch bars.   *Makes about 32 bars*

Creamy Coffee Frosting: Dissolve 1 teaspoon instant coffee granules in ¼ cup milk. In small bowl with electric mixer at high speed, beat 4 ounces cream cheese and milk mixture until creamy. Gradually beat in 1 (16-ounce) package confectioner's sugar until well blended and good spreading consistency.

FROSTED TOFFEE BARS

2 cups QUAKER® Oats (quick
    or old fashioned,
    uncooked)
½ cup firmly packed brown
    sugar

½ cup (1 stick) margarine or
    butter, melted
½ cup semi-sweet chocolate
    pieces
¼ cup chopped peanuts

Heat oven to 350°F. Lightly grease 9-inch square baking pan. In large bowl, combine oats, brown sugar and margarine; mix well. Spread into prepared pan. Bake 13 minutes or until light golden brown; cool on wire rack.

In small saucepan over low heat, melt chocolate pieces. Spread over baked oat mixture; sprinkle with peanuts. Chill 4 hours or until chocolate is set. Cut into 2×1½-inch bars. Store tightly covered in refrigerator.
                                                    Makes about 28 bars

RICH 'N' CREAMY BROWNIE BARS

BROWNIES
1 package DUNCAN HINES®
    Chocolate Lovers' Double
    Fudge Brownie Mix
2 eggs

⅓ cup water
¼ cup CRISCO® Oil or
    CRISCO® PURITAN® Oil
½ cup chopped pecans

TOPPING
1 package (8 ounces) cream
    cheese, softened
2 eggs

1 pound (3½ cups)
    confectioners sugar
1 teaspoon vanilla extract

1. Preheat oven to 350°F. Grease bottom of 13×9-inch pan.

2. **For brownies,** combine brownie mix, contents of fudge packet from Mix, 2 eggs, water and oil in large bowl. Stir with spoon until well blended, about 50 strokes. Stir in pecans. Spread evenly in pan.

3. **For topping,** beat cream cheese in large bowl at medium speed with electric mixer until smooth. Beat in 2 eggs, confectioners sugar and vanilla extract until smooth. Spread evenly over brownie mixture. Bake at 350°F for 45 to 50 minutes or until edges and top are golden brown and shiny. Cool completely. Refrigerate until well chilled. Cut into bars.

Makes 48 bars

SPICED MINCEMEAT SQUARES

½ cup all-purpose flour
½ teaspoon ground
    cinnamon
¼ teaspoon ground nutmeg
¼ teaspoon baking soda
⅓ cup BLUE BONNET®
    Margarine, softened

½ cup firmly packed light
    brown sugar
1 egg
1 cup prepared mincemeat
1 cup NABISCO® 100% Bran
    Confectioner's Sugar Glaze
    (page 53)

In small bowl, combine flour, cinnamon, nutmeg and baking soda; set aside.

In medium bowl with electric mixer at medium speed, beat margarine and brown sugar until creamy. Beat in egg. Add flour mixture, mincemeat and bran. Spread into greased 9×9-inch baking pan. Bake at 400°F for 20 to 25 minutes or until knife inserted into center comes out clean. Cool on wire rack. Drizzle with Confectioner's Sugar Glaze. Cut into 2¼-inch squares. Store in airtight container. *Makes 16 squares*

Rich 'n' Creamy Brownie Bars

YUMMY PEANUT BUTTER BARS

BARS
1 package DUNCAN HINES®
  Peanut Butter
  Cookie Mix

1 egg
1 tablespoon water
⅓ cup chopped peanuts

WHITE GLAZE
½ cup confectioners sugar

1 to 2 teaspoons water

CHOCOLATE GLAZE
¼ cup semi-sweet chocolate
  chips

2 teaspoons CRISCO®
  Shortening

1. Preheat oven to 350°F.

2. **For bars,** combine cookie mix, contents of peanut butter packet from Mix, egg and 1 tablespoon water in large bowl. Stir until thoroughly blended. Stir in peanuts. Spread in ungreased 8-inch square pan. Bake at 350°F for 23 to 25 minutes or until edges are light golden brown. Cool completely.

3. **For white glaze,** place confectioners sugar in small bowl. Add water, 1 teaspoon at a time, stirring until smooth and desired consistency. Drizzle over cooled bars.

4. **For chocolate glaze,** place chocolate chips and shortening in small resealable plastic bag; seal. Place bag in bowl of hot water for several minutes. Dry with paper towel. Knead until blended and chocolate is smooth. Snip pinpoint hole in corner of bag. Drizzle chocolate glaze over white glaze. Allow glazes to set before cutting into bars.

Makes 18 bars

Tip: For a special presentation, cut cookies into diamond or triangle shapes instead of bars.

RASPBERRY MERINGUE BARS

1 cup butter or margarine,
  softened
½ cup firmly packed brown
  sugar

1 egg
2 cups all-purpose flour
1 can SOLO® *or* 1 jar BAKER®
  Raspberry Filling

MERINGUE TOPPING
3 egg whites
¾ cup granulated sugar

½ cup shredded coconut
½ cup slivered almonds

Continued

Preheat oven to 325°F. Grease 13×9-inch baking pan. Beat butter and brown sugar in medium bowl with electric mixer at medium speed until light and fluffy. Add 1 egg; beat until blended. Stir in flour until well combined. Pat dough evenly in prepared pan. Bake 20 minutes. Remove from oven; spread raspberry filling over crust. (Do not turn oven off.)

For meringue topping, beat egg whites in medium bowl with electric mixer at high speed until soft peaks form. Add granulated sugar gradually; beat until stiff and glossy. Fold coconut and almonds into beaten egg white mixture. Spread over raspberry filling. Return to oven. Bake 20 minutes or until meringue topping is lightly browned. Cool completely in pan on wire rack. Cut into 48 bars.   *Makes 48 bars*

KAHLÚA® MUDSLIDE BROWNIES

2 cups all-purpose flour	2 tablespoons Irish cream
½ teaspoon baking powder	liqueur
½ teaspoon salt	1 tablespoon vodka
⅔ cup butter	¾ cup coarsely chopped
4 squares (1 ounce *each*)	walnuts (optional)
unsweetened chocolate,	Kahlúa® Glaze (recipe
chopped	follows)
3 eggs	Whole coffee beans
1½ cups granulated sugar	(optional)
4 tablespoons KAHLÚA®	

Combine flour, baking powder and salt in small bowl. Melt butter and chocolate in small saucepan over low heat; set aside. Beat eggs and granulated sugar in large bowl until light. Beat in flour mixture, chocolate mixture, 4 tablespoons Kahlúa, Irish cream and vodka. Fold in walnuts. Pour into greased 13×9-inch baking pan.

Bake in 350°F oven just until toothpick inserted into center comes out clean, about 25 minutes. *Do not overbake.* Cool in pan on wire rack. Spread with Kahlúa Glaze. Decorate with whole coffee beans, if desired. Cut into squares.   *Makes 24 brownies*

KAHLÚA® GLAZE

1¼ cups powdered sugar   3 tablespoons KAHLÚA®

Beat together powdered sugar and 3 tablespoons Kahlúa in small bowl until smooth.

Banana Gingerbread Bars

BANANA GINGERBREAD BARS

1 extra-ripe, medium DOLE®
    Banana, peeled
1 package (14.5 ounces)
    gingerbread cake mix
½ cup lukewarm water
1 egg
1 small DOLE® Banana,
    peeled and chopped
    (½ cup)

½ cup DOLE® Raisins
½ cup DOLE® Slivered
    Almonds
1½ cups powdered sugar
    Juice from 1 DOLE® Lemon

Continued

• Place medium banana in blender. Process until puréed; use ½ cup for recipe.

• Combine gingerbread mix, water, ½ cup puréed banana and egg in large bowl. Beat well.

• Stir in chopped banana, raisins and almonds.

• Spread batter in greased 13×9-inch baking pan. Bake in 350°F oven 20 to 25 minutes until toothpick inserted in center comes out clean.

• Mix powdered sugar and 3 tablespoons lemon juice in medium bowl to make thin glaze. Spread over warm gingerbread. Cool. Cut into bars. Sprinkle with additional powdered sugar if desired.   *Makes 32 bars*

OATMEAL EXTRAVAGANZAS

1 cup all-purpose flour
1½ teaspoons baking powder
½ teaspoon salt
1 cup firmly packed brown sugar
¾ cup (1½ sticks) butter, softened
1 teaspoon vanilla extract

1 egg
2 tablespoons water
2 cups quick oats, uncooked
One 12-ounce package (2 cups) NESTLÉ® Toll House® semi-sweet chocolate morsels

Preheat oven to 375°F. In small bowl, combine flour, baking powder and salt; set aside.

In large mixer bowl, beat brown sugar, butter and vanilla extract until creamy. Beat in egg. Gradually blend in flour mixture, then water. Stir in oats and Nestlé Toll House semi-sweet chocolate morsels. Spread in greased 9-inch square pan.

Bake 30 to 35 minutes. Cool; cut into 1½-inch squares.
          Makes 3 dozen squares

Fanciful Cookies

Beautiful to look at and great-tasting, these cookies take a little extra time to prepare—but they're worth it!

CHOCOLATE-GILDED DANISH SUGAR CONES

½ cup butter or margarine,
 softened
½ cup sugar
½ cup all-purpose flour
2 egg whites

1 teaspoon vanilla
3 ounces bittersweet
 chocolate *or* ½ cup
 semisweet chocolate
 chips

Preheat oven to 400°F. Generously grease 4 cookie sheets. Beat butter and sugar in large bowl until light and fluffy. Blend in flour. In clean, dry bowl, beat egg whites until frothy. Blend into butter mixture with vanilla.

Using measuring teaspoon, place 4 mounds of dough, 4 inches apart, on each prepared cookie sheet. Spread mounds with back of spoon dipped in water to 3-inch diameter. Bake, 1 sheet at a time, 5 to 6 minutes or until edges are just barely golden. (Do not overbake or cookies become crisp too quickly and are difficult to shape.) Remove from oven and quickly loosen each cookie from cookie sheet with thin spatula. Shape each into a cone; cones become firm as they cool. (If cookies become too firm to shape, return to oven for a few seconds to soften.)

Melt chocolate in small bowl over hot, not boiling, water. Stir until smooth. When all cookies are baked and cooled, dip flared ends into melted chocolate. Let stand until chocolate is set. If desired, serve cones by standing them in a bowl. (Adding about 1 inch of sugar to bottom of bowl may be necessary to hold them upright.) *Makes 16 cookies*

Chocolate-Gilded Danish Sugar Cones

Orange Pecan Gems

SNOW CAPS

3 egg whites
¼ teaspoon cream of tartar
¾ cup sugar
½ teaspoon vanilla extract
1 cup (6 ounces) semi-sweet
    chocolate chips

2 white chocolate baking
    bars (2 ounces each),
    chopped (optional)

Preheat oven to 200°F. Line baking sheets with parchment paper. In large mixer bowl, combine egg whites and cream of tartar. Beat at highest speed of electric mixer until mixture is just frothy. Add sugar, 1 tablespoon at a time, beating well after each addition. Beat until stiff peaks form. Add vanilla; beat 1 minute. Fold in chocolate chips. Drop mixture by teaspoonfuls, 1 inch apart, onto prepared baking sheets. Bake 2 hours or until meringues are thoroughly dry to touch but not browned, rotating baking sheets halfway through baking. Turn off heat. Leave in closed oven 3 to 4 hours or until completely dry. Remove from oven. Cool completely. Carefully remove from parchment.

Melt white chocolate in top of double boiler over hot, not boiling, water. Stir constantly until chocolate melts. Dip top of each cookie into melted chocolate, if desired. Place on waxed paper to dry. Store at room temperature in tightly covered containers.

Makes about 6 dozen cookies

ORANGE PECAN GEMS

1 package DUNCAN HINES® Moist Deluxe Orange Supreme Cake Mix	1 egg
	2 tablespoons butter or margarine, softened
1 container (8 ounces) vanilla lowfat yogurt	1 cup finely chopped pecans
	1 cup pecan halves

1. Preheat oven to 350°F. Grease baking sheets.

2. Combine cake mix, yogurt, egg, butter and chopped pecans in large bowl. Beat at low speed with electric mixer until blended. Drop by rounded teaspoonfuls 2 inches apart onto greased baking sheets. Press pecan half onto center of each cookie. Bake at 350°F for 11 to 13 minutes or until golden brown. Cool 1 minute on baking sheets. Remove to cooling racks. Cool completely. Store in airtight container.

Makes 4½ to 5 dozen cookies

Tip: Cookies may be stored in an airtight container in freezer for up to 6 months.

HOLIDAY TEATIME TREATS

2 packages (3 ounces each) cream cheese, softened	2 tablespoons sugar
	2 cups all-purpose flour
1 cup butter or margarine, softened	

FILLING

½ cup sugar	
2 eggs	1 can SOLO® *or* 1 jar BAKER® Apricot or other fruit filling
¼ cup all-purpose flour	
1 teaspoon vanilla	½ cup chopped nuts (optional)

Preheat oven to 350°F. Beat cream cheese, butter and 2 tablespoons sugar in medium bowl with electric mixer until fluffy. Stir in 2 cups flour to make soft dough. Divide dough in half. Shape each piece of dough into about 24 (1-inch) balls. Press balls into bottom and up side of ungreased miniature (1¾-inch) muffin cups. Set aside.

To make filling, beat ½ cup sugar, eggs, ¼ cup flour, vanilla and apricot filling in medium bowl with electric mixer until blended. Stir in nuts. Spoon evenly into pastry-lined muffin cups. Bake 25 to 30 minutes or until filling is set and crust is golden. Cool completely in muffin cups on wire racks.

Makes about 4 dozen cookies

CHERRY SURPRISES

1 package DUNCAN HINES®
   Golden Sugar Cookie Mix
36 to 40 candied cherries

½ cup semi-sweet chocolate
   chips
1 teaspoon CRISCO®
   Shortening

1. Preheat oven to 375°F. Grease baking sheets.

2. Prepare cookie mix following package directions. Shape thin layer of dough around each candied cherry. Place 2 inches apart on greased baking sheets. Bake at 375°F for 8 minutes or until set but not browned. Cool 1 minute on baking sheets. Remove to cooling racks. Cool completely.

3. Place chocolate chips and shortening in small resealable plastic bag; seal. Place bag in bowl of hot water for several minutes. Dry with paper towel. Knead until blended and chocolate is smooth. Snip pinpoint hole in corner of bag. Drizzle chocolate over cookies. Allow drizzle to set before storing between layers of waxed paper in airtight container.

Makes 3 to 3½ dozen cookies

Tip: Well-drained maraschino cherries may be substituted for candied cherries.

DATE ORANGE COOKIE PIZZA

½ cup margarine, softened
½ cup brown sugar, packed
1 cup all-purpose flour
1 tablespoon orange juice
1 teaspoon grated DOLE®
   Orange peel

1 package (8 ounces) DOLE®
   Pitted Dates, chopped
½ cup DOLE® Almonds,
   toasted and chopped

• Beat margarine and sugar in large bowl until light and fluffy. Gradually beat in flour until blended. Beat in orange juice and peel, then dates and almonds.

• Form dough into ball. Placed on greased 14-inch pizza pan. Pat to 12-inch cookie.

• Bake in 375°F oven 15 minutes. Cool completely. Cut into 14 to 16 wedges to serve.

Makes 14 to 16 servings

Cherry Surprises

FLORENTINE CUPS

BASE

2 cups HONEY ALMOND
DELIGHT® brand cereal,
crushed to 1 cup
1 cup flaked coconut
½ cup raisins
½ cup all-purpose flour
1½ teaspoons grated fresh
orange peel

½ teaspoon baking powder
½ teaspoon ground
cinnamon
½ cup packed brown sugar
⅓ cup butter or margarine
¼ cup honey

ICING

1 tablespoon butter or
margarine, softened
½ cup powdered sugar

1½ teaspoons orange juice
Sliced almonds

To prepare base, preheat oven to 350°F. Grease 32 miniature (1¾-inch) muffin cups. In large bowl, combine cereal, coconut, raisins, flour, orange peel, baking powder and cinnamon; mix well and set aside. In small saucepan, combine brown sugar, ⅓ cup butter and honey. Stir over medium heat until butter is melted and brown sugar is dissolved. Pour over cereal mixture; blend well. Place 1 tablespoon mixture in each prepared muffin cup; press firmly. Bake 8 to 10 minutes or until golden brown (cups will be soft). Cool in pan 15 minutes. Loosen edges. Invert onto wire racks. Cool completely.

To prepare icing, in small bowl, beat 1 tablespoon butter, powdered sugar and orange juice until smooth. With pastry tube, pipe a decorative swirl on top of each cup. Garnish with sliced almonds.

Makes 32 cups

MOCHA MINT CRISPS

1 cup butter or margarine,
softened
1 cup granulated sugar
1 egg
¼ cup light corn syrup
¼ teaspoon peppermint
extract
1 teaspoon powdered instant
coffee

1 teaspoon hot water
2 cups all-purpose flour
6 tablespoons HERSHEY'S
Cocoa
2 teaspoons baking soda
¼ teaspoon salt
Mocha Mint Sugar (page
83)

Continued

Heat oven to 350°F. In large mixer bowl, beat butter and granulated sugar until light and fluffy. Add egg, corn syrup and peppermint extract; mix thoroughly. Dissolve 1 teaspoon instant coffee in water; stir into butter mixture. Stir together flour, cocoa, baking soda and salt; gradually add to butter mixture, blending thoroughly.

Shape dough into 1-inch balls. (Dough may be refrigerated for a short time for easier handling.) Prepare Mocha Mint Sugar. Roll dough balls in sugar mixture. Place on ungreased cookie sheet, about 2 inches apart. Bake 8 to 10 minutes or until no imprint remains when touched lightly. Cool slightly. Remove from cookie sheet to wire rack. Cool completely.

Makes about 4 dozen cookies

Mocha Mint Sugar: In small bowl, stir together 1/4 cup powdered sugar, 2 tablespoons crushed hard peppermint candies (about 6 candies) and 1 1/2 teaspoons powdered instant coffee.

OATMEAL CRANBERRY-NUT COOKIES

3/4 cup BUTTER FLAVOR CRISCO®
1 cup firmly packed dark brown sugar
1/4 cup dark molasses
1 egg
2 tablespoons milk
1 1/2 teaspoons vanilla
1 cup all-purpose flour
1 1/4 teaspoons cinnamon
1/2 teaspoon baking soda
1/2 teaspoon salt
1/4 teaspoon allspice
1 cup crushed whole-berry cranberry sauce
1/2 cup sliced almonds, broken
3 cups quick oats (not instant or old fashioned), uncooked

1. Heat oven to 375°F. Grease baking sheet with Butter Flavor Crisco.

2. Combine Butter Flavor Crisco and brown sugar in large bowl. Beat at medium speed of electric mixer until well blended. Beat in molasses, egg, milk and vanilla.

3. Combine flour, cinnamon, baking soda, salt and allspice. Mix into creamed mixture at low speed until just blended. Stir in cranberry sauce and nuts. Stir in oats with spoon. Drop tablespoonfuls of dough 2 inches apart onto prepared baking sheet.

4. Bake at 375°F for 12 minutes or until set. Cool 2 minutes on baking sheet. Remove to cooling rack. *Makes about 4 dozen cookies*

CANDY SHOP PIZZA

1½ cups all-purpose flour
½ teaspoon baking soda
½ teaspoon salt
10 tablespoons (1¼ sticks)
    butter, softened
½ cup granulated sugar
½ cup firmly packed brown
    sugar
1 egg
½ teaspoon vanilla extract
One 12-ounce package (2 cups)
    NESTLÉ® Toll House®
    semi-sweet chocolate
    morsels, divided

½ cup peanut butter
About 1 cup cut-up fruit,
    such as bananas and
    strawberries (optional)
About 1 cup chopped
    candy bars, such as
    NESTLÉ® CRUNCH® bars,
    BUTTERFINGER® bars,
    ALPINE WHITE® bars,
    GOOBERS® and
    RAISINETS®

Preheat oven to 375°F. In small bowl, combine flour, baking soda and salt; set aside.

In large mixer bowl, beat butter, granulated sugar and brown sugar until creamy. Beat in egg and vanilla extract. Gradually beat in flour mixture. Stir in 1 cup Nestlé Toll House semi-sweet chocolate morsels. Spread batter in lightly greased 12- to 14-inch pizza pan or 15½×10½-inch jelly-roll pan. Bake 20 to 24 minutes or until lightly browned.

Immediately sprinkle remaining 1 cup semi-sweet chocolate morsels over crust; drop peanut butter by spoonfuls onto morsels. Let stand 5 minutes or until soft and shiny. Gently spread chocolate and peanut butter over crust. Top with fruit and candy. Cut into wedges. Serve warm.

Makes about 12 servings

Candy Shop Pizza

PARTY!

For: THE WHOLE CLASS
Place: SCHOOL GYM
Date: JUNE
RSVP:

PINECONE COOKIES

6 tablespoons butter or
   margarine
⅓ cup HERSHEY'S Cocoa
1 cup sugar
2 eggs
1 teaspoon vanilla extract

2 cups all-purpose flour
½ teaspoon baking powder
½ teaspoon salt
¼ teaspoon baking soda
Light corn syrup
Sliced almonds

In small saucepan, melt butter over low heat; remove from heat. Add cocoa; blend well. In large mixer bowl, combine sugar, eggs and vanilla; blend in cocoa mixture. Stir together flour, baking powder, salt and baking soda; add to cocoa-sugar mixture, beating until smooth. Refrigerate dough about 1 hour or until firm enough to roll.

Heat oven to 350°F. Roll out small portion of dough between two pieces of waxed paper to ⅛-inch thickness. Cut into pinecone shapes using 2- or 2½-inch oval cookie cutter. Place on lightly greased cookie sheet; lightly brush cookies with corn syrup. Arrange almonds in pinecone fashion; lightly drizzle or brush almonds with corn syrup. Repeat with remaining dough. Bake 7 to 8 minutes or until set. Cool slightly; remove from cookie sheet to wire rack. Cool completely. *Makes about 4 dozen cookies*

ALMOND-RASPBERRY THUMBPRINT COOKIES

1 cup butter or margarine,
   softened
1 cup sugar
1 can SOLO® *or* 1 jar BAKER®
   Almond Filling
2 egg yolks
1 teaspoon almond extract

2½ cups all-purpose flour
½ teaspoon baking powder
½ teaspoon salt
1 can SOLO® *or* 1 jar BAKER®
   Raspberry or Strawberry
   Filling

Beat butter and sugar in medium bowl with electric mixer until light and fluffy. Add almond filling, egg yolks and almond extract; beat until blended. Stir in flour, baking powder and salt with wooden spoon to make soft dough. Cover; refrigerate at least 3 hours or overnight.

Preheat oven to 350°F. Shape dough into 1-inch balls. Place on ungreased baking sheets, about 1½ inches apart. Press thumb into center of each ball to make indentation. Spoon ½ teaspoon raspberry filling into each indentation. Bake 11 to 13 minutes or until edges of cookies are golden brown. Cool on baking sheets 1 minute. Remove from baking sheets; cool completely on wire racks. *Makes about 5 dozen cookies*

SPECIAL CHOCOLATE CHIP SANDWICHES

1 package DUNCAN HINES®
Chocolate Chip
Cookie Mix
1 egg
2 teaspoons water

8 ounces chocolate-flavored
candy coating
¼ cup chopped sliced natural
almonds

1. Preheat oven to 375°F.

2. Combine cookie mix, contents of buttery flavor packet from Mix, egg and water in large bowl. Stir until thoroughly blended. Drop by rounded teaspoonfuls 2 inches apart onto ungreased baking sheets. Bake at 375°F for 8 to 10 minutes or until light golden brown. Cool 1 minute on baking sheets. Remove to cooling racks. Cool completely.

3. Place chocolate candy coating in small saucepan. Melt on low heat, stirring frequently until smooth.

4. To assemble, spread about ½ teaspoon melted coating on bottom of one cookie; top with second cookie. Press together to make sandwiches. Repeat with remaining cookies. Dip one-third of each sandwich cookie in remaining melted coating and sprinkle with almonds. Place on cooling racks until coating is set. Store between layers of waxed paper in airtight containers.   *Makes 18 sandwich cookies*

Special Chocolate Chip Sandwiches

CHECKERBOARD COOKIES

¾ cup plus 1 tablespoon
   butter or margarine,
   softened and divided
2 egg yolks
½ teaspoon vanilla extract

1 package DUNCAN HINES®
   Moist Deluxe Fudge
   Marble Cake Mix
1 egg, lightly beaten

1. Combine ¾ cup butter, egg yolks and vanilla extract in large bowl. Beat at low speed with electric mixer until blended. Set aside cocoa packet from Mix. Gradually add cake mix. Blend well.

2. Divide dough in half. Add cocoa packet and remaining 1 tablespoon butter to half the dough. Knead until well blended and chocolate colored.

3. Roll out yellow dough between two pieces of waxed paper into a 6-inch square. Repeat with chocolate dough. Remove top pieces of waxed paper from yellow and chocolate doughs. Cut each square into twelve ½-inch-wide strips.

4. To assemble, place one strip chocolate dough on plastic wrap. Brush edge with beaten egg. Place one strip yellow dough next to chocolate dough. Brush edge with egg. Repeat with a second chocolate strip, egg and a second yellow strip to make first row. Brush top of row with egg. Prepare second row by stacking strips on first row, alternating yellow over chocolate strips. Brush edge and top of each strip with egg. Repeat for third row to complete one checkerboard bar. Repeat with remaining strips to make second bar. Cover with plastic wrap. Refrigerate 1 hour or until firm enough to slice.

5. Preheat oven to 350°F. Grease baking sheets.

6. Cut checkerboard bars into ¼-inch slices. Place 2 inches apart on greased baking sheets. Bake at 350°F for 7 to 9 minutes or until edges are light golden brown. Cool 1 minute on baking sheets. Remove to cooling racks. Cool completely. Store in airtight containers.

Makes 4 dozen cookies

DELICATE LACE NUT COOKIES

2 (2-ounce) packages
   PLANTERS® Nut Topping
½ cup firmly packed light
   brown sugar
⅓ cup BLUE BONNET®
   Margarine

3 tablespoons all-purpose
   flour
1 tablespoon milk
1 teaspoon vanilla extract

Continued

Line baking sheets with foil; grease foil. In medium saucepan, combine nut topping, brown sugar, margarine, flour and milk. Cook over low heat, stirring until margarine is melted and mixture is blended. Stir in vanilla; keep warm over low heat. Drop mixture by slightly rounded teaspoonfuls onto prepared baking sheets, about 2½ inches apart.

Bake at 375°F for 4 to 5 minutes or until golden brown. Cool on sheets on wire racks. Carefully peel cooled cookies off foil. Store in airtight containers. *Makes about 4 dozen cookies*

MINIATURE FRUITCAKE JEWELS

FRUITCAKES
- 1 cup all-purpose flour
- ⅓ cup BUTTER FLAVOR CRISCO®
- ⅓ cup granulated sugar
- ¼ cup orange juice
- ½ teaspoon baking powder
- 2 eggs
- 1 cup diced mixed candied fruit
- ½ cup quartered red candied cherries
- ½ cup quartered green candied cherries
- 1 cup golden raisins
- ½ cup diced dates
- ½ cup coarsely chopped pecans

GLAZE
- ⅓ cup confectioners sugar
- 2 teaspoons brandy or orange juice

1. Preheat oven to 350°F. Place 22 (2½-inch) foil baking cups in muffin pan cups.

2. **For fruitcakes,** combine flour, Butter Flavor Crisco, granulated sugar, orange juice, baking powder and eggs in large bowl. Beat at low speed of electric mixer until blended. Increase speed to medium. Beat until light and fluffy. Stir in mixed fruit, red and green cherries, raisins, dates and pecans. Spoon into prepared muffin cups, filling about ¾ full.

3. Bake at 350°F for 25 to 27 minutes or until toothpick inserted into center comes out clean. Leave fruitcakes in muffin pans.

4. **For glaze,** combine confectioners sugar and brandy in small bowl. Stir until smooth. Brush lightly over tops of warm baked fruitcakes. Cool in pans. *Makes 22 miniature fruitcakes*

Note: Can also be made in 2-inch baking cups. Place 36 foil baking cups in muffin pan cups. Prepare batter and fill cups as directed in step 2. Bake at 350°F for 18 to 20 minutes or until toothpick inserted into center comes out clean. Makes 36 fruitcakes.

Fancy Walnut Brownies

FANCY WALNUT BROWNIES

BROWNIES
    1 package DUNCAN HINES®
        Chocolate Lovers' Walnut
        Brownie Mix
    1 egg

$^1/_3$ cup water
$^1/_3$ cup CRISCO® Oil or
        CRISCO® PURITAN® Oil

GLAZE
    4$^1/_2$ cups confectioners sugar
    $^1/_2$ cup milk or water

24 walnut halves, for garnish

CHOCOLATE DRIZZLE
    $^1/_3$ cup semi-sweet chocolate
        chips

1 tablespoon CRISCO®
        Shortening

Continued

90

1. Preheat oven to 350°F. Place 24 (2-inch) foil liners on baking sheets.

2. **For brownies,** combine brownie mix, egg, water and oil in large bowl. Stir with spoon until well blended, about 50 strokes. Stir in contents of walnut packet from Mix. Fill each foil liner with 2 generous tablespoons batter. Bake at 350°F for 20 to 25 minutes or until set. Cool completely. Remove liners. Turn brownies upside down on cooling racks.

3. **For glaze,** combine confectioners sugar and milk in medium bowl. Blend until smooth. Spoon glaze over first brownie to completely cover. Top immediately with walnut half. Repeat with remaining brownies. Allow glaze to set.

4. **For chocolate drizzle,** place chocolate chips and shortening in small resealable plastic bag; seal. Place bag in bowl of hot water for several minutes. Dry with paper towel. Knead until blended and chocolate is smooth. Snip pinpoint hole in corner of bag. Drizzle chocolate over brownies. Allow chocolate drizzle to set before storing in single layer in airtight containers. *Makes 24 brownies*

CHERRY PINWHEEL SLICES

2 cups all-purpose flour
½ teaspoon salt
1 cup butter or margarine, softened
1 cup dairy sour cream

1 can SOLO® *or* 1 jar BAKER® Cherry, Raspberry or Strawberry Filling
1 cup flaked coconut
1 cup finely chopped pecans Confectioner's sugar

Place flour and salt in medium bowl. Cut in butter until mixture resembles coarse crumbs. Add sour cream; stir until blended. Divide dough into 4 pieces. Wrap each piece separately in plastic wrap or waxed paper; refrigerate 2 to 4 hours.

Preheat oven to 350°F. Roll out dough, 1 piece at a time, on lightly floured surface into 12×6-inch rectangle. Spread one fourth of filling over dough and sprinkle with ¼ cup coconut and ¼ cup pecans. Roll up, jelly-roll style, starting from short side. Pinch seam to seal. Place, seam side down, on ungreased baking sheet. Repeat with remaining dough, filling, coconut and pecans.

Bake 40 to 45 minutes or until rolls are golden brown. Remove from baking sheets to wire racks. Dust liberally with confectioner's sugar while still warm. Cool completely. Cut into 1-inch slices.
Makes about 2 dozen cookies

FUDGE-FILLED CREAM WAFERS

2 cups all-purpose flour
3/4 cup butter or margarine,
     softened
1/2 cup heavy cream

Granulated sugar
Fudge Filling (recipe
     follows)

Preheat oven to 375°F. Line cookie sheets with parchment paper or leave ungreased. Place flour in large bowl. Using electric mixer, blend 3/4 butter into flour until it forms pea-size pieces. Drizzle cream over the butter mixture; toss by hand just until mixed (mixture will look curdled).

Turn dough out onto lightly floured surface; press together to form ball. (If dough is too soft to handle, cover and refrigerate until firm.) Roll out dough, 1/3 at a time, to 1/8-inch thickness on lightly floured surface. Cut out with 1 1/4-inch round cutter. Dip top of each dough circle in granulated sugar. Place sugared side up, 2 inches apart, on prepared cookie sheets. Pierce each cookie with fork.

Bake 9 to 11 minutes or just until edges are very lightly browned. Remove to wire racks to cool. Prepare Fudge Filling. Spread filling on bottoms of half the cookies. Top with remaining cookies, bottom sides down, forming sandwiches.   *Makes about 10 dozen sandwich cookies*

FUDGE FILLING

1/4 cup butter or margarine
2 squares (1 ounce each)
     unsweetened chocolate
1 cup powdered sugar

1 teaspoon vanilla or dark
     rum
1 to 2 tablespoons hot coffee
     or water

Melt 1/4 cup butter and chocolate in small bowl over hot water. Stir until smooth. Blend in powdered sugar and vanilla. Stir in coffee until filling is spreadable, but not too soft.

ACKNOWLEDGMENTS

The publishers would like to thank the companies
and organizations listed below for the use
of their recipes in this publication.

Checkerboard Kitchens, Ralston Purina Company
Dole Food Company, Inc.
Filippo Berio Olive Oil
Hershey Chocolate U.S.A.
Kahlúa Liqueur
Kraft General Foods, Inc.
Nabisco Foods Group
Nestlé Foods Company
The Procter & Gamble Company
The Quaker Oats Company
Sokol and Company
Walnut Marketing Board
Wisconsin Milk Marketing Board

PHOTO CREDITS

The publishers would like to thank the companies
and organizations listed below for the use of
their photographs in this publication.

Dole Food Company, Inc.
Hershey Chocolate U.S.A.
Kraft General Foods, Inc.
Nestlé Foods Company
The Procter & Gamble Company

Index

Festive
HOLIDAY
COOKIES

From Your Favorite Brand Name Companies

Duncan Hines®   HERSHEY'S®   Nestlé®   Crisco® BUTTER FLAVOR

and many more

Festive
HOLIDAY
COOKIES

PUBLICATIONS INTERNATIONAL, LTD.

Front and back cover photography and photography on pages 5, 17, 21, 33,
39, 59, 73, 77 and 89 by Sanders Studios, Inc./Chicago
Photographer: Kathy Sanders
Food Stylist: Lenni Gilbert
Assistant Food Stylist: Carol Pearson

Pictured on the cover: Cherry Coconut Cookies (page 32), Cherry Rum
Cookies (page 20), Chocolate Scotcheroos (page 88), Chocolate
Thumbprints (page 34), Cornflake Macaroons (page 23), Cream Cheese
Cookies (page 32), Double Crunch Biscotti (page 4), Frosted Butter Cookies
(page 38), Frosty Cherry Cookies (page 7), Lemon Pecan Crescents
(page 19), Peanut Butter Stars (page 16), Pecan Crunchies (page 72),
Peppermint Refrigerator Slices (page 18), Snickerdoodles (page 72),
Snowpuff Cookies (page 7), Spicy Pumpkin Cookies (page 58), Spritz
Christmas Trees (page 16).

8 7 6 5 4 3 2 1

Manufactured in U.S.A.

Microwave Cooking: Microwave ovens vary in wattage. The cooking times
given in this publication are approximate. Use the cooking times as guidelines
and check for doneness before adding any more time.

Festive
HOLIDAY COOKIES

Holiday Specialties

DOUBLE CRUNCH BISCOTTI

⅓ cup vegetable oil
¾ cup sugar
3 eggs, beaten
½ teaspoon almond extract
½ teaspoon vanilla extract
2½ cups all-purpose flour
2 cups HONEY ALMOND
    DELIGHT® brand cereal,
    crushed to 1 cup

2 teaspoons baking powder
12 ounces chocolate, melted
    (optional)
¼ cup chopped almonds
    (optional)

Preheat oven to 350°F. Lightly grease cookie sheet. In large bowl, combine oil and sugar. Beat in eggs, almond extract and vanilla. Gradually stir in flour, cereal and baking powder. Divide dough in half. Place each half of dough on prepared cookie sheet; shape each into a 3½-inch by 11-inch log. Bake 25 to 28 minutes or until lightly browned. Remove from oven; immediately cut into ½-inch-thick slices. Place slices, cut side down, on clean ungreased cookie sheet. Bake 13 minutes, turning cookies over after 8 minutes. Cool on wire rack. If desired, spread chocolate on one end of each cookie; sprinkle with almonds. *Makes 44 cookies*

Top to bottom: Frosty Cherry Cookies (page 7),
Double Crunch Biscotti, Snow Puff Cookies (page 7)

ALMOND CREAM COOKIES

¾ cup (1½ sticks) margarine,
    softened
¾ cup granulated sugar
½ cup plus 2 tablespoons
    soft-style cream cheese
1 egg
1 teaspoon almond extract
1¼ cups all-purpose flour

¾ cup QUAKER® Corn Meal
½ teaspoon baking powder
½ cup coarsely chopped
    almonds
1 cup powdered sugar
1 tablespoon milk or water
Red or green candied
    cherries

Preheat oven to 350°F. Beat margarine, granulated sugar and ½ cup cream cheese at medium speed of electric mixer until fluffy. Add egg and almond extract; mix until well blended. Gradually add combined flour, corn meal and baking powder; mix well. Stir in almonds. Drop by rounded teaspoonfuls onto ungreased cookie sheet. Bake 12 to 14 minutes or until edges are golden brown. Cool on cookie sheet for 2 minutes; remove to wire rack. Cool completely.

Mix remaining 2 tablespoons cream cheese and powdered sugar until blended. Add milk; mix until smooth. Spread over cookies. Garnish with halved red or green candied cherries, if desired. Store tightly covered.

Makes about 4 dozen cookies

Almond Cream Cookies

FROSTY CHERRY COOKIES

½ cup (1 stick) butter or
    margarine
1 cup plus 3 tablespoons
    sugar, divided
1 egg, slightly beaten
½ teaspoon almond extract
1½ cups all-purpose flour

½ teaspoon salt
½ teaspoon baking soda
½ teaspoon baking powder
2 cups Rice CHEX® brand
    cereal, crushed to 1 cup
½ cup chopped green and red
    glacé cherries

Preheat oven to 350°F. In large bowl, combine butter and 1 cup sugar. Stir in egg and almond extract. Stir in flour, salt, baking soda and baking powder; mix well. Stir in cereal and cherries. Shape into ¾-inch balls. In small bowl, place remaining 3 tablespoons sugar. Roll balls in sugar. Place, 2 inches apart, on baking sheet. Bake 8 to 10 minutes or until bottoms are lightly browned. *Makes 6 dozen cookies*

SNOW PUFF COOKIES

1 cup (2 sticks) butter or
    margarine, softened
1 cup sifted confectioners'
    sugar
2 teaspoons vanilla

2 cups all-purpose flour
1 cup Wheat CHEX® brand
    cereal, crushed to ⅓ cup
½ teaspoon salt
    Confectioners' sugar

Preheat oven to 325°F. In large bowl, combine butter and 1 cup sugar until well blended. Stir in vanilla. Stir in flour, cereal and salt, mixing well. Shape into 1-inch balls. Place, 2 inches apart, on ungreased baking sheet. Bake 14 to 16 minutes or until bottoms are lightly browned. Cool. Roll in confectioners' sugar. *Makes 3 dozen cookies*

CHOCOLATE-DIPPED ALMOND HORNS

1½ cups powdered sugar
1 cup butter or margarine,
  softened
2 egg yolks
1½ teaspoons vanilla
2 cups all-purpose flour

½ cup ground almonds
1 teaspoon cream of tartar
1 teaspoon baking soda
1 cup semisweet chocolate
  chips, melted
Powdered sugar

Preheat oven to 325°F. In large mixer bowl, combine powdered sugar and butter. Beat at medium speed, scraping bowl often, until creamy, 1 to 2 minutes. Add egg yolks and vanilla; continue beating until well blended, 1 to 2 minutes. Reduce speed to low. Add flour, almonds, cream of tartar and baking soda. Continue beating, scraping bowl often, until well mixed, 1 to 2 minutes. Shape into 1-inch balls. Roll balls into 2-inch ropes; shape into crescents. Place, 2 inches apart, on cookie sheets. Flatten slightly with glass bottom covered in waxed paper. Bake for 8 to 10 minutes or until set. (Cookies do not brown.) Cool completely. Dip half of each cookie into chocolate; sprinkle remaining half with powdered sugar. Refrigerate until set.   *Makes about 3 dozen cookies*

CHERRY DOT COOKIES

2¼ cups all-purpose flour
2 teaspoons baking powder
½ teaspoon salt
¾ cup margarine, softened
1 cup sugar
2 eggs
2 tablespoons skim milk
1 teaspoon vanilla
1 cup chopped nuts

1 cup finely cut pitted dates
⅓ cup finely chopped
  maraschino cherries
2⅔ cups KELLOGGS'® CORN
  FLAKES® cereal, crushed
  to 1⅓ cups
15 maraschino cherries, cut
  into quarters

1. Preheat oven to 350°F. Stir together flour, baking powder and salt. Set aside.

2. In large mixing bowl, beat margarine and sugar until light and fluffy. Add eggs. Beat well. Stir in milk and vanilla. Add flour mixture. Mix well. Stir in nuts, dates and ⅓ cup chopped cherries.

3. Shape level measuring tablespoons of dough into balls. Roll in Kelloggs'® Corn Flakes® cereal. Place on cookie sheets coated with cooking spray. Top each cookie with cherry quarter.

4. Bake about 12 minutes or until lightly browned.
                                        Makes about 5 dozen cookies

Chocolate-Dipped Almond Horns

HOLIDAY SHORTBREAD WITH VARIATIONS

| 1 cup (2 sticks) butter | 2½ cups all-purpose flour |
| ½ cup sugar | ¼ teaspoon salt |

Preheat oven to 375°F. Cream butter in large mixer bowl until fluffy. Add sugar; beat until light and fluffy. Gradually blend in flour and salt. Roll out on lightly floured surface to 11 × 7-inch rectangle, ½ inch thick. Cut into 1-inch squares. Bake on unbuttered cookie sheets 12 to 15 minutes or until a pale golden color. Cool completely on wire racks. Store at room temperature in container with tight fitting lid.   *Makes about 6 dozen*

Variations

Anise Stars: Prepare Basic Shortbread, stirring in ¾ teaspoon anise extract and ¼ teaspoon nutmeg with flour and salt. Wrap dough in plastic wrap. Refrigerate 1 to 2 hours. Roll dough to ¼-inch thickness on lightly floured surface. Cut into star shape using floured cutter. Bake in preheated 375°F oven on unbuttered cookie sheets 13 to 15 minutes or until very pale golden color. Cool completely on wire rack. Decorate with red and green frosting and small silver dragées. Makes 3 to 4 dozen.

Rum Raisin Balls: Prepare Basic Shortbread, stirring in 1 cup golden seedless raisins and 1 teaspoon rum extract with flour and salt. Form into 1-inch balls. Bake in preheated 375°F oven on unbuttered cookie sheets 15 to 18 minutes or until pale golden color. Remove from cookie sheets; cool completely on wire racks. Dust lightly with confectioners' sugar before serving. Makes 5 dozen.

Noel Tarts: Prepare Basic Shortbread, stirring in 1 teaspoon vanilla extract with flour and salt. Press rounded tablespoonfuls of dough into 1¾-inch muffin cups. Bake in preheated 375°F oven 18 to 20 minutes or until pale golden in color. Cool in pan 10 minutes. Carefully remove from pan; cool completely on wire rack. Fill as desired with pie filling, pudding, mincemeat, etc. Makes 3 dozen.

Chocolate-Frosted Almond Bars: Prepare Basic Shortbread, reducing flour to 2 cups. Add ½ cup finely ground almonds and 1 teaspoon almond extract with flour and salt. Press into unbuttered 13 × 9-inch baking pan. Bake in preheated 375°F oven 20 to 25 minutes or until pale golden color. Cool completely in pan on wire rack. Frost with 1 package (6 oz.) semisweet chocolate morsels, melted, and combined with ½ cup dairy sour cream and 1 teaspoon vanilla extract. Cut into bars. Decorate with sliced almonds. Makes 4 dozen.

Favorite recipe from American Dairy Industry Association

Top to bottom: Anise Stars, Rum Raisin Balls, Noel Tarts, Chocolate-Frosted Almond Bars

DOUBLE SURPRISE COOKIES

⅔ cup butter or margarine
⅓ cup sugar
2 egg yolks
½ teaspoon vanilla
⅛ teaspoon almond extract
1½ cups all-purpose flour
¼ teaspoon salt
36 "M&M's"® Peanut, Peanut
    Butter or Almond
    Chocolate Candies

¼ cup confectioners'
    (powdered) sugar
1½ teaspoons water
¾ cup "M&M's"® Semi-Sweet
    Chocolate Candies*

Preheat oven to 350°F. In mixer, beat butter 30 seconds. Gradually add sugar; beat until light and fluffy. Add egg yolks, vanilla and almond extract; beat thoroughly. Stir together flour and salt. Add to creamed mixture; mix well. Cover and chill at least 1 hour. For each cookie, shape, with floured hands, a rounded teaspoonful dough around each Peanut, Peanut Butter or Almond "M&M's"® to form a ball, about 1 inch in diameter. Place, 1 inch apart, on ungreased baking sheet. Bake 12 to 15 minutes until dough springs back when touched and cookie is lightly browned on bottom. Remove to wire rack; cool completely. To decorate, mix together confectioners' sugar and water until smooth. Spread on tops of cookies; immediately sprinkle generously with "M&M's"® Semi-Sweet Chocolate Candies, pressing in lightly.

Makes 36 cookies

*Found in baking section.

PEPPERMINT MACAROONS

2 egg whites
1 cup sugar
2 cups KELLOGGS'® SPECIAL
    K® cereal
½ cup (about 4 ozs.)
    peppermint candy canes,
    crushed (about 5 candy
    canes)

½ teaspoon vanilla
Vegetable cooking spray

1. In the bowl of an electric mixer, beat egg whites until foamy. Gradually add sugar, beating until stiff and glossy.

2. Add Kelloggs'® Special K® cereal, crushed candy canes and vanilla, mixing until blended. Drop by rounded teaspoonfuls onto baking sheets lightly coated with cooking spray.

3. Bake at 350°F about 12 minutes. Remove immediately from baking sheets. Let cool on wire racks. Store in airtight container.

Makes about 3½ dozen cookies

Kolacky

KOLACKY

½ cup butter or margarine,
   softened
3 ounces cream cheese,
   softened
1 teaspoon vanilla
1 cup all-purpose flour

⅛ teaspoon salt
6 teaspoons fruit preserves,
   assorted flavors
1 egg
1 teaspoon cold water
   Powdered sugar (optional)

Combine butter and cream cheese in large bowl; beat until smooth and
creamy. Blend in vanilla. Combine flour and salt; gradually add to butter
mixture, mixing until mixture forms soft dough. Divide dough in half;
wrap each half in plastic wrap. Refrigerate until firm.

Preheat oven to 375°F. Roll out half of dough on lightly floured pastry
cloth or board to ⅛-inch thickness. Cut with top of glass or biscuit cutter
into 3-inch rounds. Spoon ½ teaspoon preserves onto center of each
dough circle. Beat egg with water; lightly brush onto edges of dough
circles. Bring three edges of dough up over fruit spread; pinch edges
together to seal. Place on ungreased cookie sheets; brush with egg
mixture. Repeat with remaining dough, fruit spread and egg mixture.
Bake 12 minutes or until golden brown. Let stand on cookie sheets 1
minute; transfer to wire rack. Cool completely. Sprinkle with powdered
sugar, if desired. Store in tightly covered container. *Makes 2 dozen*

Anise Cookie Cordials

ANISE COOKIE CORDIALS

2¾ cups all-purpose flour
1½ teaspoons baking powder
1 cup sugar
½ cup butter, softened
3 eggs
2 tablespoons anise-flavored
    liqueur
2 tablespoons water

1 tablespoon anise seeds
½ of 12-ounce package
    (1 cup) NESTLÉ® Toll
    House® Mini Morsels
    Semi-Sweet Chocolate
1 cup coarsely chopped
    toasted almonds

In medium bowl, combine flour and baking powder; set aside. In large
bowl, combine sugar and butter; beat until creamy. Add eggs, anise-
flavored liqueur, water and anise seeds; beat until well blended. Gradually
beat in flour mixture. Stir in mini morsels and almonds. Cover; chill
several hours.

Preheat oven to 375°F. Divide dough into four pieces. With floured hands,
shape each piece into 15½ × 2 × ½-inch loaf. Place loaves, 4 inches apart,
on greased cookie sheets. Bake at 375°F for 15 minutes. Remove from
oven. Cut into 1-inch slices. Place slices back on cookie sheets. Bake at
375°F for 7 minutes. Turn cookies over. Bake at 375°F for 7 minutes. Cool
completely on wire racks.

Makes about 4½ dozen (1-inch) cookies

TWO-TONED SPRITZ COOKIES

1 square (1 ounce)
  unsweetened chocolate,
  coarsely chopped
2¼ cups all-purpose flour
¼ teaspoon salt

1 cup butter or margarine,
  softened
1 cup sugar
1 large egg
1 teaspoon vanilla

Melt chocolate in small, heavy saucepan over low heat, stirring constantly; set aside. Combine flour and salt; set aside. Beat butter and sugar in large bowl until light and fluffy. Beat in egg and vanilla. Gradually add flour mixture. Remove and reserve 2 cups dough. Beat chocolate into dough in bowl until smooth. Cover both doughs and refrigerate until easy to handle, about 20 minutes.

Preheat oven to 400°F. Roll out vanilla dough between two sheets of waxed paper to ½-inch thickness. Cut into 5×4-inch rectangles. Place chocolate dough on sheet of waxed paper. Using waxed paper to hold dough, roll it back and forth to form a log about 1-inch in diameter. Cut into 5-inch-long logs. Place chocolate log in center of vanilla rectangle. Wrap vanilla dough around log and fit into cookie press fitted with star disc. Press dough onto cookie sheets 1½ inches apart. Bake about 10 minutes or until just set. Remove cookies with spatula to wire racks; cool completely.   *Makes about 4 dozen cookies*

LEMON BUTTER COOKIES

2 cups all-purpose flour
½ teaspoon baking soda
1 cup BLUE BONNET®
  Margarine, softened
1 cup sugar

1 teaspoon vanilla extract
1 teaspoon grated lemon
  peel
1 egg
Sugar

Preheat oven to 375°F.

In small bowl, combine flour and baking soda; set aside.

In medium bowl, with electric mixer at medium speed, beat margarine, sugar, vanilla and lemon peel just until blended. Beat in egg until light and fluffy. Gradually blend in flour mixture. Drop dough by rounded teaspoonfuls, 2 inches apart, onto ungreased cookie sheets. Grease bottom of small glass; dip into sugar. Press onto dough to flatten slightly. Bake for 8 to 10 minutes. Remove from sheets; cool on wire racks. Store in airtight container.   *Makes about 4½ dozen cookies*

SPRITZ CHRISTMAS TREES

⅓ cup (3½ ounces) almond paste
1 egg
1 package DUNCAN HINES® Golden Sugar Cookie Mix
8 drops green food coloring

1 container DUNCAN HINES® Vanilla Layer Cake Frosting
Cinnamon candies, for garnish

1. Preheat oven to 375°F.

2. Combine almond paste and egg in large bowl. Beat at low speed with electric mixer until blended. Add contents of buttery flavor packet from Mix and green food coloring. Beat until smooth and evenly tinted. Add cookie mix. Beat at low speed until thoroughly blended.

3. Fit cookie press with Christmas tree plate; fill with dough. Force dough through press, 2 inches apart, onto ungreased cookie sheets. Bake at 375°F for 6 to 7 minutes or until set but not browned. Cool 1 minute on cookie sheets. Remove to cooling racks. Cool completely.

4. To decorate, fill resealable plastic bag half full with vanilla frosting. Do not seal bag. Cut pinpoint hole in bottom corner of bag. Pipe small dot of frosting onto tip of one cookie tree and top with cinnamon candy. Repeat with remaining cookies. Pipe remaining frosting to form garland on cookie trees. Allow frosting to set before storing between layers of waxed paper in airtight container. *Makes about 5 dozen cookies*

PEANUT BUTTER STARS

1 package DUNCAN HINES® Peanut Butter Cookie Mix
1 egg
2 packages (3½ ounces each) chocolate sprinkles

2 packages (7 ounces each) milk chocolate candy stars

1. Preheat oven to 375°F.

2. Combine cookie mix, contents of peanut butter packet from Mix and egg in large bowl. Stir until thoroughly blended. Shape dough into ¾-inch balls. Roll in chocolate sprinkles. Place, 2 inches apart, on ungreased cookie sheets. Bake at 375°F for 8 to 9 minutes or until set. Immediately place milk chocolate candy stars on top of hot cookies. Cool 1 minute on cookie sheets. Remove to cooling racks. Cool completely. Store in airtight containers. *Makes 7½ to 8 dozen cookies*

Counter-clockwise from top: Peppermint Refrigerator Slices (page 18), Lemon Pecan Crescents (page 19), Spritz Christmas Trees, Peanut Butter Stars

PEPPERMINT REFRIGERATOR SLICES

3 packages DUNCAN HINES®
   Golden Sugar Cookie Mix,
   divided
3 eggs, divided
3 to 4 drops red food
   coloring

¾ teaspoon peppermint
   extract, divided
3 to 4 drops green food
   coloring

1. **For pink cookie dough,** combine contents of one buttery flavor packet from Mix, one egg, red food coloring and ¼ teaspoon peppermint extract in large bowl. Stir until evenly tinted. Add one cookie mix and stir until thoroughly blended. Set aside.

2. **For green cookie dough,** combine contents of one buttery flavor packet from Mix, one egg, green food coloring and ¼ teaspoon peppermint extract in large bowl. Stir until evenly tinted. Add one cookie mix and stir until thoroughly blended. Set aside.

3. **For plain cookie dough,** combine remaining cookie mix, contents of buttery flavor packet from Mix, egg and ¼ teaspoon peppermint extract in large bowl. Stir until thoroughly blended.

4. **To assemble,** divide each batch of cookie dough into four equal portions. Shape each portion into 12-inch-long roll on waxed paper. Lay one pink roll beside one green roll; press together slightly. Place one plain roll on top. Press rolls together to form one tri-colored roll; wrap in waxed paper or plastic wrap. Repeat with remaining rolls to form three more tri-colored rolls; wrap separately in waxed paper or plastic wrap. Refrigerate rolls for several hours or overnight.

5. Preheat oven to 375°F.

6. Cut chilled rolls into ¼-inch-thick slices. Place, 2 inches apart, on ungreased cookie sheets. Bake at 375°F for 7 to 8 minutes or until set but not browned. Cool 1 minute on cookie sheets. Remove to cooling racks. Cool completely. Store in airtight containers.

Makes about 15 dozen small cookies

CHERRY THUMBPRINT COOKIES

¾ cup sugar
½ cup HELLMANN'S® or BEST
   FOODS® Real Mayonnaise
½ cup MAZOLA® Margarine
2 eggs, separated
1 teaspoon vanilla

2 cups all-purpose flour
¼ teaspoon ground nutmeg
1½ cups finely chopped
   walnuts or almonds
Red and green candied
   cherries

In large bowl, beat sugar, mayonnaise, margarine, egg yolks and vanilla. Beat in flour and nutmeg until well blended. Cover; refrigerate until firm, at least 3 hours.

Preheat oven to 350°F. Shape dough into ¾-inch balls. In small bowl, beat egg whites with fork until foamy. Dip each ball into egg whites; roll in nuts. Place, 1½ inches apart, on greased cookie sheets. Press thumb into centers of balls. Place one whole cherry in each center. Bake 15 to 17 minutes or until bottoms are browned. Let cookies cool slightly before removing them from cookie sheets to wire racks.

Makes about 5 dozen cookies

LEMON PECAN CRESCENTS

1 package DUNCAN HINES®
    Golden Sugar Cookie Mix
2 egg whites
¾ cup toasted pecans,
    chopped

¼ cup all-purpose flour
1 tablespoon grated lemon
    peel
Confectioners sugar

1. Preheat oven to 375°F.

2. Combine cookie mix, contents of buttery flavor packet from Mix, egg whites, pecans, flour and lemon peel in large bowl. Stir until thoroughly blended. Form level ½ measuring tablespoonfuls dough into crescent shapes. Place, 2 inches apart, on ungreased baking sheets. Bake at 375°F for 7 to 8 minutes or until set but not browned. Cool 2 minutes on baking sheets. Remove to cooling racks. Roll warm cookies in confectioners sugar. Cool completely. Roll cookies again in confectioners sugar. Store between layers of waxed paper in airtight container.

Makes about 5 dozen cookies

DATE-NUT MACAROONS

1 (8-ounce) package pitted
    dates, chopped
1½ cups flaked coconut
1 cup PLANTERS® Pecan
    Halves, chopped

¾ cup sweetened condensed
    milk (not evaporated
    milk)
½ teaspoon vanilla extract

Preheat oven to 350°F.

In medium bowl, combine dates, coconut and nuts; blend in sweetened condensed milk and vanilla. Drop by rounded tablespoonfuls onto greased and floured cookie sheets. Bake for 10 to 12 minutes or until light golden brown. Carefully remove from cookie sheets; cool completely on wire racks. Store in airtight container.

Makes about 2 dozen cookies

Cookie Exchange Favorites

CHERRY RUM COOKIES

4 cups KELLOGGS'®
    SPECIAL K® cereal,
    crushed to 1½ cups,
    divided
2¼ cups all-purpose flour
  1 teaspoon baking powder
¼ teaspoon salt (optional)

½ cup margarine, softened
⅔ cup sugar
 1 egg
 1 teaspoon rum flavoring
10 to 12 maraschino cherries,
    cut into quarters

1. Stir together 1 cup of the crushed Kelloggs'® Special K® cereal, flour, baking powder and salt. Set aside.

2. In large mixing bowl, beat margarine and sugar until light and fluffy. Add egg and rum flavoring. Beat well. Add dry ingredients. Mix well.

3. Shape dough into balls using rounded measuring teaspoon. Roll in remaining ½ cup crushed cereal. Place on ungreased baking sheets. Top each cookie with cherry quarter.

4. Bake at 375°F about 12 minutes or until lightly browned. Remove immediately from baking sheets. Cool on wire racks. Store in airtight container. *Makes 3½ dozen*

Top to bottom: Corn Flake Macaroons (page 23),
Cherry Rum Cookies

CHOCOLATE-DIPPED BRANDY SNAPS

½ cup butter
½ cup sugar
⅓ cup dark corn syrup
½ teaspoon cinnamon
¼ teaspoon ginger
1 cup all-purpose flour
2 teaspoons brandy

1 cup (6-ounce package)
NESTLÉ® Toll House®
Semi-Sweet Chocolate
Morsels
1 tablespoon vegetable
shortening
⅓ cup finely chopped nuts

Preheat oven to 300°F. In heavy saucepan, combine butter, sugar, dark corn syrup, cinnamon and ginger; cook over medium heat, stirring constantly, until melted and smooth. Remove from heat; stir in flour and brandy. Drop mixture by rounded teaspoonfuls, about 3 inches apart, onto ungreased cookie sheets. (Do not bake more than 6 cookies at one time.)

Bake at 300°F for 10 to 12 minutes. Let stand a few seconds. Remove from cookie sheets and immediately roll around wooden spoon handle; cool completely. Combine over hot (not boiling) water, semi-sweet chocolate morsels and vegetable shortening; stir until morsels are melted and mixture is smooth. Dip each Brandy Snap halfway into melted chocolate. Sprinkle with nuts; set on waxed paper-lined cookie sheets. Chill until set. Store in airtight container in refrigerator.

Makes about 3 dozen (2½-inch) snaps

Chocolate-Dipped Brandy Snaps

CORN FLAKE MACAROONS

4 egg whites	1 cup chopped pecans
1 teaspoon vanilla	1 cup shredded coconut
¼ teaspoon cream of tartar	3 cups KELLOGGS'® CORN
1⅓ cups sugar	FLAKES® cereal

1. Preheat oven to 325°F. In large mixing bowl, beat egg whites until foamy. Stir in vanilla and cream of tartar. Gradually add sugar, beating until stiff and glossy. Fold in pecans, coconut and Kellogg's® Corn Flakes® cereal. Drop mixture by rounded measuring tablespoons onto cookie sheets sprayed with vegetable cooking spray.

2. Bake about 15 minutes or until lightly browned. Remove immediately from cookie sheets. Cool on wire racks.

Makes about 3 dozen cookies

Variation: Fold in ½ cup crushed peppermint candy with pecans and coconut.

RASPBERRY ALMOND SANDWICH COOKIES

SANDWICH COOKIES

1 package DUNCAN HINES®	½ teaspoon almond extract
Golden Sugar Cookie Mix	¾ cup sliced natural almonds,
1 egg	broken
1 tablespoon water	Seedless red raspberry jam

1. Preheat oven to 375°F.

2. Combine cookie mix, buttery flavor packet from Mix, egg, water and almond extract in large bowl. Stir until thoroughly blended. Drop half the dough by level measuring teaspoons, 2 inches apart, onto ungreased cookie sheets. (It is a small amount of dough but will spread during baking to 1½ to 1¾ inches.)

3. Place almonds on waxed paper. Drop other half of dough by level measuring teaspoons onto nuts. Place, almond-side up, 2 inches apart on cookie sheets.

4. Bake both plain and almond cookies at 375°F for 6 minutes or until set but not browned. Cool 1 minute on cookie sheets. Remove to cooling racks. Cool completely.

5. Spread bottoms of plain cookies with jam; top with almond cookies. Press together to make sandwiches. Store in airtight container.

Makes 4½ to 5 dozen cookies

NO-BAKE PEANUTTY COOKIES

2 cups Roasted Honey Nut
    SKIPPY® Creamy or
    SUPER CHUNK® Peanut
    Butter
2 cups graham cracker
    crumbs
1 cup confectioners' sugar

½ cup KARO® Light or Dark
    Corn Syrup
¼ cup semisweet chocolate
    chips, melted
Colored sprinkles
    (optional)

In large bowl, combine peanut butter, graham cracker crumbs, confectioners' sugar and corn syrup. Mix until smooth. Shape into 1-inch balls. Place on waxed paper-lined cookie sheets. Drizzle melted chocolate over balls or roll in colored sprinkles. Store covered in refrigerator.

Makes about 5 dozen cookies

MELTING MOMENTS

1 cup flour
½ cup ARGO® or
    KINGSFORD'S® Corn
    Starch

½ cup confectioners sugar
¾ cup MAZOLA® Margarine,
    softened
1 teaspoon vanilla

In medium bowl, combine flour, corn starch and confectioners sugar. In large bowl with mixer at medium speed, beat margarine until smooth. Add flour mixture and vanilla; beat until well blended. If necessary, refrigerate dough 1 hour or until easy to handle.

Preheat oven to 350°F. Shape dough into 1-inch balls. Place, 1½ inches apart, on ungreased cookie sheets; flatten with lightly floured fork. Bake 10 to 12 minutes or until edges are lightly browned. Remove from cookie sheets; cool completely on wire racks. Store in tightly covered container.

Makes about 3 dozen cookies

Almond Melting Moments: Add 1 cup finely chopped almonds to flour mixture.

Food Processor Method: In bowl of food processor with metal blade, combine flour, corn starch and confectioners sugar. Cut cold margarine into 1-inch pieces. Add to flour mixture. Process, adding vanilla through feed tube, 15 seconds or until mixture forms a ball. Continue as above.

CHOCOLATE CHIP & MINT MERINGUE COOKIES

3 egg whites
½ teaspoon cream of tartar
  Pinch of salt
¾ cup sugar
4 drops green food coloring

4 drops mint extract
1 (6-ounce) package
    miniature semisweet
    chocolate chips

Preheat oven to 375°F. Grease and lightly flour two cookie sheets. Beat egg whites with cream of tartar and salt until foamy. Gradually beat in sugar, 2 tablespoons at a time, until soft peaks form. Stir in food coloring and mint extract. Fold in chocolate chips. Drop meringue by teaspoonfuls, 1 inch apart, onto prepared cookie sheets. Place in preheated oven. Turn off heat; let meringues set in oven 8 to 12 hours.

Makes about 4 dozen cookies

Chocolate Chip & Mint Meringue Cookies

CHOCO-CHERRY COOKIES SUPREME

⅔ cup all-purpose flour
½ cup unsweetened cocoa
1½ teaspoons baking powder
½ teaspoon salt
⅓ cup butter or margarine,
softened
½ cup granulated sugar
½ cup packed light brown
sugar
⅓ cup milk

1 large egg
1 teaspoon vanilla
2 cups uncooked quick-
cooking or old-fashioned
oats
3 ounces white baking bar *or*
white chocolate candy
bar, cut into ¼-inch
pieces
½ cup candied cherries

Preheat oven to 375°F. Combine flour, cocoa, baking powder and salt; set aside. Beat butter and sugars in large bowl with electric mixer at medium speed until light and fluffy. Beat in milk, egg and vanilla, scraping down side of bowl once. Gradually add flour mixture. Stir in oats until well blended. Stir in baking bar pieces and cherries. Drop heaping teaspoonfuls of dough, 2 inches apart, onto greased cookie sheets. Bake 10 minutes or until set. Let stand on cookie sheets 1 minute. Remove cookies to wire racks; cool completely.   *Makes about 3 dozen cookies*

PECAN DROPS

¾ cup sugar
½ cup FLEISCHMANN'S®
Margarine, softened
¼ cup EGG BEATERS® 99% Egg
Product
1 teaspoon vanilla extract

2 cups all-purpose flour
⅔ cup PLANTERS® Pecans,
finely chopped
3 tablespoons jam, jelly or
preserves, any flavor

In small bowl, with electric mixer at medium speed, cream sugar and margarine. Add egg product and vanilla; beat for 1 minute. Stir in flour until blended. Chill dough for 1 hour.

Preheat oven to 350°F. Form dough into 36 (1¼-inch) balls; roll in pecans, pressing into dough. Place, 2 inches apart, on greased cookie sheets. Indent center of each ball with thumb or back of wooden spoon. Bake for 10 minutes; remove from oven. Spoon ¼ teaspoon jam into each cookie indentation. Bake for 2 to 5 more minutes or until lightly browned. Remove from sheets; cool on wire racks.
Makes about 3 dozen cookies

DATE MENENAS

2¾ cups all-purpose flour
½ teaspoon DAVIS® Baking
   Powder
¾ cup sugar, divided
⅔ cup FLEISCHMANN'S®
   Margarine, softened
1 teaspoon vanilla extract

¼ cup EGG BEATERS® 99%
   Real Egg Product
8 ounces pitted dates, finely
   chopped
½ cup water
1 tablespoon lemon juice

In medium bowl, combine flour and baking powder. Set aside. Reserve
2 tablespoons sugar for date filling. In large bowl of electric mixer, on
medium speed, beat margarine and remaining sugar until creamy. On low
speed, add vanilla and Egg Beaters® alternately with flour mixture. Beat
until well combined. Form into flattened disk; wrap in plastic wrap.
Refrigerate 1 hour.

To make date filling, place dates, water, reserved sugar and lemon juice in
medium saucepan. Bring to a boil. Reduce heat; simmer, covered, 10
minutes. Remove from heat; let cool to room temperature.

Preheat oven to 400°F. Cut dough in half. On floured waxed paper, roll
each half of dough to 12×10-inch rectangle. Spread half the filling (½
cup) onto each dough piece. From long side, roll up as a jelly roll. With
thread, cut log into ⅜-inch slices. Place on greased cookie sheets. Repeat
with remaining dough and filling.

Bake at 10 minutes or until bottoms are lightly browned. Remove to wire
rack to cool. Store in airtight container.

Makes about 5 dozen cookies

CHOCOLATE CHERRY DROPS

FUDGE FILLING
1 package (6 ounces) semi-
   sweet chocolate chips
½ cup sweetened condensed
   milk

2 tablespoons maraschino
   cherry juice

COOKIES
1 package DUNCAN HINES®
   Chocolate Chip Cookie
   Mix
1 egg

⅓ cup chopped maraschino
   cherries, well drained
42 maraschino cherry halves,
   well drained, for garnish

Chocolate Cherry Drops

1. Preheat oven to 350°F.

2. **For Fudge Filling,** combine chocolate chips, sweetened condensed milk and maraschino cherry juice in small saucepan. Heat on low heat until chocolate chips are melted, stirring until smooth. Set aside.

3. **For Cookies,** combine cookie mix, contents of buttery flavor packet from Mix and egg in large bowl. Stir until thoroughly blended. Stir in chopped maraschino cherries. Drop dough by rounded teaspoonfuls, 2 inches apart, onto ungreased cookie sheets. Bake at 350°F for 5 minutes. Remove from oven. Drop 1 rounded teaspoonful fudge filling onto top of each partially baked cookie. Top each with maraschino cherry half. Bake 4 to 5 minutes longer or until edges are light golden brown. Cool 2 minutes on cookie sheets. Remove to cooling racks. Cool completely. Store between layers of waxed paper in airtight container.

Makes about 3½ dozen cookies

Chocolate Peanut Butter Cup Cookies

CHOCOLATE PEANUT BUTTER CUP COOKIES

COOKIES
   1 cup semi-sweet chocolate
      chips
   2 squares (1 ounce each)
      unsweetened baking
      chocolate
   1 cup sugar
   ½ cup BUTTER FLAVOR
      CRISCO®
   2 eggs

   1 teaspoon salt
   1 teaspoon vanilla
   1½ cups plus 2 tablespoons
      all-purpose flour
   ½ teaspoon baking soda
   ¾ cup finely chopped
      peanuts
   36 miniature peanut butter
      cups, unwrapped

DRIZZLE
   1 cup peanut butter chips

1. Heat oven to 350°F.

2. **For Cookies,** combine chocolate chips and chocolate squares in microwave-safe measuring cup or bowl. Microwave at 50% (MEDIUM) 2 minutes; stir. Repeat until smooth (or melt on rangetop in small saucepan on very low heat). Cool slightly.

3. Combine sugar and Butter Flavor Crisco® in large bowl. Beat at medium speed of electric mixer until blended and crumbly. Beat in eggs, one at a time, then salt and vanilla. Reduce speed to low. Add chocolate slowly. Mix until well blended. Stir in flour and baking soda with spoon until well blended. Shape dough into 1¼-inch balls. Roll in nuts. Place, 2 inches apart, on ungreased cookie sheet.

4. Bake at 350°F for 8 to 10 minutes or until set. Immediately press peanut butter cup into center of each cookie. Press sides of cookie up against cup. Cool 2 minutes on cookie sheet before removing to cooling rack. Cool completely.

5. **For Drizzle,** place peanut butter chips in heavy resealable sandwich bag. Seal. Microwave at 50% (MEDIUM) 1 minute. Knead bag. Repeat until smooth (or melt by placing bag in hot water). Cut tiny tip off bottom corner of bag. Squeeze out and drizzle over cookies.

Makes about 3 dozen cookies

TOFFEE TASSIES

½ cup margarine or butter	1 egg
1 (3-ounce) package cream cheese, softened	1 tablespoon margarine or butter, melted
1 cup all-purpose flour	½ cup chopped pecans
¼ cup ground pecans	½ cup HEATH® Bits
¾ cup packed brown sugar	

For pastry, in a mixing bowl beat ½ cup margarine or butter and cream cheese until thoroughly combined. Stir in flour and ground pecans. Press a rounded teaspoon of pastry evenly into the bottom and up sides of 24 ungreased 1¾-inch miniature muffin cups. Set aside.

For filling, beat together brown sugar, egg and 1 tablespoon melted margarine or butter. Stir in chopped pecans. Spoon 1 teaspoon filling into each pastry-lined cup. Sprinkle about 1 teaspoon Heath® Bits over each. Bake in a 325°F oven about 30 minutes or until pastry is golden and filling is puffed. Cool slightly in pans on wire racks. Remove and cool completely on wire racks.

Makes 24 tassies

CHERRY COCONUT COOKIES

¾ cup sugar
¾ cup BUTTER FLAVOR
   CRISCO®
1 egg
1 teaspoon grated lemon
   peel
¾ teaspoon almond extract
½ teaspoon salt
1¾ cups all-purpose flour

1 teaspoon baking powder
½ teaspoon baking soda
¾ cup flaked coconut
½ cup coarsely chopped
   pecans
⅓ cup quartered maraschino
   cherries, well drained on
   paper towel

1. Preheat oven to 350°F.

2. Combine sugar, Butter Flavor Crisco®, egg, lemon peel, almond extract and salt in large bowl. Beat at medium speed of electric mixer until well blended.

3. Combine flour, baking powder and baking soda. Add gradually to creamed mixture, mixing at low speed until blended. Stir in coconut, nuts and cherries with spoon. Shape dough into 1-inch balls. Place, 2 inches apart, on ungreased cookie sheet.

4. Bake at 350°F for 11 to 12 minutes. Cool on cookie sheet 1 minute before removing to cooling rack.   *Makes about 3½ dozen cookies*

CREAM CHEESE COOKIES

½ cup BUTTER FLAVOR
   CRISCO®
1 package (3 ounces) cream
   cheese, softened
1 tablespoon milk

1 cup sugar
½ teaspoon vanilla
1 cup all-purpose flour
½ cup chopped pecans

1. Preheat oven to 375°F.

2. Combine Butter Flavor Crisco®, cream cheese and milk in medium bowl. Beat at medium speed of electric mixer until well blended. Beat in sugar and vanilla. Mix in flour. Add nuts. Drop dough by level measuring tablespoonfuls, 2 inches apart, onto ungreased cookie sheet.

3. Bake at 375°F for 10 minutes. Remove to cooling rack.
                              Makes about 3 dozen cookies

Top to bottom: Cherry Coconut Cookies, Cream Cheese Cookies, Chocolate Thumbprints (page 34)

CHOCOLATE THUMBPRINTS

COOKIES

½ cup BUTTER FLAVOR CRISCO®
½ cup granulated sugar
1 tablespoon milk
½ teaspoon vanilla
1 egg yolk
1 square (1 ounce) unsweetened baking chocolate, melted and cooled

1 cup all-purpose flour
¼ teaspoon salt
⅓ cup mini semisweet chocolate chips

PEANUT BUTTER CREAM FILLING

2 tablespoons BUTTER FLAVOR CRISCO®
⅓ cup JIF® Creamy Peanut Butter

1 cup confectioners sugar
2 tablespoons milk
½ teaspoon vanilla

1. Preheat oven to 350°F. Grease cookie sheet with Butter Flavor Crisco®.

2. **For Cookies,** combine ½ cup Butter Flavor Crisco®, granulated sugar, milk, vanilla and egg yolk in large bowl. Beat at medium speed of electric mixer until well blended. Add melted chocolate. Mix well.

3. Combine flour and salt. Add gradually to chocolate mixture while mixing at low speed until blended. Add chocolate chips. Shape dough into 1-inch balls. Place, 2 inches apart, on greased cookie sheet. Press thumb gently into center of each cookie.

4. Bake at 350°F for 8 minutes. Press centers again with small measuring spoon. Remove to cooling rack. Cool completely.

5. **For Peanut Butter Cream Filling,** combine 2 tablespoons Butter Flavor Crisco® and peanut butter in medium bowl. Stir with spoon until blended. Add confectioners sugar. Stir well. Add 2 tablespoons milk and vanilla. Stir until smooth. Spoon into centers of cookies.

Makes about 2½ dozen cookies

WALNUT JAM CRESCENTS

⅔ cup butter or margarine
1⅓ cups all-purpose flour
½ cup dairy sour cream
⅔ cup raspberry jam or orange marmalade

⅔ cup DIAMOND® Walnuts, finely chopped, divided

Preheat oven to 350°F. In medium bowl, cut butter into flour until mixture resembles fine crumbs. Add sour cream; mix until stiff dough is formed. Divide dough in half. Shape each half into a ball; flatten slightly. Wrap balls in waxed paper; chill well. Working with one half of dough at a time, roll dough into 11-inch round on lightly floured pastry cloth or board. Spread with ⅓ cup jam; sprinkle with ⅓ cup walnuts. Cut into quarters; cut each quarter into three wedges. Roll up, one at a time, starting from outer edge; place on lightly greased cookie sheets. Repeat with remaining half of dough. Bake 25 to 30 minutes or until lightly browned. Remove to wire racks to cool.

Makes about 2 dozen crescents

AUSTRIAN TEA COOKIES

1½ cups sugar, divided
½ cup butter, softened
½ cup shortening
1 egg, beaten
½ teaspoon vanilla extract
2 cups all-purpose flour
2 cups HONEY ALMOND DELIGHT® Brand Cereal, crushed to 1 cup

½ teaspoon baking powder
¼ teaspoon ground cinnamon
14 ounces almond paste
2 egg whites
5 tablespoons raspberry or apricot jam, warmed

In large bowl, beat 1 cup sugar, butter and shortening. Add egg and vanilla; mix well. Stir in flour, cereal, baking powder and cinnamon until well blended. Refrigerate 1 to 2 hours or until firm.

Preheat oven to 350°F. Roll dough out on lightly floured surface to ¼-inch thickness; cut into 2-inch circles with floured cookie cutter. Place on ungreased cookie sheet; set aside.

In small bowl, beat almond paste, egg whites and remaining ½ cup sugar until smooth. With pastry tube fitted with medium-sized star tip, pipe almond paste mixture, ½ inch thick, along outside edge of top of each cookie. Spoon ¼ teaspoon jam into center of each cookie.

Bake 8 to 10 minutes or until lightly browned. Let stand 1 minute before removing from cookie sheet. Cool on wire rack.

Makes about 3½ dozen cookies

No-Bake Cherry Crisps

NO-BAKE CHERRY CRISPS

¼ cup butter or margarine,
  softened
1 cup powdered sugar
1 cup peanut butter
1⅓ cups crisp rice cereal
¼ cup plus 2 tablespoons
  mini semisweet
  chocolate chips

¼ cup chopped pecans
½ cup maraschino cherries,
  drained, dried and
  chopped
1 to 2 cups flaked coconut
  (for rolling)

In large mixing bowl, cream butter, sugar and peanut butter. Stir in
cereal, chips, pecans and cherries. Mix well. Shape teaspoonfuls of dough
into 1-inch balls. Roll in coconut. Put on cookie sheet; chill in refrigerator
1 hour. Store refrigerated.   *Makes about 3 dozen treats*

CHOCOLATE ALMOND SNOWBALLS

1¾ cups all-purpose flour
⅔ cup NESTLÉ® Cocoa
2 teaspoons baking powder
¼ teaspoon salt
¾ cup granulated sugar

½ cup (1 stick) butter, melted
   and cooled
2 eggs
1 teaspoon almond extract
Confectioners' sugar

Preheat oven to 350°F. In small bowl, combine flour, Nestlé® cocoa, baking powder and salt; set aside.

In large mixer bowl, beat granulated sugar, butter, eggs and almond extract until creamy. Gradually add flour mixture, beating until well blended. Roll measuring tablespoonfuls of dough into balls. Place on ungreased cookie sheet.

Bake 6 to 8 minutes. Cool completely on wire racks. Sprinkle with confectioners' sugar.

Makes about 2½ dozen cookies

ORANGE DROP COOKIES

COOKIES

1 package DUNCAN HINES®
   Golden Sugar Cookie Mix
1 egg
1 tablespoon orange juice

½ teaspoon grated orange
   peel
¾ cup flaked coconut
½ cup chopped pecans

GLAZE

1 cup confectioners sugar
2 teaspoons lemon juice
2 teaspoons orange juice

1 teaspoon grated orange
   peel

1. Preheat oven to 375°F.

2. **For Cookies,** combine cookie mix, contents of buttery flavor packet from Mix, egg, 1 tablespoon orange juice and ½ teaspoon orange peel in large bowl. Stir with spoon until well blended. Stir in coconut and pecans. Drop by rounded teaspoonfuls, 2 inches apart, onto ungreased cookie sheets. Bake at 375°F for 7 to 8 minutes or until set. Cool 1 minute on baking sheets. Remove to cooling racks. Cool completely.

3. **For Glaze,** combine confectioners sugar, lemon juice, 2 teaspoons orange juice and 1 teaspoon orange peel in small bowl. Stir until blended. Drizzle over tops of cooled cookies. Allow glaze to set before storing between layers of waxed paper in airtight container.

Makes about 3 dozen cookies

Creative Cutouts

FROSTED BUTTER COOKIES

COOKIES
1½ cups butter, softened
¾ cup granulated sugar
3 egg yolks
3 cups all-purpose flour

1 teaspoon baking powder
2 tablespoons orange juice
1 teaspoon vanilla

FROSTING
4 cups powdered sugar
½ cup butter, softened
3 to 4 tablespoons milk
2 teaspoons vanilla

Food coloring (optional)
Colored sugars, flaked
coconut and cinnamon
candies for decoration

For Cookies, in large bowl, cream butter and granulated sugar. Add yolks; beat until light and fluffy. Add flour, baking powder, orange juice and vanilla; beat until well mixed. Cover; refrigerate until firm, 2 to 3 hours.

Preheat oven to 350°F. Roll out dough, one half at a time, to ¼-inch thickness on well-floured surface. Cut out with holiday cookie cutters. Place, 1 inch apart, on ungreased cookie sheets. Bake 6 to 10 minutes or until edges are golden brown. Remove to wire racks to cool completely.

For Frosting, in medium bowl, combine all frosting ingredients except food coloring and decorations; beat until fluffy. If desired, divide frosting into small bowls; tint with food coloring. Frost cookies and decorate with colored sugars, coconut and candies.   *Makes about 3 dozen cookies*

Frosted Butter Cookies

Cinnamon Stars

CINNAMON STARS

2 tablespoons sugar	2 egg yolks
¾ teaspoon ground cinnamon	1 teaspoon vanilla extract
¾ cup butter or margarine, softened	1 package DUNCAN HINES® Moist Deluxe French Vanilla Cake Mix

1. Preheat oven to 375°F.

2. Combine sugar and cinnamon in small bowl. Set aside.

3. Combine butter, egg yolks and vanilla extract in large bowl. Blend in cake mix gradually. Roll to ⅛-inch thickness on lightly floured surface. Cut with 2½-inch star cookie cutter. Place, 2 inches apart, on ungreased cookie sheets. Sprinkle cookies with cinnamon-sugar mixture. Bake at 375°F for 6 to 8 minutes or until edges are light golden brown. Cool 1 minute on cookie sheets. Remove to cooling racks. Cool completely. Store in airtight container. *Makes 3 to 3½ dozen cookies*

COCOA ALMOND CUT-OUT COOKIES

¾ cup margarine or butter,
  softened
1 (14-ounce) can EAGLE®
  Brand Sweetened
  Condensed Milk (NOT
  evaporated milk)
2 eggs
1 teaspoon vanilla extract

½ teaspoon almond extract
2¾ cups unsifted flour
⅔ cup HERSHEY'S Cocoa
2 teaspoons baking powder
½ teaspoon baking soda
½ cup finely chopped
  almonds
Chocolate Glaze

In large mixer bowl, beat margarine, sweetened condensed milk, eggs and extracts until well blended. Combine dry ingredients; add to margarine mixture, beating until well blended. Stir in almonds. Divide dough into four equal portions. Wrap each in plastic wrap; flatten. Chill until firm enough to roll, about 2 hours.

Preheat oven to 350°F. Working with one portion at a time (keep remaining dough in refrigerator), on floured surface, roll to about ⅛-inch thickness. Cut into desired shapes. Place on lightly greased baking sheets. Bake 6 to 8 minutes or until set. Remove from baking sheets. Cool completely. Drizzle with Chocolate Glaze. Store tightly covered at room temperature.

Makes about 6 dozen (3-inch) cookies

Chocolate Glaze: Melt 1 cup (6 ounces) HERSHEY'S Semi-Sweet Chocolate Chips with 2 tablespoon shortening. Makes about ⅔ cup.

HOLIDAY GINGERBREAD PEOPLE

1 (14½ oz.) package
  gingerbread mix
⅓ cup orange juice
1 tablespoon grated orange
  rind
½ teaspoon ground
  cinnamon

1 cup confectioners' sugar
4 teaspoons milk
½ cup "M&M's"® Plain
  Chocolate Candies

Preheat oven to 375°F. In mixing bowl, blend gingerbread mix, orange juice, rind and cinnamon until smooth. Turn dough onto floured surface; knead until smooth. Form into a ball; divide in half. Roll out half of dough to ⅛-inch thickness. With a 6-inch cookie cutter, cut three or four cookie people, carefully placing on lightly greased baking sheet. Re-roll dough scraps; cut to make eight cookies in all. Repeat with remaining half of dough. Bake 6 to 8 minutes or until firm. Cool slightly; remove to wire rack to cool completely. Combine confectioners' sugar and milk; mix until well blended. Spoon into icing bag fitted with writing tip. Outline cookies with powdered sugar frosting. Decorate with candies.

Makes 16 cookies

PEANUT BUTTER SUGAR COOKIES

1 (6-oz.) pkg. (3 foil-wrapped bars) NESTLÉ® Premier White® Baking Bars, divided
2½ cups all-purpose flour
¾ teaspoon salt
¾ cup (1½ sticks) butter or margarine, softened

¾ cup peanut butter
1 cup sugar
1 egg
1 teaspoon vanilla extract
Assorted NESTLÉ® Toll House® Morsels

In small saucepan over low heat, melt 1 foil-wrapped (2 oz.) baking bar; set aside. In small bowl, combine flour and salt; set aside.

In large mixer bowl, beat butter, peanut butter and sugar until creamy. Blend in egg and vanilla extract. Beat in melted baking bar. Gradually beat in flour mixture. Divide dough in half. Shape each half into ball. Wrap with plastic wrap. Refrigerate 3 to 4 hours until firm enough to roll.

Preheat oven to 350°F. Between two sheets of waxed paper, roll each ball to ⅛-inch thickness. Peel off top sheets of waxed paper; cut with 2½- to 3-inch cookie cutters. Slide waxed paper onto ungreased cookie sheets; refrigerate 10 minutes. Transfer cutouts to ungreased cookie sheets. Decorate with assorted morsels.

Bake 10 to 12 minutes until set. Let stand 2 minutes. Remove from cookie sheets; cool completely.

In small saucepan over low heat, melt remaining 2 foil-wrapped (4 oz.) baking bars. Drizzle over cookies.   *Makes about 5 dozen cookies*

BUTTER COOKIES

¾ cup butter, softened
¼ cup granulated sugar
¼ cup packed brown sugar
1 egg yolk

1¾ cups all-purpose flour
¾ teaspoon baking powder
⅛ teaspoon salt

1. Combine butter, sugars and egg yolk in medium bowl. Add dry ingredients; mix well. Cover; chill until firm, about 4 hours or overnight.

2. Preheat oven to 350°F. Roll dough on floured surface to ¼-inch thickness. Cut into desired shapes with cookie cutters. Place on ungreased cookie sheets.

3. Bake 8 to 10 minutes or until edges begin to brown. Remove to wire racks; cool completely.   *Makes about 2 dozen cookies*

Kittens and Mittens

KITTENS AND MITTENS

1 recipe Chocolate Cookie
  dough (see next page)
1 recipe Cookie Glaze
  (see next page)

Assorted food colors
Assorted candies

1. Preheat oven to 325°F. Grease cookie sheets.

2. Roll dough on floured surface to ⅛-inch thickness. Using diagrams
1 and 2 on next page as guides, cut out kitten and mitten cookies. Place
cookies on prepared cookie sheets. With plastic straw, make holes in tops
of cookies, about ½ inch from top edges.

3. Bake 8 to 10 minutes until edges begin to brown. Remove to wire
racks; cool completely. If necessary, push straw through warm cookies to
remake holes.

4. Place cookies on racks on waxed paper-lined baking sheets. Spoon
Cookie Glaze into several small bowls. Color as desired with food color.
Spoon glaze over cookies. Place some of remaining glaze in small plastic
food storage bag. Cut tiny tip from corner of bag. Use to pipe decorations
as shown in photo. Decorate with candies as shown. Let stand until glaze
has set.

4. Thread yarn or ribbon through holes to make garland.
Makes about 2 dozen cookies

CHOCOLATE COOKIES

1 cup butter or margarine,
   softened
1 cup sugar
1 egg
1 teaspoon vanilla

2 ounces semisweet
   chocolate, melted
2¼ cups all-purpose flour
1 teaspoon baking powder
¼ teaspoon salt

1. Beat butter and sugar in large bowl at high speed of electric mixer until fluffy. Beat in egg and vanilla. Add melted chocolate; mix well. Add flour, baking powder and salt; mix well. Cover; refrigerate until firm, about 2 hours.

2. Preheat oven to 325°F. Grease cookie sheets. Roll dough on floured surface to ⅛-inch thickness. Cut into desired shapes with cookie cutters. Place on prepared cookie sheets.

3. Bake 8 to 10 minutes or until set. Remove to wire racks; cool completely.

Makes about 3 dozen cookies

COOKIE GLAZE

4 cups confectioners' sugar
4 to 6 tablespoons milk

Assorted food color

1. Combine confectioners' sugar and enough milk to make a medium-thick pourable glaze. Color as desired with food color.

2. Place cookies on wire rack on waxed paper-lined baking sheet. Spoon glaze over cookies; allow to dry completely.

Makes about 4 cups glaze

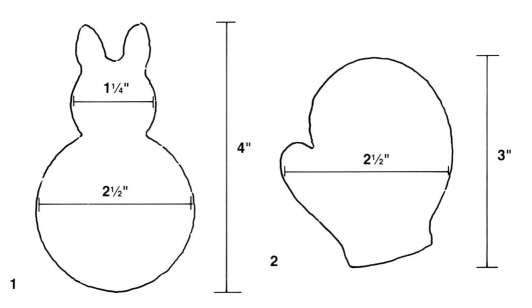

HANUKKAH COOKIES

COOKIES
- ¾ cup butter or margarine, softened
- 2 egg yolks
- 2 tablespoons grated orange peel

- 1 package DUNCAN HINES® Moist Deluxe White Cake Mix

FROSTING
- 1 container (16 ounces) DUNCAN HINES® Vanilla Layer Cake Frosting

- 3 to 4 drops blue food coloring
- 3 to 4 drops yellow food coloring

1. **For Cookies,** combine butter, egg yolks and orange peel in large bowl. Beat at low speed with electric mixer until blended. Add cake mix gradually, beating until thoroughly blended. Form dough into ball. Cover with plastic wrap and refrigerate for 1 to 2 hours or until chilled but not firm.

2. Preheat oven to 375°F.

3. Roll dough to ⅛-inch thickness on lightly floured surface. Cut with Hanukkah cookie cutters. Place, 2 inches apart, on ungreased cookie sheets. Bake at 375°F for 6 to 7 minutes or until edges are light golden brown. Cool 1 minute on cookie sheets. Remove to cooling racks. Cool completely.

4. **For Frosting,** tint ½ cup vanilla frosting with blue food coloring. Warm frosting in microwave oven at HIGH (100% power) for 5 to 10 seconds, if desired. Place writing tip in pastry bag. Fill with tinted frosting. Pipe outline pattern on cookies (see photo). Tint ½ cup frosting with yellow food coloring and leave ½ cup frosting untinted; decorate as desired. Allow frosting to set before storing cookies between layers of waxed paper in airtight container. *Makes 3½ to 4 dozen cookies*

Hanukkah Cookies

CHRISTMAS STAINED GLASS COOKIES

Hard candies (in assorted
   colors)
¾ cup butter, softened
¾ cup white granulated sugar
2 eggs

1 teaspoon vanilla extract
3 cups all-purpose flour
1 teaspoon baking powder
Frosting (optional)
Candy (optional)

Separate colors of hard candy. Place each color of candy in small freezer-weight plastic food storage bag; crush with a wooden mallet.* In a mixing bowl, beat together butter and sugar. Beat in eggs and vanilla. Combine flour and baking powder. Gradually stir into butter mixture until dough is very stiff. Wrap in plastic wrap; chill about 3 hours.

Preheat oven to 375°F. Roll out dough to ⅛-inch thickness on lightly floured surface. Additional flour can be added, if necessary. Cut out cookies using large Christmas cookie cutters. Transfer cookies to a foil-lined baking sheet. Using a small Christmas cookie cutter of the same shape as the large one, cut out and remove dough from center of each cookie.** Fill cut-out sections with crushed candy. If using cookies as hanging ornaments, make holes with a chopstick at top of cookies for string. Bake 7 to 9 minutes or until cookies are lightly browned and candy is melted. Slide foil off baking sheets. When cool, carefully loosen cookies from foil. If desired, decorate with frosting and other candies.

Makes about 2½ dozen medium cookies

*You will need a total measurement of about ⅓ cup crushed.

**Other shapes can be used to cut out center to make different designs.

Favorite recipe from The Sugar Association, Inc.

CHOCOLATE GINGERBREAD COOKIES

COOKIES
2¼ cups all-purpose flour
¾ cup NESTLÉ® Cocoa
1 teaspoon baking soda
1 teaspoon ginger
½ teaspoon baking powder
½ teaspoon cinnamon
½ teaspoon cloves

¼ teaspoon salt
½ cup (1 stick) butter or
   margarine, softened
1 cup granulated sugar
1 egg
½ cup molasses

GLAZE
1 cup confectioners' sugar
2 to 3 tablespoons milk

1 foil-wrapped bar
   (2 oz.) NESTLÉ® Semi-
   Sweet Chocolate Baking
   Bar, broken up

Cookies: In small bowl, combine flour, cocoa, baking soda, ginger, baking powder, cinnamon, cloves and salt; set aside.

In large mixer bowl, beat butter and granulated sugar until creamy. Blend in egg and molasses. Gradually beat in flour mixture. Divide dough into four equal pieces; wrap in plastic wrap. Refrigerate at least 2 hours until firm.

Preheat oven to 350°F. Lightly grease two large cookie sheets. On floured board, roll dough, one piece at a time, to ⅛-inch thickness. Cut with 4½-inch cookie cutters. With metal spatula, transfer cutouts to prepared cookie sheets. Repeat with remaining dough.

Bake 8 to 10 minutes until set. Let stand 2 minutes. Remove from cookie sheets; cool completely.

Glaze: In small bowl, combine confectioners' sugar and 2 tablespoons milk; stir until smooth. (Add additional 1 tablespoon milk if necessary for desired consistency.) Set aside.

In small saucepan over low heat, melt baking bar. Pipe cookies with Glaze or decorate with melted semi-sweet chocolate baking bar.

Makes about 2 dozen cookies

Chocolate Gingerbread Cookies

SPICY GINGERBREAD COOKIES

COOKIES

½ cup firmly packed brown
sugar
¾ cup (1¼ sticks) butter or
margarine, softened
⅔ cup light molasses
1 egg
1½ teaspoons grated lemon
peel
2½ cups all-purpose flour

1¼ teaspoons ground
cinnamon
1 teaspoon vanilla
1 teaspoon ground allspice
½ teaspoon ground ginger
½ teaspoon baking soda
½ teaspoon salt
¼ teaspoon baking powder

FROSTING

4 cups powdered sugar
½ cup butter, softened
4 tablespoons milk

2 teaspoons vanilla
Food coloring

For Cookies, in large mixer bowl, combine brown sugar, butter, molasses, egg and lemon peel. Beat at medium speed, scraping bowl often, until smooth and creamy, 1 to 2 minutes. Add all remaining cookie ingredients. Reduce speed to low. Continue beating, scraping bowl often, until well mixed, 1 to 2 minutes. Cover; refrigerate at least 2 hours.

Preheat oven to 350°F. On well floured surface, roll out dough, one half at a time (keeping remaining dough refrigerated), to ¼-inch thickness. Cut with 3- to 4-inch cookie cutters. Place, 1 inch apart, on greased cookie sheets. Bake for 6 to 8 minutes or until no indentation remains when touched. Remove immediately. Cool completely.

For Frosting, in small mixer bowl combine powdered sugar, butter, milk and vanilla. Beat at low speed, scraping bowl often, until fluffy, 1 to 2 minutes. If desired, color frosting with food coloring. Decorate cookies with frosting.   *Makes about 4 dozen cookies*

Spicy Gingerbread Cookies

VERSATILE CUT-OUT COOKIES

3½ cups unsifted flour
1 tablespoon baking powder
½ teaspoon salt
1 (14-ounce) can EAGLE®
  Brand Sweetened
  Condensed Milk (NOT
  evaporated milk)

¾ cup margarine or butter,
  softened
2 eggs
1 tablespoon vanilla extract
  or 2 teaspoons almond or
  lemon extract

Combine flour, baking powder and salt. In large mixer bowl, beat sweetened condensed milk, margarine, eggs and vanilla until well blended. Add dry ingredients; mix well. Cover; chill 2 hours.

Preheat oven to 350°F. On floured surface, knead dough to form a smooth ball. Divide into thirds. On well-floured surface, roll out each portion to ⅛-inch thickness. Cut with floured cookie cutter. Reroll as necessary to use all dough. Place, 1 inch apart, on greased cookie sheets. Bake 7 to 9 minutes or until lightly browned around edges (do not overbake). Cool. Frost and decorate as desired. Store loosely covered at room temperature.

Makes about 6½ dozen cookies

Chocolate Cookies: Decrease flour to 3 cups. Add ½ cup HERSHEY'S Cocoa to dry ingredients. Chill and roll dough as directed. Makes about 6½ dozen cookies.

Versatile Cut-Out Cookies

Sandwich Cookies: Prepare, chill and roll dough as directed. Use 2½-inch floured cookie cutter. Bake as directed. Sandwich two cookies together with ready-to-spread frosting. Sprinkle tops with confectioners' sugar, if desired. Makes about 3 dozen cookies.

Cookie Pecan Critters: Prepare and chill dough as directed. For each critter, arrange three pecan halves together on ungreased cookie sheets. Shape 1 teaspoonful dough into 1-inch ball. Press firmly onto center of arranged pecans. Repeat until all dough is used. Bake 12 to 14 minutes. Spread tops with Chocolate Frosting.* Makes about 6½ dozen cookies.

***Chocolate Frosting:** In small saucepan, melt ¼ cup margarine or butter with ¼ cup water. Stir in ½ cup HERSHEY'S Cocoa. Remove saucepan from heat; beat in 2 cups confectioners' sugar and 1 teaspoon vanilla until smooth. Stir in additional water for a thinner consistency if desired. Makes about 1 cup.

Mincemeat Peek-a-Boo Cookies: Prepare, chill and roll dough as directed. Use 3-inch floured round cookie cutter. Using sharp knife, cut "X" in center of half the rounds. Place 1 teaspoon mincemeat in center of remaining rounds. Top with cut rounds. Bake 8 to 10 minutes. Cool. Sprinkle with confectioners' sugar, if desired. Makes about 4 dozen cookies.

Stained Glass Cookies: Prepare, chill and roll dough as directed. Use 3-inch floured cookie cutter to cut into desired shapes. Cut out holes for "stained glass" in each cookie with small cutters or knife. Place on aluminum foil-lined cookie sheets. Fill holes with crushed hard candies. (If planning to hang cookies, make hole in each cookie in dough near edge with straw.) Bake 6 to 8 minutes or until candy has melted. Cool 10 minutes; remove from foil. Makes about 8 dozen cookies.

Cinnamon Pinwheel Cookies: Decrease baking powder to 2 teaspoons. Prepare and chill dough as directed. Divide into quarters. Roll each quarter of dough into a 16 × 8-inch rectangle. Brush with melted margarine or butter. Top each with 2 tablespoons sugar combined with ½ teaspoon ground cinnamon. Roll up tightly, beginning at 8-inch side. Wrap tightly; freeze until firm, about 20 minutes. Unwrap; cut into ¼-inch slices. Place on ungreased cookie sheets. Bake 12 to 14 minutes or until lightly browned. Makes about 6½ dozen cookies.

Chocolate Snow Balls: Prepare dough as directed for Chocolate Cookies, increasing eggs to three; add 1 cup finely chopped nuts. Chill. Shape into 1-inch balls. Roll in confectioners' sugar. Bake 8 to 10 minutes. Cool. Roll again in confectioners' sugar. Makes about 7½ dozen cookies.

GINGERBREAD COOKIES

½ cup shortening
⅓ cup packed light brown
    sugar
¼ cup dark molasses
1 egg white
½ teaspoon vanilla
1½ cups all-purpose flour

½ teaspoon baking soda
½ teaspoon salt
¼ teaspoon baking powder
1 teaspoon ground
    cinnamon
½ teaspoon ground ginger

1. Beat shortening, brown sugar, molasses, egg white and vanilla in large bowl at high speed of electric mixer until smooth. Combine flour, baking soda, salt, baking powder and spices in small bowl. Add to shortening mixture; mix well. Cover; refrigerate until firm, about 8 hours or overnight.

2. Preheat oven to 350°F. Grease cookie sheets.

3. Roll dough on floured surface to ⅛-inch thickness. Cut into desired shapes with cookie cutters. Place on prepared cookie sheets.

4. Bake 6 to 8 minutes or until edges begin to brown. Remove to wire racks; cool completely.   *Makes about 2½ dozen cookies*

BLACK AND WHITE CUT-OUTS

2¾ cups *plus* 2 tablespoons
    all-purpose flour, divided
1 teaspoon baking soda
¾ teaspoon salt
1 cup butter or margarine,
    softened
¾ cup granulated sugar
¾ cup packed light brown
    sugar
2 large eggs

1 teaspoon vanilla
¼ cup unsweetened cocoa
4 ounces white baking bar,
    broken into ½-inch
    pieces
4 ounces semisweet
    chocolate chips
Assorted decorative
    candies (optional)

Combine 2¾ cups flour, baking soda and salt in medium bowl; mix well. Beat butter and sugars in large bowl until light and fluffy. Beat in eggs, one at a time. Beat in vanilla. Gradually add flour mixture. Beat until well blended. Remove half of dough from bowl; reserve. To make chocolate dough, beat cocoa into remaining dough with spoon until well blended. To make butter cookie dough, beat remaining 2 tablespoons flour into reserved dough. Flatten each piece of dough into a disc; wrap in plastic wrap and refrigerate about 1½ hours or until firm. (Dough may be refrigerated up to 3 days before baking.)

Black and White Cut-Outs

Preheat oven to 375°F. Working with one type of dough at a time, place dough on lightly floured surface. Roll out dough to ¼-inch thickness. Cut dough into desired shapes with cookie cutters. Place cut-outs, 1 inch apart, on cookie sheets. Bake 9 to 11 minutes or until set. Let cookies stand on cookie sheets 2 minutes. Remove cookies to wire rack; cool completely.

For white chocolate drizzle, place baking bar pieces in small resealable plastic freezer bag; seal bag. Heat in microwave oven at MEDIUM (50% power) 2 minutes. Turn bag over; heat at MEDIUM (50% power) 2 to 3 minutes or until melted. Knead bag until baking bar is completely smooth. Cut very tiny corner off bottom of bag; pipe or drizzle baking bar onto chocolate cookies. Decorate as desired with assorted candies. Let stand until white chocolate is set, about 30 minutes.

For chocolate drizzle, place chocolate chips in small resealable plastic freezer bag; seal bag. Heat in microwave oven at HIGH 1 minute. Turn bag over; heat at HIGH 1 to 2 minutes or until chocolate is melted. Knead bag until chocolate is completely smooth. Cut tiny corner off bottom of bag; pipe or drizzle chocolate onto butter cookies. Decorate as desired with assorted candies. Let stand until chocolate is set, about 40 minutes.
Makes 3 to 4 dozen cookies

Black and White Sandwiches: Cut cookies out with same cookie cutter. Spread thin layer of prepared frosting onto bottom side of chocolate cookie. Place bottom side of butter cookie over frosting. Drizzle either side of cookie with melted chocolate or white chocolate.

PEEK-A-BOO APRICOT COOKIES

4 ounces bittersweet
   chocolate candy bar,
   broken into pieces
3 cups all-purpose flour
½ teaspoon baking soda
½ teaspoon salt

⅔ cup butter or margarine,
   softened
¾ cup sugar
2 large eggs
2 teaspoons vanilla
   Apricot preserves

Melt chocolate in small bowl set in bowl of very hot water, stirring twice. Set aside to cool. Combine flour, baking soda and salt in medium bowl; mix well. Set aside. Beat butter and sugar in large bowl until light and fluffy. Beat in eggs, one at a time, scraping down side of bowl after each addition. Beat in vanilla and chocolate. Gradually add flour mixture. Divide dough into two rounds; wrap in plastic wrap. Refrigerate 2 hours or until firm.

Preheat oven to 350°F. Roll out dough on lightly floured surface to ¼- to ⅛-inch thickness. Cut out dough with 2½-inch round cutter. Cut 1-inch centers out of half of circles. Remove scraps of dough from around and within circles; reserve. Place on ungreased cookie sheets. Repeat rolling and cutting with remaining scraps of dough. Bake cookies 9 to 10 minutes or until set. Let cookies stand on cookie sheets 2 minutes. Remove cookies to wire racks; cool completely. To assemble cookies, spread about 1½ teaspoons preserves over each cookie circle; close with cut-out cookies to form a sandwich.   *Makes about 1½ dozen cookies*

LINZER HEARTS

1 package DUNCAN HINES®
   Golden Sugar Cookie Mix
½ cup all-purpose flour
½ cup finely ground almonds
1 egg
1 tablespoon water

3 tablespoons confectioners
   sugar
½ cup plus 1 tablespoon
   seedless red raspberry
   jam, warmed

1. Preheat oven to 375°F.

2. Combine cookie mix, contents of buttery flavor packet from Mix, flour, almonds, egg and water in large bowl. Stir with spoon until blended. Roll dough to ⅛-inch thickness on lightly floured board. Cut out 3-inch hearts with floured cookie cutter. Cut out centers of half the hearts with smaller heart cookie cutter. Reroll dough as needed. Place, 2 inches apart, on ungreased cookie sheets. Bake whole hearts at 375°F for 8 to 9 minutes and cut-out hearts for 6 to 7 minutes or until edges are lightly browned. Cool 1 minute on cookie sheets. Remove to cooling racks. Cool completely.

3. To assemble, dust cut-out hearts with sifted confectioners sugar. Spread warm jam over whole hearts almost to edges; top with cut-out hearts. Press together to make sandwiches. Fill center with ¼ teaspoon jam. Store between layers of waxed paper in airtight container.

Makes 22 (3-inch) sandwich cookies

YULE TREE NAMESAKES

1 recipe Gingerbread Cookie
    dough (page 54)
1 recipe Cookie Glaze
    (page 45)
Green food color
Confectioners' sugar

Assorted candies
3 packages (12 ounces each)
    semisweet chocolate
    chips, melted
1 cup flaked coconut, tinted
    green*

1. Preheat oven to 350°F. Roll dough on floured surface to ⅛-inch thickness. Cut out cookies using tree-shaped cookie cutter. Place, 2 inches apart, on ungreased cookie sheets.

2. Bake 12 to 14 minutes until edges begin to brown. Remove to wire racks; cool completely.

3. Reserve ⅓ cup Cookie Glaze; color remaining glaze green with food color. Place cookies on wire rack over waxed paper-lined baking sheet. Spoon green glaze over cookies.

4. Add 1 to 2 tablespoons confectioners' sugar to reserved Cookie Glaze. Spoon into pastry bag fitted with small writing tip. Pipe names onto trees. Decorate with assorted candies. Let stand until glaze is set.

5. Spoon melted chocolate into baking cups or tartlet pans, filling evenly. Let stand until chocolate is very thick and partially set. Place trees, standing upright, in chocolate.

6. Sprinkle tinted coconut over chocolate.   *Makes 24 place cards*

*Tinting coconut: Dilute a few drops of food color with ½ teaspoon water in a large plastic food storage bag. Add 1 to 1⅓ cups flaked coconut. Close bag and shake well until the coconut is evenly coated. If a deeper color is desired, add more diluted food color and shake again.

Cookie Jar Classics

SPICY PUMPKIN COOKIES

2 cups CRISCO® Shortening
2 cups sugar
1 can (16 ounces) pumpkin
2 eggs
2 teaspoons vanilla
4 cups all-purpose flour
2 teaspoons baking powder
2 teaspoons ground
  cinnamon

1 teaspoon salt
1 teaspoon baking soda
1 teaspoon ground nutmeg
½ teaspoon ground allspice
2 cups raisins
1 cup chopped nuts

1. Preheat oven to 350°F.

2. Combine Crisco®, sugar, pumpkin, eggs and vanilla in large bowl; beat well.

3. Combine flour, baking powder, cinnamon, salt, baking soda, nutmeg and allspice. Add to batter; mix well. Stir in raisins and nuts. Drop rounded teaspoonfuls of dough, 2 inches apart, onto greased cookie sheet.

4. Bake at 350°F for 12 to 15 minutes. Cool on rack. If desired, frost with vanilla frosting.   *Makes about 7 dozen cookies*

Top to bottom: Drop Sugar Cookies (page 61),
Spicy Pumpkin Cookies

Top to bottom: Chocolate Orange Granola Cookies,
Double Chocolate Cookies

DOUBLE CHOCOLATE COOKIES

2¼ cups all-purpose flour
1 teaspoon baking soda
1 teaspoon salt
1 cup butter, softened
¾ cup granulated sugar
¾ cup firmly packed brown
   sugar
1 teaspoon vanilla extract
2 eggs

Two envelopes (2 ounces)
  NESTLÉ® Choco-Bake®
  Unsweetened Baking
  Chocolate Flavor
One 12-ounce package (2 cups)
  NESTLÉ® Toll House®
  Semi-Sweet Chocolate
  Morsels
1 cup chopped walnuts

Preheat oven to 375°F. In medium bowl, combine flour, baking soda and salt; set aside. In large bowl, combine butter, granulated sugar, brown sugar and vanilla extract; beat until creamy. Beat in eggs and unsweetened baking chocolate flavor. Gradually beat in flour mixture. Stir in morsels and nuts. Drop by rounded teaspoonfuls onto ungreased cookie sheets. Bake at 375°F for 8 to 10 minutes. Cool completely on wire racks. *Makes about 6 dozen (2½-inch) cookies*

CHOCOLATE ORANGE GRANOLA COOKIES

1 cup all-purpose flour
½ teaspoon baking powder
½ teaspoon allspice
½ teaspoon salt
⅔ cup firmly packed brown sugar
½ cup butter, softened
1 egg
1 teaspoon vanilla extract

½ teaspoon grated orange rind
1¼ cups granola cereal
One 6-ounce package (1 cup) NESTLÉ® Toll House® Semi-Sweet Chocolate Morsels
½ cup flaked coconut
¼ cup chopped nuts

Preheat oven to 350°F. In small bowl, combine flour, baking powder, allspice and salt; set aside. In large bowl, combine brown sugar and butter; beat until creamy. Add egg, vanilla extract and orange rind; beat well. Gradually beat in flour mixture. Stir in granola cereal, morsels, coconut and nuts. Drop by rounded tablespoonfuls onto ungreased cookie sheets. Sprinkle with additional coconut, if desired. Bake at 350°F for 9 to 11 minutes. Cool completely on wire racks.

Makes about 1½ dozen (2-inch) cookies

DROP SUGAR COOKIES

⅓ cup CRISCO® Oil
1 cup sugar
1 tablespoon vanilla
1 egg

2½ cups all-purpose flour
¾ teaspoon salt
½ teaspoon baking soda
¼ cup skim milk

1. Preheat oven to 400°F. Oil cookie sheet lightly.

2. Combine ⅓ cup Crisco® Oil, sugar and vanilla in large bowl. Add egg. Beat at medium speed of electric mixer until blended. Stir in flour, salt and baking soda with spoon. Stir until mixture is smooth. Add milk. Stir until well blended.

3. Drop dough by teaspoonfuls, 2 inches apart, onto cookie sheet. Flatten cookies with bottom of glass lightly oiled and dipped in sugar (or colored sugar).

4. Bake at 400°F for 6 to 8 minutes or until barely browned around edges. *Do not overbake.* Remove to cooling rack.

Makes about 3 dozen cookies

SOFT SPICY MOLASSES COOKIES

2 cups all-purpose flour
1 cup sugar
¾ cup butter, softened
⅓ cup light molasses
3 tablespoons milk
1 egg
½ teaspoon baking soda

½ teaspoon ground ginger
½ teaspoon ground
  cinnamon
½ teaspoon ground cloves
⅛ teaspoon salt
Sugar for rolling

In large mixer bowl, combine flour, 1 cup sugar, butter, molasses, milk, egg, baking soda, ginger, cinnamon, cloves and salt. Beat at low speed, scraping bowl often, until well mixed, 2 to 3 minutes. Cover; refrigerate until firm, at least 4 hours or overnight.

Preheat oven to 350°F. Shape rounded teaspoonfuls of dough into 1-inch balls. Roll in sugar. Place, 2 inches apart, on ungreased cookie sheets. Bake 10 to 12 minutes or until slightly firm to the touch. Remove immediately.   *Makes about 4 dozen cookies*

BUTTER-FLAVORED BRICKLE DRIZZLES

COOKIES

1 cup BUTTER FLAVOR
  CRISCO®
1 cup granulated sugar
1 cup firmly packed brown
  sugar
1 can (14 ounces) sweetened
  condensed milk (not
  evaporated milk)

1 teaspoon vanilla
1¾ cups all-purpose flour
1 teaspoon salt
½ teaspoon baking soda
3 cups quick oats, uncooked
1 cup almond brickle chips

DRIZZLE

1 cup milk chocolate chips

1. Preheat oven to 350°F. Grease cookie sheet with Butter Flavor Crisco®.

2. **For Cookies,** combine 1 cup Butter Flavor Crisco®, granulated sugar and brown sugar in large bowl. Stir with spoon until well blended and creamy. Stir in condensed milk and vanilla. Mix well.

3. Combine flour, salt and baking soda. Stir into creamed mixture. Stir in oats.

4. Shape dough into 1-inch balls. Press tops into brickle chips. Place, brickle side up, 2 inches apart on greased cookie sheet.

5. Bake at 350°F for 9 to 10 minutes or until set but not browned. Remove to cooling rack. Cool completely.

6. **For Drizzle,** place chocolate chips in heavy resealable sandwich bag. Seal. Microwave at 50% (MEDIUM). Knead bag after 1 minute. Repeat until smooth (or melt by placing in bowl of hot water). Cut tiny tip off bottom corner of bag. Squeeze out and drizzle over cookies.

Makes about 6 dozen cookies

Butter-Flavored Brickle Drizzles

ALMOND MILK CHOCOLATE CHIPPERS

1¼ cups all-purpose flour
½ teaspoon baking soda
½ teaspoon salt
½ cup butter or margarine,
   softened
½ cup packed light brown
   sugar

⅓ cup granulated sugar
1 large egg
2 tablespoons almond-
   flavored liqueur
1 cup milk chocolate chips
½ cup slivered almonds,
   toasted

Preheat oven to 375°F. Combine dry ingredients; mix until well blended. Set aside. Beat butter, brown sugar and granulated sugar in large bowl until light and fluffy. Beat in egg until well blended. Beat in liqueur. Gradually add dry ingredients. Beat until well blended. Stir in chips and almonds. Drop dough by rounded teaspoonfuls, 2 inches apart, onto ungreased cookie sheets. Bake 9 to 10 minutes or until edges are golden brown. Let cookies stand on cookies sheets 2 minutes. Remove cookies with spatula to wire racks; cool completely.

Makes about 3 dozen cookies

RAISIN SPICE DROPS

¾ cup (1½ sticks) margarine,
   softened
⅔ cup firmly packed brown
   sugar
⅔ cup granulated sugar
2 eggs
1 teaspoon vanilla
2½ cups QUAKER® Oats (quick
   or old fashioned,
   uncooked)

1¼ cups all-purpose flour
1 teaspoon cinnamon
½ teaspoon baking soda
½ teaspoon salt (optional)
¼ teaspoon nutmeg
⅔ cup raisins
½ cup chopped nuts

Preheat oven to 350°F. Beat margarine and sugars until fluffy. Blend in eggs and vanilla. Add remaining ingredients; mix well. Drop dough by rounded teaspoonfuls onto ungreased cookie sheet. Bake 8 to 10 minutes or until light golden brown. Cool on wire rack. Store tightly covered.

Makes about 4½ dozen cookies

Almond Milk Chocolate Chippers

PINEAPPLE CARROT COOKIES

2 cans (8 ounces *each*)
  DOLE® Crushed
  Pineapple in Juice
¾ cup margarine, softened
½ cup brown sugar, packed
½ cup granulated sugar
1 egg
1 teaspoon vanilla extract
1 cup shredded DOLE®
  Carrots

1 cup chopped walnuts
1 cup DOLE® Raisins
1½ cups all-purpose flour
1 teaspoon ground
  cinnamon
½ teaspoon ground ginger
½ teaspoon baking powder
¼ teaspoon salt

Preheat oven to 375°F.

Drain pineapple well, reserving juice for beverage or another use.

Beat margarine and sugars until light and fluffy. Beat in egg and vanilla.
Beat in pineapple, carrots, nuts and raisins.

Combine remaining ingredients; beat into pineapple mixture until well
blended.

Drop dough by heaping tablespoonfuls onto greased cookie sheets.
Flatten tops with spoon. Bake 15 to 20 minutes.

Makes about 3 dozen cookies

Prep Time: 20 minutes
Bake Time: 20 minutes per batch

OATMEAL MACAROONS

1 cup (2 sticks) margarine or
  butter, softened
1 cup firmly packed brown
  sugar
2 eggs
½ teaspoon almond extract
1¼ cups all-purpose flour

1 teaspoon baking soda
3 cups QUAKER® Oats (quick
  or old fashioned),
  uncooked
1⅓ cups (4-ounce package)
  flaked or shredded
  coconut

Preheat oven to 350°F. Lightly grease cookie sheet. Beat margarine and
sugar until fluffy. Blend in eggs and almond extract. Add combined flour
and baking soda; mix well. Stir in oats and coconut. Drop dough by
rounded teaspoonfuls onto prepared cookie sheet. Bake 10 minutes or
until light golden brown. Cool 2 minutes on cookie sheet; remove to wire
rack. Cool completely. Store tightly covered.

Makes about 4½ dozen cookies

Choco-Scutterbotch

CHOCO-SCUTTERBOTCH

⅔ cup BUTTER FLAVOR
    CRISCO®
½ cup firmly packed brown
    sugar
2 eggs
1 package DUNCAN HINES®
    Moist Deluxe Yellow
    Cake Mix

1 cup toasted rice cereal
½ cup milk chocolate chunks
½ cup butterscotch chips
½ cup semi-sweet chocolate
    chips
½ cup coarsely chopped
    walnuts or pecans

1. Preheat oven to 375°F.

2. Combine Butter Flavor Crisco® and brown sugar in large bowl. Beat at medium speed of electric mixer until well blended. Beat in eggs.

3. Add cake mix gradually at low speed. Mix until well blended. Stir in cereal, chocolate chunks, butterscotch chips, chocolate chips and nuts with spoon until well blended. Shape dough into 1¼-inch balls. Place, 2 inches apart, on ungreased cookie sheet. Flatten slightly. Shape sides to form circle, if necessary.

4. Bake at 375°F for 7 to 9 minutes or until lightly browned around edges. Cool 2 minutes before removing to paper towels to cool completely.
Makes about 3 dozen cookies

PEANUT BUTTER SENSATIONS

1 cup JIF® Creamy Peanut
  Butter
¾ cup granulated sugar
½ cup firmly packed brown
  sugar
½ cup BUTTER FLAVOR
  CRISCO®

1 tablespoon milk
1 teaspoon vanilla
1 egg
1¼ cups all-purpose flour
¾ teaspoon baking soda
½ teaspoon baking powder
¼ teaspoon salt

1. Preheat oven to 375°F.

2. Combine peanut butter, granulated sugar, brown sugar, Butter Flavor Crisco®, milk and vanilla in large bowl. Beat at medium speed of electric mixer until well blended. Beat in egg.

3. Combine flour, baking soda, baking powder and salt. Add gradually to creamed mixture at low speed. Mix just until blended. Drop by rounded tablespoonfuls, 2 inches apart, onto ungreased cookie sheet. Make crisscross marks on top of dough with floured fork tines.

4. Bake at 375°F for 8 to 10 minutes. Cool 2 minutes on cookie sheet before removing to cooling rack.   *Makes about 2 dozen cookies*

Clockwise from top: Old-Fashioned Oatmeal Cookies (page 70), Peanut Butter Sensations, Ultimate Chocolate Chip Cookies

ULTIMATE CHOCOLATE CHIP COOKIES

¾ cup BUTTER FLAVOR
  CRISCO®
1¼ cups firmly packed brown
  sugar
2 tablespoons milk
1 tablespoon vanilla
1 egg

1¾ cups all-purpose flour
1 teaspoon salt
¾ teaspoon baking soda
1 cup semi-sweet chocolate
  chips
1 cup coarsely chopped
  pecans*

1. Preheat oven to 375°F.

2. Combine Butter Flavor Crisco®, sugar, milk and vanilla in large bowl.
Beat at medium speed of electric mixer until well blended. Beat in egg.

3. Combine flour, salt and baking soda. Mix into creamed mixture at low
speed until just blended. Stir in chocolate chips and nuts.

4. Drop rounded tablespoonfuls of dough, 3 inches apart, onto ungreased
cookie sheet.

5. Bake at 375°F for 8 to 10 minutes for chewy cookies (they will look
light and moist—do not overbake), 11 to 13 minutes for crisp cookies.
Cool 2 minutes on cookie sheet. Remove to cooling rack.

Makes about 3 dozen cookies

*You may substitute an additional ½ cup semi-sweet chocolate chips for
the pecans.

Variations

Drizzle: Combine 1 teaspoon BUTTER FLAVOR CRISCO® and 1 cup
semi-sweet chocolate chips or 1 cup white melting chocolate, cut into
small pieces, in microwave-safe measuring cup. Microwave at 50%
(MEDIUM) 1 minute. Stir. Repeat until smooth (or melt on rangetop in
small saucepan on very low heat). To thin, add a little more Butter Flavor
Crisco®. Drizzle back and forth over cookie. Sprinkle with nuts before
chocolate hardens, if desired. To quickly harden chocolate, place cookies
in refrigerator for a few minutes.

Chocolate Dipped: Melt chocolate as directed for Drizzle. Dip one end
of each cooled cookie halfway into chocolate. Sprinkle with finely
chopped nuts before chocolate hardens. Place on waxed paper until
chocolate is firm. To quickly harden chocolate, place cookies in
refrigerator for a few minutes.

OLD-FASHIONED OATMEAL COOKIES

¾ cup BUTTER FLAVOR
    CRISCO®
1¼ cups firmly packed brown
    sugar
  1 egg
⅓ cup milk
1½ teaspoons vanilla
  1 cup all-purpose flour

½ teaspoon baking soda
½ teaspoon salt
¼ teaspoon cinnamon
3 cups quick oats (not instant
    or old fashioned)
1 cup raisins
1 cup coarsely chopped
    walnuts

1. Preheat oven to 375°F. Grease cookie sheet with Butter Flavor Crisco®.

2. Combine ¾ cup Butter Flavor Crisco®, sugar, egg, milk and vanilla in large bowl. Beat at medium speed of electric mixer until well blended.

3. Combine flour, baking soda, salt and cinnamon. Mix into creamed mixture at low speed until just blended. Stir in oats, raisins and nuts with spoon.

4. Drop rounded tablespoonfuls of dough, 2 inches apart, onto prepared cookie sheet.

5. Bake at 375°F for 10 to 12 minutes or until lightly browned. Cool 2 minutes on cookie sheet. Remove to cooling rack.

Makes about 2½ dozen cookies

PEANUT BUTTER REFRIGERATOR COOKIES

2½ cups flour
  1 teaspoon baking powder
  1 teaspoon baking soda
¼ teaspoon salt
  1 cup MAZOLA® Margarine
  1 cup SKIPPY® Creamy or
    Super Chunk® Peanut
    Butter

1 cup granulated sugar
1 cup packed brown sugar
2 eggs
1 teaspoon vanilla

In small bowl, combine flour, baking powder, baking soda and salt. In large bowl with mixer at medium speed, beat margarine and peanut butter until smooth. Beat in sugars until blended. Beat in eggs and vanilla. Add flour mixture; beat until well blended. Shape dough into two rolls, 1½ inches in diameter. Wrap in plastic wrap; refrigerate until firm.

Preheat oven to 350°F. Slice rolls into ¼-inch-thick slices. Place, 2 inches apart, on ungreased cookie sheets. Bake 12 minutes or until lightly browned. Remove; cool completely on wire racks. Store in tightly covered container.

Makes about 8 dozen cookies

APPLESAUCE OATMEAL COOKIES

1 cup all-purpose flour
1 teaspoon baking powder
1 teaspoon ground allspice
1 teaspoon cinnamon
½ teaspoon nutmeg
½ teaspoon cloves
¼ teaspoon salt

½ cup margarine
½ cup packed brown sugar
2 egg whites
2 cups rolled oats
1 cup unsweetened
   applesauce
½ cup chopped raisins

Preheat oven to 375°F. Grease baking sheet. Mix flour, baking power, spices and salt. Beat margarine and sugar until creamy. Add egg whites; beat well. Add dry ingredients. Stir in oats, applesauce and raisins. Drop by level tablespoonfuls onto baking sheet. Bake 10 to 12 minutes or until edges are lightly browned. Cool on rack before serving.

Makes about 4 dozen cookies

Favorite recipe from Western New York Apple Growers Association, Inc.

BUTTERSCOTCH FRUIT DROPS

2 cups all-purpose flour
1 teaspoon baking soda
½ teaspoon salt
½ cup (1 stick) butter or
   margarine, softened
¾ cup firmly packed brown
   sugar
1 egg

2 tablespoons milk
1 teaspoon grated lemon
   rind, optional
2 cups (12-oz. pkg.) NESTLÉ®
   Toll House® Butterscotch
   Flavored Morsels
1 cup diced mixed dried fruit
   bits or raisins

Preheat oven to 350°F. In small bowl, combine flour, baking soda and salt; set aside.

In large mixer bowl, beat butter and brown sugar until creamy. Blend in egg, milk and lemon rind. Gradually beat in flour mixture. Stir in morsels and fruit. Drop by rounded measuring teaspoonfuls onto ungreased cookie sheets.

Bake 9 to 11 minutes until golden brown. Let stand 2 minutes. Remove from cookie sheets; cool on wire racks.

Makes about 6 dozen cookies

SNICKERDOODLES

3 tablespoons sugar
1 teaspoon ground
   cinnamon
1 package (18.25 ounces)
   DUNCAN HINES® Moist
   Deluxe Yellow Cake Mix

2 eggs
¼ cup CRISCO® Oil

1. Preheat oven to 375°F. Grease cookie sheet.

2. Combine sugar and cinnamon in small bowl.

3. Combine cake mix, eggs and Crisco® Oil in large bowl. Stir until well blended. Shape dough into one-inch balls. Roll in cinnamon-sugar mixture. Place balls, 2 inches apart, on cookie sheet. Flatten balls with bottom of glass.

4. Bake at 375°F for 8 to 9 minutes or until set. Cool one minute on cookie sheet before removing to wire rack.

Makes about 3 dozen cookies

PECAN CRUNCHIES

1 package DUNCAN HINES®
   Golden Sugar Cookie Mix
1 egg
1 tablespoon water

1½ cups crushed potato chips,
   divided
½ cup chopped pecans

1. Preheat oven to 375°F. Grease cookie sheets lightly.

2. Combine cookie mix, contents of buttery flavor packet from Mix, egg, water, ½ cup potato chips and pecans in large bowl. Stir until thoroughly blended. Form dough into 36 (1-inch) balls. Roll in remaining 1 cup crushed potato chips. Place, 2 inches apart, on cookie sheets. Flatten dough with fork.

3. Bake at 375°F for 8 to 10 minutes or until golden brown. Cool 1 minute on cookie sheets. Remove to cooling racks. Cool completely. Store in airtight container.

Makes about 3 dozen cookies

Top to bottom: Snickerdoodles, Pecan Crunchies

Banana Drop Cookies

BANANA DROP COOKIES

2 ripe, medium DOLE®
   Bananas
1 cup margarine, softened
1 cup granulated sugar
½ cup packed brown sugar
2 eggs
1 teaspoon vanilla
2 cups all-purpose flour

1 teaspoon baking soda
1 teaspoon ground
   cinnamon (optional)
½ teaspoon salt
1 cup peanut butter chips
1 cup chopped walnuts
1 cup raisins

Preheat oven to 375°F.

Cut bananas into chunks. In food processor or blender, process bananas
until smooth. In large bowl, cream margarine and sugars. Beat in
bananas, eggs and vanilla. In small bowl, combine flour, baking soda,
cinnamon and salt. Gradually beat flour mixture into banana mixture.
Stir in chips, nuts and raisins. Drop dough by tablespoonfuls, 2 inches
apart, onto greased cookie sheets. Bake 12 minutes or until golden
brown. Cool on wire racks. *Makes about 4 dozen cookies*

ALMOND DELIGHTFUL COOKIES

¼ cup (½ stick) margarine or
  butter, softened
¼ cup vegetable shortening
½ cup packed brown sugar
¼ cup sugar
1 egg, beaten
1 teaspoon vanilla extract

1 cup all-purpose flour
1 teaspoon baking powder
3 cups HONEY ALMOND
  DELIGHT® brand cereal,
  crushed to 1½ cups
½ cup semi-sweet chocolate
  pieces *or* raisins

Preheat oven to 350°F. Lightly grease cookie sheet. In large bowl, cream margarine, shortening and sugars. Add egg and vanilla; mix well. Stir in flour and baking powder until well combined. Add cereal and chocolate pieces; mix well. Drop by level tablespoons onto prepared cookie sheet. Bake 10 to 12 minutes or until lightly browned. Let stand 1 minute before removing from cookie sheet. Cool on wire rack.

Makes about 2½ dozen cookies

CHOCO PEANUT BUTTER DREAMS

1½ cups firmly packed brown
  sugar
1 cup creamy or chunk-style
  peanut butter
¾ cup (1½ sticks) margarine
⅓ cup water
1 egg
1 teaspoon vanilla
3 cups QUAKER® Oats (quick
  or old fashioned,
  uncooked)

1½ cups all-purpose flour
½ teaspoon baking soda
1½ cups semi-sweet chocolate
  pieces
4 teaspoons vegetable
  shortening
⅓ cup chopped peanuts
  (optional)

Preheat oven to 350°F. Beat brown sugar, peanut butter and margarine until fluffy. Blend in water, egg and vanilla. Add combined oats, flour and baking soda; mix well. Shape into 1-inch balls. Place on ungreased cookie sheet. Using bottom of glass dipped in sugar, press into ¼-inch-thick circles. Bake 8 to 10 minutes or until edges are golden brown. Remove to wire rack; cool completely.

In saucepan over low heat, melt chocolate pieces and shortening, stirring until smooth.* Top each cookie with ½ teaspoon melted chocolate; sprinkle with chopped peanuts. Chill until set. Store tightly covered.

Makes about 6 dozen cookies

*Microwave Directions: Place chocolate pieces and shortening in microwavable bowl. Microwave at HIGH 1 to 2 minutes, stirring after 1 minute and then every 30 seconds until smooth.

Brownie & Bar Bonanza

APPLE CRUMB SQUARES

2 cups QUAKER® Oats (Quick or Old Fashioned), uncooked
1½ cups all-purpose flour
1 cup packed brown sugar
1 teaspoon ground cinnamon
½ teaspoon salt (optional)

½ teaspoon baking soda
¼ teaspoon ground nutmeg
¾ cup butter or margarine, melted
1 cup commercially prepared applesauce
½ cup chopped nuts

Preheat oven to 350°F. In large bowl, combine all ingredients except applesauce and nuts; mix until crumbly. Reserve 1 cup oats mixture. Press remaining oats mixture onto bottom of greased 13×9-inch pan. Bake 13 to 15 minutes; cool. Spread applesauce over partially baked crust; sprinkle with nuts. Sprinkle reserved 1 cup oats mixture over top. Bake 13 to 15 minutes or until golden brown. Cool in pan on wire rack; cut into 2-inch squares.   *Makes about 24 squares*

Apple Crumb Squares

FUDGY WALNUT COOKIE WEDGES

1 (20-ounce) package
   refrigerated cookie
   dough, any flavor
1 (12-ounce) package
   semisweet chocolate
   chips
2 tablespoons margarine or
   butter

1 (14-ounce) can EAGLE®
   Brand Sweetened
   Condensed Milk (NOT
   evaporated milk)
1 teaspoon vanilla extract
½ cup chopped walnuts

Preheat oven to 350°F. Divide cookie dough into thirds. With floured hands, press onto bottom of three aluminum foil-lined 9-inch round cake pans or press into 9-inch circles on ungreased baking sheets. Bake 10 to 20 minutes or until golden. Cool. In heavy saucepan, over medium heat, melt chips and margarine with sweetened condensed milk. Cook and stir until thickened, about 5 minutes; add vanilla. Spread over cookie circles. Top with walnuts. Chill. Cut into wedges. Store loosely covered at room temperature.   *Makes about 36 wedges*

Fudgy Walnut Cookie Wedges

PUMPKIN JINGLE BARS

¾ cup MIRACLE WHIP® Salad
   Dressing
1 two-layer spice cake mix
1 (16-oz.) can pumpkin
3 eggs

Confectioners' sugar
Vanilla frosting
Red and green gum drops,
   sliced

Preheat oven to 350°F. Mix first 4 ingredients in large bowl at medium speed of electric mixer until well blended. Pour into greased 15½×10½-inch jelly roll pan. Bake 18 to 20 minutes or until edges pull away from sides of pan. Cool. Sprinkle with sugar. Cut into bars. Decorate with frosting and gum drops. *Makes about 36 bars*

Preparation time: 5 minutes
Baking time: 20 minutes

LEMON CRUNCHIES

1 (14- or 15-ounce) can
   sweetened condensed
   milk
½ cup lemon juice
1 teaspoon grated lemon
   peel
2 to 3 drops yellow food
   coloring
1½ cups sifted all-purpose
   flour

1 teaspoon DAVIS® Baking
   Powder
1 teaspoon salt
⅔ cup BLUE BONNET®
   Margarine, softened
1 cup firmly packed light
   brown sugar
1 cup quick-cooking oats

Blend milk, juice, lemon peel and food coloring; set aside.

Sift together flour, baking powder and salt. With mixer, beat margarine and sugar until creamy; mix in flour mixture and oats until crumbly.

Pat half the oat mixture onto bottom of a well greased 8 × 8-inch pan. Spread milk mixture over crust; sprinkle with remaining oat mixture. Bake 30 minutes or until browned around pan edges. Cool in pan on wire rack for about 15 minutes; cut into bars. Chill until firm. *Makes about 24 bars*

ULTIMATE DESIGNER BROWNIES

¾ cup **HERSHEY'S Cocoa**
½ teaspoon baking soda
⅔ cup butter or margarine,
    melted and divided
½ cup boiling water
2 cups sugar
2 eggs
1⅓ cups all-purpose flour
1 teaspoon vanilla extract
¼ teaspoon salt

¾ cup (3½-ounce jar)
    macadamia nuts,
    coarsely chopped
2 cups (12-ounce package)
    HERSHEY'S Semi-Sweet
    Chocolate Chips, divided
½ teaspoon shortening (not
    butter, margarine or oil)
Vanilla Glaze (recipe
    follows)

Preheat oven to 350°F. Grease 13×9-inch baking pan or two 8-inch square baking pans. In medium bowl, stir together cocoa and baking soda; blend in ⅓ cup melted butter. Add boiling water; stir until mixture thickens. Stir in sugar, eggs and remaining ⅓ cup melted butter; stir until smooth. Add flour, vanilla and salt; blend well. Stir in nuts and 1½ cups chocolate chips. Pour into prepared pan(s). Bake 30 to 35 minutes for square pans or 35 to 40 minutes for rectangular pan or until brownie begins to pull away from sides of pan. Cool completely in pan on wire rack.

Prepare Vanilla Glaze; spread Vanilla Glaze on top of brownies. Cut brownies into triangles. Place remaining ½ cup chips and shortening in top of double boiler over hot, not boiling, water; stir until melted. Put into pastry bag fitted with small writing tip. Pipe design on each brownie.

Makes about 24 brownies

VANILLA GLAZE

2 tablespoons butter or
    margarine
4 teaspoons milk

¼ teaspoon brandy extract
¼ teaspoon rum extract
1 cup powdered sugar

In small saucepan over low heat, melt butter in milk. Remove from heat; add brandy and rum extracts. Gradually add powdered sugar, beating with wire whisk until smooth. Makes about ½ cup glaze.

Streusel Caramel Bars

STREUSEL CARAMEL BARS

2 cups unsifted flour
¾ cup firmly packed light brown sugar
1 egg, beaten
¾ cup cold margarine or butter
¾ cup chopped nuts

24 EAGLE™ Brand Caramels, unwrapped
1 (14-ounce) can EAGLE® Brand Sweetened Condensed Milk (NOT evaporated milk)

Preheat oven to 350°F. In large bowl, combine flour, sugar and egg; cut in *½ cup* margarine until crumbly. Stir in nuts. Reserving 2 cups crumb mixture, press remainder firmly onto bottom of greased 13×9-inch baking pan. Bake 15 minutes. Meanwhile, in heavy saucepan, over low heat, melt caramels with sweetened condensed milk and remaining *¼ cup* margarine. Pour over prepared crust. Top with reserved crumb mixture. Bake 20 minutes or until bubbly. Cool. Cut into bars. Store loosely covered at room temperature.   *Makes 24 to 36 bars*

Chocolate Caramel Bars: Melt 2 (1-ounce) squares unsweetened chocolate with caramels, sweetened condensed milk and margarine. Proceed as above.

CHOCOLATE CARAMEL-PECAN BARS

2 cups butter, softened,
　　divided
½ cup granulated sugar
1 large egg
2¾ cups all-purpose flour
⅔ cup packed light brown
　　sugar

¼ cup light corn syrup
2½ cups coarsely chopped
　　pecans
1 cup semisweet chocolate
　　chips

Preheat oven to 375°F. Grease 15×10-inch jelly-roll pan; set aside. Beat 1 cup butter and granulated sugar in large bowl until light and fluffy. Beat in egg. Add flour. Beat until well combined. Spread dough with rubber spatula into prepared pan. Bake 20 minutes or until light golden brown.

While bars are baking, prepare topping. Combine remaining 1 cup butter, brown sugar and corn syrup in medium, heavy saucepan. Cook over medium heat until mixture boils, stirring frequently. Boil gently 2 minutes, without stirring. Quickly stir in pecans; spread evenly over base. Return to oven. Bake 20 minutes or until dark golden brown and bubbling. Immediately sprinkle chocolate chips evenly over hot caramel. Gently press chips into caramel topping with spatula. Loosen caramel from edges of pan with a thin spatula or knife. Remove pan to wire rack; cool completely. Cut into 3×1½-inch bars. *Makes about 40 bars*

BUTTERSCOTCH BROWNIES

2 cups all-purpose flour
2 teaspoons baking powder
1½ teaspoons salt
One 12-oz. pkg. (2 cups)
　　NESTLÉ® Toll House®
　　Butterscotch Flavored
　　Morsels

½ cup (1 stick) butter
1 cup firmly packed brown
　　sugar
4 eggs
1 teaspoon vanilla extract
1 cup chopped nuts

Preheat oven to 350°F. In small bowl, combine flour, baking powder and salt; set aside. Combine over hot (not boiling) water, butterscotch flavored morsels and butter. Stir until morsels are melted and mixture is smooth. Transfer to large mixer bowl. Stir in brown sugar; cool 5 minutes. Beat in eggs and vanilla extract. Blend in flour mixture. Stir in nuts. Spread in greased 15½×10½-inch baking pan.

Bake 20 minutes. Cool. Cut into 2-inch squares.
Makes about 35 brownies

Chocolate Caramel-Pecan Bars

PINEAPPLE ALMOND SHORTBREAD BARS

CRUST

1½ cups all-purpose flour
½ cup DOLE® Almonds,
 toasted, ground

¼ cup sugar
½ cup cold margarine

TOPPING

1 can (20 ounces) DOLE®
 Crushed Pineapple,
 drained
3 eggs
¼ cup sugar

¼ cup honey
1 tablespoon grated lemon
 peel
1½ cups DOLE® Slivered
 Almonds, toasted

For Crust, preheat oven to 350°F. In large bowl, combine flour, ground almonds and sugar. Cut in margarine until crumbly. Form dough into a ball; press into ungreased 13 × 9-inch baking pan. Bake 10 minutes. Cool slightly.

For Topping, in medium bowl, combine pineapple, eggs, sugar, honey and lemon peel. Stir in toasted almonds. Pour topping over partially baked crust. Bake an additional 30 to 35 minutes. Cool completely in pan on wire rack. Cut into bars. *Makes about 2 dozen bars*

APPLE MACADAMIA NUT BAR

3 Golden Delicious apples,
 chopped small
1 tablespoon lemon juice
1 (16-ounce) box pound cake
 mix
1 cup milk
1 teaspoon grated lemon
 peel

½ teaspoon almond extract
1 cup flaked, sweetened
 coconut
3½ ounces macadamia nuts,
 coarsely chopped
3½ ounces white chocolate,
 coarsely chopped

1. Heat oven to 350°F. Grease and flour 13×9-inch baking pan. Combine apples and lemon juice; set aside.

2. In large bowl, with electric mixer, beat together dry pound cake mix, milk, lemon peel and almond extract. Stir in coconut, macadamia nuts, white chocolate and the reserved apples; mix well.

3. Spoon batter into prepared pan. Bake 50 to 55 minutes or until center springs back when gently pressed. Cool in pan 5 minutes; cut into bars.
Makes 12 bars

Favorite recipe from Washington Apple Commission

MAGIC COOKIE BARS

½ cup margarine or butter
1½ cups graham cracker
  crumbs
1 (14-ounce) can EAGLE®
  Brand Sweetened
  Condensed Milk (NOT
  evaporated milk)

1 (6-ounce) package semi-
  sweet chocolate chips
1 (3½-ounce) can flaked
  coconut (1½ cups)
1 cup chopped nuts

Preheat oven to 350°F (325°F for glass dish). In 13×9-inch baking pan, melt margarine in oven. Sprinkle crumbs over margarine; pour sweetened condensed milk evenly over crumbs. Top with remaining ingredients; press down firmly. Bake 25 to 30 minutes or until lightly browned. Cool. Chill if desired. Cut into bars. Store loosely covered at room temperature. *Makes 24 to 36 bars*

Seven Layer Magic Cookie Bars: Add 1 (6-ounce) package butterscotch flavored chips after chocolate chips.

Magic Peanut Cookie Bars: Omit chocolate chips and chopped nuts. Top sweetened condensed milk with 2 cups (about ¾ pound) chocolate-covered peanuts, then coconut. Proceed as above.

Magic Cookie Bars

Cherry Chewbilees

CHERRY CHEWBILEES

CRUST
1 cup walnut pieces, divided
1¼ cups all-purpose flour
½ cup firmly packed brown sugar

½ cup BUTTER FLAVOR CRISCO®
½ cup flaked coconut

FILLING
2 packages (8 ounces each) cream cheese, softened
⅔ cup granulated sugar
2 eggs

2 teaspoons vanilla
1 can (21 ounces) cherry pie filling

1. Preheat oven to 350°F. Grease 13×9-inch pan with Butter Flavor Crisco®. Set aside. Chop ½ cup nuts coarsely for topping. Set aside. Chop remaining ½ cup nuts finely.

2. **For Crust,** combine flour and brown sugar. Cut in ½ cup Butter Flavor Crisco® until fine crumbs form. Add ½ cup finely chopped nuts and coconut. Mix well. Remove ½ cup coconut mixture. Set aside. Press remaining coconut mixture onto bottom of pan. Bake at 350°F for 12 to 15 minutes, until edges are lightly browned.

3. **For Filling,** beat cream cheese, granulated sugar, eggs and vanilla in small bowl at medium speed of electric mixer until smooth. Spread over hot baked crust. Return to oven. Bake 15 minutes longer or until set. Spread cherry pie filling over cheese layer. Combine reserved coarsely chopped nuts and reserved coconut mixture. Sprinkle evenly over cherries. Return to oven. Bake 15 minutes longer. Chill. Refrigerate several hours. Cut into 2×1½-inch bars.   *Makes about 36 bars*

GERMAN SWEET CHOCOLATE CREAM CHEESE BROWNIES

BROWNIE LAYER
  1 package (4 ounces)
    BAKER'S® GERMAN'S®
    Sweet Chocolate
  ¼ cup (½ stick) margarine or
    butter

  ¾ cup sugar
  2 eggs
  1 teaspoon vanilla
  ½ cup all-purpose flour
  ½ cup chopped nuts

CREAM CHEESE LAYER
  4 ounces PHILADELPHIA
    BRAND® Cream Cheese,
    softened
  ¼ cup sugar

  1 egg
  1 tablespoon all-purpose
    flour

Preheat oven to 350°F.

Microwave chocolate and margarine in large microwavable bowl on HIGH 2 minutes or until margarine is melted. Stir until chocolate is completely melted.

Stir ¾ cup sugar into melted chocolate mixture. Mix in 2 eggs and vanilla until well blended. Stir in ½ cup flour and nuts. Spread in greased 8-inch square pan.

Mix cream cheese, ¼ cup sugar, 1 egg and 1 tablespoon flour in same bowl until smooth. Place spoonfuls over brownie batter. Swirl with knife to marbleize.

Bake for 35 minutes or until toothpick inserted into center comes out with fudgy crumbs. Do not overbake. Cool in pan; cut into squares.
Makes about 16 brownies

Prep time: 20 minutes
Baking time: 35 minutes

CHOCOLATE SCOTCHEROOS

1 cup light corn syrup
1 cup sugar
1 cup peanut butter
6 cups KELLOGGS'® RICE
    KRISPIES® Cereal
  Vegetable cooking spray

1 package (6 ounces, 1 cup)
    semi-sweet chocolate
    morsels
1 package (6 ounces, 1 cup)
    butterscotch morsels

1. Measure corn syrup and sugar into large saucepan. Cook over medium heat, stirring frequently, until sugar dissolves and mixture begins to boil. Remove from heat. Stir in peanut butter. Mix well. Add Kellogg's® Rice Krispies® Cereal. Stir until well coated. Press mixture into 13 × 9-inch pan coated with cooking spray. Set aside.

2. Melt chocolate and butterscotch morsels together in small saucepan over low heat, stirring constantly. Spread evenly over cereal mixture. Let stand until firm. Cut into 2 × 1-inch bars to serve.

Makes about 48 bars

CHOCOLATE CHUNK BLONDE BROWNIES

½ cup (1 stick) margarine or
    butter, softened
1 cup firmly packed brown
    sugar
1 cup granulated sugar
4 eggs
2 teaspoons vanilla
2 cups all-purpose flour

1 teaspoon CALUMET®
    Baking Powder
¼ teaspoon salt
1 package (8 ounces)
    BAKER'S® Semi-Sweet
    Chocolate, coarsely
    chopped
1 cup chopped nuts

Preheat oven to 350°F.

Beat margarine, sugars, eggs and vanilla until light and fluffy. Mix in flour, baking powder and salt until well blended. Stir in chocolate and nuts. Spread into greased 13 × 9-inch pan.

Bake for 30 minutes or until toothpick inserted into center comes out with moist crumbs. Do not overbake. Cool in pan; cut into squares.

Makes about 24 brownies

Prep time: 20 minutes
Baking time: 30 minutes

Chocolate Scotcheroos

PEACHY OATMEAL BARS

CRUMB MIXTURE
1½ cups all-purpose flour
   1 cup quick cooking oats
   ½ cup sugar
   ½ teaspoon baking soda

¼ teaspoon salt
¾ cup margarine, melted
2 teaspoons almond extract

FILLING
   ¾ cup peach or apricot
      preserves

⅓ cup flaked coconut

Preheat oven to 350°F.

For Crumb Mixture, combine all crumb mixture ingredients in large mixer bowl. Beat at low speed, scraping bowl often, until mixture is crumbly, 1 to 2 minutes. *Reserve ¾ cup crumb mixture;* press remaining crumb mixture onto bottom of greased 9-inch square baking pan.

For Filling, spread preserves to within ½ inch of edge of crust; sprinkle with reserved crumb mixture and coconut. Bake for 20 to 25 minutes or until edges are lightly browned. Cool completely. Cut into bars.
Makes about 24 bars

STREUSEL STRAWBERRY BARS

1 cup butter or margarine,
   softened
1 cup sugar
1 egg
2 cups all-purpose flour

¾ cup pecans, coarsely
   chopped
1 jar (10 ounces) strawberry
   or raspberry preserves

Preheat oven to 350°F. Combine butter and sugar in large mixer bowl. Beat at low speed, scraping bowl often, until well blended. Add egg and flour. Beat until mixture is crumbly, 2 to 3 minutes. Stir in pecans. Reserve 1 cup crumb mixture; press remaining crumb mixture onto bottom of greased 9-inch square baking pan. Spread preserves to within ½ inch of edge of crust. Crumble reserved crumb mixture over preserves. Bake for 40 to 50 minutes or until lightly browned. Cool completely. Cut into bars.
Makes about 24 bars

Top to bottom: Peachy Oatmeal Bars, Streusel Strawberry Bars

CRANBERRY JEWEL BARS

2 cups unsifted flour
1½ cups quick-cooking or
    old-fashioned oats
¾ cup plus 1 tablespoon
    firmly packed brown
    sugar
1 cup *cold* margarine or
    butter
1 (14-ounce) can EAGLE®
    Brand Sweetened
    Condensed Milk (NOT
    evaporated milk)

1 cup ricotta cheese
2 eggs
1½ teaspoons vanilla extract
1 teaspoon grated orange
    rind
2 tablespoons cornstarch
1 (16-ounce) can whole berry
    cranberry sauce

Preheat oven to 350°F. In large bowl, combine flour, oats and ¾ *cup* sugar.
Cut in *cold* margarine until crumbly. Reserving 2 cups crumb mixture,
press remainder firmly onto bottom of 13×9-inch baking pan. Bake 15
minutes.

Meanwhile, in small mixer bowl, beat sweetened condensed milk,
cheese, eggs, vanilla and rind until smooth. Spread evenly over baked
crust. In small bowl, combine remaining *1 tablespoon* sugar and
cornstarch; stir in cranberry sauce. Spoon over cheese layer. Top with
reserved crumb mixture. Bake 40 minutes or until lightly browned. Cool.
Chill. Garnish as desired. Cut into bars. Store covered in refrigerator.
Makes 36 to 40 bars

EXTRA MOIST & CHUNKY BROWNIES

1 (8-ounce) package cream
    cheese, softened
1 cup sugar
1 egg
1 teaspoon vanilla extract
¾ cup all-purpose flour

1 (3⅜-ounce) package
    ROYAL® Chocolate or
    Dark 'N' Sweet Chocolate
    Pudding & Pie Filling
4 (1-ounce) semisweet
    chocolate squares,
    chopped

In large bowl, with electric mixer at high speed, beat cream cheese,
sugar, egg and vanilla until smooth; blend in flour and pudding mix.
Spread batter into greased 8 × 8-inch microwavable dish; sprinkle with
chocolate. Shield corners of dish with foil. Microwave at HIGH (100%
power) for 8 to 10 minutes or until toothpick inserted in center comes
out clean, rotating dish ½ turn every 2 minutes. Cool completely in pan.
Cut into squares. *Makes about 16 brownies*

MINTED CHOCOLATE CHIP BROWNIES

¾ cup granulated sugar
½ cup butter or margarine
2 tablespoons water
1 cup semisweet chocolate
    chips or mini chocolate
    chips
1½ teaspoons vanilla

2 large eggs
1¼ cups all-purpose flour
½ teaspoon baking soda
½ teaspoon salt
1 cup mint chocolate chips
    Powdered sugar for garnish

Preheat oven to 350°F. Combine sugar, butter and water in medium microwavable bowl. Microwave on HIGH 2½ to 3 minutes or until butter is melted. Stir in semisweet chips; stir gently until chips are melted and mixture is well blended. Stir in vanilla; let stand 5 minutes to cool. Beat eggs into chocolate mixture, one at a time. Add combined flour, baking soda and salt; stir in mint chips. Spread into greased 9-inch square baking pan.

Bake 25 minutes for fudgy brownies or 30 to 35 minutes for cake-like brownies. Remove pan to wire rack; cool completely. Cut into 2¼-inch squares. Sprinkle with powdered sugar, if desired.

Makes 16 brownies

Minted Chocolate Chip Brownies

Acknowledgments

The publishers would like to thank the companies and organizations
listed below for the use of their recipes in this publication.

American Dairy Industry Association
Best Foods, a Division of CPC International Inc.
Borden Kitchens, Borden, Inc.
Checkerboard Kitchens, Ralston Purina Company
Diamond Walnut Growers, Inc.
Dole Food Company, Inc.
Hershey Chocolate U.S.A.
Kellogg Company
Kraft General Foods, Inc.
Leaf, Inc.
M&M/Mars
Nabisco Foods Group
Nestlé Food Company
The Procter & Gamble Company
The Quaker Oats Company
The Sugar Association, Inc.
Washington Apple Commission
Western New York Apple Growers Association, Inc.

Photo Credits

The publishers would like to thank the companies and organizations
listed below for the use of their photographs in this publication.

American Dairy Industry Association
Borden Kitchens, Borden, Inc.
Dole Food Company, Inc.
Nestlé Food Company
The Procter & Gamble Company
The Quaker Oats Company

Index